Evangelical Faith and
Public Zeal

Evangelical Faith and Public Zeal

Evangelicals and Society in Britain 1780–1980

edited by
JOHN WOLFFE

First published in Great Britain in 1995
SPCK,
Holy Trinity Church,
Marylebone Road,
London NW1 4DU

British Library Cataloguing-in-Publication Data
A catalogue record for this book is available from the British Library

ISBN 0-281-04782-0

Typeset by Pioneer Associates, Perthshire, Scotland
Printed in Great Britain by
Redwood Books Ltd, Trowbridge, Wiltshire

Contents

Notes on Contributors

David Bebbington is Reader in History at the University of Stirling and the author of *Evangelicalism in Modern Britain: A History from the 1730s to the 1980s* (new edn, Routledge, 1994), *William Ewart Gladstone: Faith and Politics in Victorian Britain* (Eerdmans, 1993) and other books.

Kenneth Brown is Professor of Economic and Social History at The Queen's University of Belfast, and an elder of Kingsway Community Church in south Belfast. He has published widely, including *A Social History of the Nonconformist Ministry In England and Wales 1800–1939* (Oxford UP, 1988).

Clive Calver is Director General of the Evangelical Alliance.

Brian Dickey is Reader in History at The Flinders University of South Australia. He is editor of *The Australian Dictionary of Evangelical Biography* (Evangelical History Association, 1994), author of *No Charity There: A Short History of Social Welfare in Australia* (Allen and Unwin, 1987) and other books.

Jane Garnett is Fellow and Tutor in Modern History at Wadham College, Oxford. She has published on Victorian and Edwardian evangelicalism, social ethics and moral philosophy.

David Hempton is Professor of Modern History at The Queen's University of Belfast. He has written *Methodism and Politics in British Society 1750–1850* (Hutchinson, 1984) and (with Myrtle Hill) *Evangelical Protestantism in Ulster Society 1740–1890* (Routledge, 1992).

Jocelyn Murray, for some years a teacher and pastoral worker in Kenya with the Church Missionary Society, worked in the Department of Religious Studies at the University of Aberdeen, and is now a free-lance writer and editor. She is the author of *Proclaim the Good News: A Short History of the CMS* (Hodder and Stoughton, 1985).

Ian Randall is a Baptist minister and Tutor in Church History at Spurgeon's College, London. He is engaged on research on evangelical spirituality in England in the inter-war years.

Edward Royle is Reader in History at the University of York. He is the author of *Modern Britain: A Social History 1750–1985* (Edward Arnold, 1987) and numerous publications on popular religion and irreligion.

Brian Stanley is Lecturer in Church History at Trinity College, Bristol. He has published *The Bible and the Flag* (Leicester: Apollos, 1990) and *The History of the Baptist Missionary Society 1792–1992* (Edinburgh: T & T Clark, 1992).

John Wolffe is Lecturer in Religious Studies at The Open University. He has published *The Protestant Crusade in Great Britain 1829–1860* (Oxford UP, 1991) and *God and Greater Britain: Religion and National Life in Britain and Ireland, 1843–1945* (Routledge, 1994).

Introduction
JOHN WOLFFE

'Evangelicalism', wrote George Eliot in 1857, 'brought into palpable existence and operation' the 'idea of duty, that recognition of something to be lived for beyond the mere satisfaction of self'.[1] This tribute to the moral and social benefits stemming from evangelicalism came from the pen of one of the movement's greatest critics and was offered at the peak of its Victorian ascendancy. Relentless though she was in exposing the shallowness and hypocrisy she perceived in evangelicalism, Eliot also had the insight to appreciate its essential role in forming the social conscience of the era in which she lived.

By contrast, more recent images of evangelicalism have tended to see it as an escapist religious movement, offering a sense of eternal security but little constructive engagement with contemporary society. In some respects evangelicals themselves have relished that sense of apartness, feeling themselves chosen by the grace of God in the intensely personal and spiritual experience of conversion, and living under the authority of the Bible in a world self-evidently in thrall to very different standards and outlooks. Accordingly the initiative in Christian social concern has often appeared to lie with liberal Protestants, with their more favourable attitude to 'secular' thought, and with Catholics, whether Anglican or Roman, holding a stronger sense of the corporate dimensions of belief.

Nevertheless recent developments in both the religious and scholarly worlds have served to re-awaken an awareness of the social implications of evangelicalism. Indeed when one begins to probe the historical record it rapidly becomes apparent that these aspects of the movement never disappeared, but only became obscured. The personal 'vital religion' of evangelicals, their sense of a faith that transformed their lives, very frequently stimulated a corresponding public zeal for change in society. The purpose of this book is to explore some features of that past experience in the belief that such a perspective has a valuable role to play in producing informed discussion in the present, among evangelicals and non-evangelicals, academics, students and general readers alike. The intention is not uncritical celebration, but the careful painting of a complex picture which is likely to challenge many preconceptions, while demonstrating the extensive and long-standing commitment of many British evangelicals to the welfare of community, nation and world.

In some respects the events that have led to the publication of this book can be seen as part of the continuing history of the movements with which it is concerned. The Evangelical Alliance was formed at a major international conference in 1846 as a focus for interdenominational evangelicalism. In the early decades of its existence its conferences and publications were a major focus for reflection by evangelicals on their relationship to society. Like other long established organizations it subsequently passed through fluctuating fortunes, but in the last ten years it has enjoyed a substantial resurgence, associated with an endeavour to return to some of its nineteenth-century roots. In November 1988 it held a major consultation on 'Evangelical Social Action' at Swanwick in Derbyshire. A further smaller scale meeting was held in Oxford in September 1990. During these discussions there was a growing awareness of a need for contemporary debate on evangelical social involvement to be set in historical perspective in a manner accessible to non-specialists. Accordingly the Evangelical Alliance provided financial and practical support for a group of historians who met for a symposium at the University of York in September 1992 to discuss their work. This book is the fruit of their labours.

While senior members of the Evangelical Alliance staff took part in the York symposium, the content of the volume has been wholly under the control of the editor and the contributors. The authors, whose own attitudes to evangelicalism might be characterized as a mixture of the sympathetically critical and the critically sympathetic, approach their task with a straight-forward desire to understand and interpret. Their concern is to place the historical record of evangelicalism on the neutral ground of scholarly investigation, providing a resource for both believers and sceptics. Others may wish to build on these foun-dations, either on the one hand in informing an explicitly providentialist view of evangelical history; or on the other in integrating an understanding of evangelicalism into an essen-tially secular view of history. The authors are most grateful to the Evangelical Alliance for making this project possible and also to John Briggs, Diane Drummond, Martyn Eden, David Jeremy, Michael Morris, Timothy Larsen, and John Walsh who either participated in their discussions or commented on drafts of chapters.

The work presented here also reflects an increase in schol-arly historical interest in evangelicalism and its social conse-quences during the last decade.[2] Some of the contributors to this volume have already added their own offerings to this accumulation of literature; others are relative newcomers to the field. Together they hope to achieve a kind of collective stock-taking, and also point the way into some new fields of research and inquiry.

This enterprise is thus designed to cross two often well-entrenched boundaries. The first is that between the past and present. The flowering of the 'heritage' industry during the 1980s has ensured that cultural interest in the past is at a high level, but this has in many respects been based on a sense that it is a 'foreign country', a channel for escapism and fantasy. This book by contrast is intended to provide a vantage point for critical re-engagement with contemporary issues. It would be rash, however, to pretend that the undertaking is without its dangers. History may inspire, but, given changing circum-stances, it cannot provide exact models for imitation; it may also offer cautionary tales, but their precise moral can be infuriatingly elusive. Nevertheless what is provided here is a long-term perspective on current conditions and issues; a sense of the range of options that existed in previous generations; and an examination of the circumstances that limited the effectiveness of action. If applied sensitively this should be of considerable service.

Second, there is the boundary between history and theology.

During recent decades these two originally closely linked disciplines have diverged: the increasing prominence of ethics, philosophical and pastoral theology on the one hand, and of social history on the other, have weakened support for their traditional points of contact in church history and historical theology. It is true that the history of religion has attracted increasing attention among historians in recent years, but their understandable tendency to 'market' their activities by setting them in the context of social and cultural history has seemingly moved them further from the interests of those starting from a theological background. At the same time this process does offer a hope of closing the circle, which is what is attempted here. If the link with theology is made through the study of practical pastoral and ethical issues rather than through contextualization of the work of great theologians of the past, or the examination of the history of the institutional church, it may well be found that insights derived from history can be a valuable complement to those coming from the social sciences.

The word 'evangelical' has had a complex history – it must be clearly distinguished from the related but different word 'evangelistic' – but it is here used to denote those movements in the Protestant churches that derived their original inspiration from the upsurge of revivalistic movements that broke out across the north Atlantic world in the 1730s. Their characteristic tenets have been examined in some detail by David Bebbington in his *Evangelicalism in Modern Britain* (1989) and have been helpfully summarized by Kenneth Brown in his contribution to the present volume: 'the need for individual salvation, a particular regard for the Bible, a stress on the centrality of Christ's atoning work on the cross, and a belief that the gospel needed to be actively expressed'. Bebbington denotes these as, respectively, conversionism, biblicism, crucicentrism and activism.[3]

While evangelicals have given birth to two major religious groups, the Methodists and Pentecostalists, and had a profound impact on numerous others, including Anglicans, Baptists, Congregationalists and Presbyterians, they have in essence been a movement rather than an institution. Hence problems of definition arise, especially when one moves from the history of individuals to that of the range of ideas associated with them, 'evangelicalism'. However, the very difficulties of defining the limits of evangelical influence are themselves indicative of the pervasiveness of the movement's interactions with the wider society.

Although the classification of individuals as evangelicals is often a straightforward matter, uncertainties also frequently arise. Sometimes these can be a result of inadequate evidence, but sometimes the presence of extensive information only serves to heighten ambiguities. Many people maintained the same general framework of belief throughout adult life but others were evangelical for only relatively short periods. Dramatic movement in views, such as that of John Henry Newman away from his youthful evangelicalism to High Anglicanism and eventually to Roman Catholicism, clearly placed an individual outside the remit of this book. Less radical changes of opinion, however, raise the question of whether the people concerned were engaged in creative and consistent reinterpretation of the evangelical tradition or whether they were gradually drifting away from it. This problem is especially acute when one is considering social involvements which did not necessarily explicitly relate to central matters of theological identity. Given the tendency of evangelicals to 'unchurch' those with whom they disagree, it will be important here to treat the compatibility of evangelicalism with particular political and social positions, whether of the right or of the left, as an open question. At the same time it is entirely legitimate to enquire whether those who espoused, say, feminist or socialist views, did so in spite of or because of their evangelicalism. The answer may well differ from one individual to another.

Furthermore it is essential to recognize that sincere deep-seated adoption of evangelical religious views did not detach individuals from their social and cultural context. For example, Lord Ashley (later Earl of Shaftesbury) was indisputably an evangelical from his mid-thirties until his death half a century later, but one cannot understand his social views adequately unless one is also aware that he was an aristocratic landowner whose assumptions about the basic structure of society were profoundly conservative.

Similar ambiguities arise in relation to the institutional expressions of evangelicalism. In its formative period in the eighteenth and early nineteenth centuries Methodism was consistently evangelical in character, but by the twentieth century its theological position was a much more variegated one. Some para-church bodies, such as the Evangelical Alliance and the Inter-Varsity Fellowship (later Universities and Colleges Christian Fellowship), founded in 1928, had evangelical doctrinal statements written into their constitutional structure, but this was relatively unusual. Other organizations committed to specifically religious purposes, such as the Church Missionary Society (1799) and the London City Mission (1835), maintained an evangelical character by long-standing custom and circumstances.

In the social and political sphere, however, identification has seldom been so clear-cut. Causes tended to be defined by the practical purposes that they served rather than by abstract theological agendas, and co-operation with non-evangelicals who shared the same specific objectives was widespread. As Brian Dickey shows in Chapter Two, there were large numbers of societies in which evangelicals readily worked with non-evangelicals. Moreover, as time passed, the character of organizations could change. For example, the Young Men's Christian Association began life in 1844 with an unambiguous evangelical character, but this gradually became less sharply defined as the social service aspect of its work developed. In politics, above all, it is seldom possible to identify hard-edged distinct evangelical activity. Even the so-called 'saints' of the Clapham Sect in Parliament in the early nineteenth century were a loose grouping rather than an organized party and as time went on the successive consolidation of Conservative, Liberal and Labour parties left (as Kenneth Brown demonstrates) less and less scope for such independent faction and pressure-group politics. Evangelical influence within the major parties might be significant, but it cannot be readily distinguished from broader political trends.

If assessment of the impact of evangelicalism through the study of individuals and institutions presents problems, even greater difficulties arise in studying the diffusion of ideas judged to be distinctively evangelical. It has recently been argued that evangelicalism, as mediated by men such as John Bird Sumner (Bishop of Chester 1828–48; Archbishop of Canterbury

1848–62) and the leading Scottish churchman Thomas Chalmers, combined with 'enlightenment rationalism' to produce the 'dominant mode of thought' of the first half of the nineteenth century.[4] The suggestion is a bold one, which deserves to be taken seriously, but it depends on debatable judgements about whether particular sets of ideas can be regarded as evangelical in any defensible sense. The same evidence could be interpreted in a very different way to argue that evangelicalism reflected 'the spirit of the age' much more than it shaped it.

Mindful of the pervasive but often unfocused nature of evangelical engagement with the world, we have accordingly in the title of this book preferred the broad description implied by the phrase 'evangelicals and society'. Concepts such as 'social action', 'social reform' and even 'social involvement' were all considered but rejected on the grounds that they both limited the scope of our investigations and implied a degree of coherence inconsistent with historical reality. Even those evangelicals most committed to emphasizing an exclusively spiritual evangelistic message did not exist in a social vacuum and their efforts often had profound, if unintended, social consequences. To have imposed on the past a twentieth-century concept of 'social action' distinct from evangelism would have been to carry the burden of a very substantial anachronism.

The chronological range of this book extends from the second major phase of evangelical revivalism and growth around 1800 up to the present day. The period of greatest evangelical influence in the mid-nineteenth century is thus set in a long-run historical perspective which will enhance appreciation of the more enduring dynamics of the movement's interaction with society. Most of the chapters are focused on a particular period, but three, those concerned with women, education and overseas involvement, pursue a particular theme across longer time spans. The overall coverage is designed to be illustrative rather than comprehensive. In particular, while the intention has been to draw material from all parts of Britain, it has not been feasible within the space available always to address distinctive features of Scottish, Welsh and regional experience.

John Wesley is usually perceived much more as a preacher of personal conversion than as a source of social transformation. Nevertheless, from the very beginnings of the movement the

social implications of Christian commitment were given considerable weight. Wesley himself advocated the adoption by
contemporary believers of the sharing of possessions which
had been practised by the early Jerusalem Church.[5] Such high
aspirations proved too idealistic for actual implementation, but
in the eighteenth and early nineteenth centuries, when revival
came to local communities it could lead to a transformation of
social and cultural relationships.[6] At the centre of national
affairs too, when in 1797 William Wilberforce called upon 'the
higher and middle classes of professed Christians' to turn to a
living faith and practice, he perceived the religious state of the
nation as having profound consequences for its moral and
social condition. 'All, therefore,' he wrote, 'who are concerned
over our country's welfare, should make every effort to revive
the Christianity that we once knew.'[7] In Chapter One David
Hempton provides extensive illustrations of particular inter-
linkages between religious revival and social change in that
formative period.

As Brian Dickey indicates in Chapter Two, active social
involvement continued to be widespread among evangelicals as
the movement moved towards its high Victorian maturity. The
essential voluntarism of their approach did not commend itself
in a later era of extensive state provision, but it still requires
sympathetic evaluation on its own terms. Indeed, as Jane Garnett shows from a different perspective in Chapter Three, while
evangelicals might support the free market, they were fully
alert to its potential dangers. Their exhortations and example
were influential in mitigating its worst excesses. There is an
analogy here with the evangelical response to British overseas
involvements outlined by Brian Stanley in Chapter Four. The
empire was enthusiastically welcomed, particularly because of
the potential that it offered for missionary activity, but its less
acceptable face was softened by the influence of evangelicals.
They were concerned that imperialism should not degenerate
into oppression and the pursuing of naked self-interest.

As time went on, however, the formative force of evangelicalism receded. This tendency was nowhere more apparent
than in relation to the situation of women. In Chapter Five
Jocelyn Murray describes how, although initial evangelical
revivals gave new opportunities and dignity to women, as the
movement became institutionalized and respectable in the

Victorian era, the more patriarchal aspects of biblical teaching came to receive greater and arguably excessive emphasis. Only as a later generation of women rediscovered scriptural legitimacy for a greater degree of active participation in ministry, did the pendulum begin to swing back again. By this period, however, evangelicals appeared merely to be reflecting wider trends rather than shaping them. Similarly in Chapter Six, Edward Royle shows how the distinctive contribution to educational endeavour made by evangelicals in early days became in the second half of the nineteenth century fractured by the rivalry of church and chapel and ultimately superseded by the essentially secular provision made by the state. As time went on evangelical efforts appeared increasingly marginal and derivative, and the tension between maintaining internal purity and influencing society as a whole became more acute.

In Chapter Seven Kenneth Brown does much to explain why the social and political impact of evangelicals receded in the later part of the nineteenth century. To some extent this was attributable to cultural and theological trends which rendered their beliefs less credible to others and induced a certain loss of confidence within the movement itself. Meanwhile, as Nonconformity came of age, both politically and socially, the distinctiveness of its evangelicalism diminished. Moreover the consolidation of two-party politics and the growing power of the state left less room for the exertion of independent influence and voluntary initiative.

Nevertheless the final two chapters in the book point to ways in which significant engagement with society continued. Ian Randall's claim in Chapter Eight that the period around 1900 was one of 'creative change' might seem to sit uneasily with Brown's more negative assessment. It can be inferred, however, that the flowering of Nonconformist social thought and activity associated with F. B. Meyer, Hugh Price Hughes, Samuel Keeble and others was their generation's substitute for the direct socially and politically transforming impact of evangelical Nonconformity in the middle decades of the nineteenth century. As such it suggested a more limited but more realistic agenda for the twentieth century. The difficulty was, as David Bebbington shows in Chapter Nine, that the succeeding interwar generation failed significantly to build on these foundations. Furthermore the political eclipse of the Liberal Party removed the traditional channel for the exercise of parliamentary influence by evangelical Nonconformists. From the middle of the twentieth century, on the other hand, evangelicalism began to regain a sense of wider social relevance. Moreover, as Clive Calver describes in the Afterword, this trend has become more pronounced since 1980, stimulated by movements and organizations such as the Shaftesbury Society, Care Trust, the Evangelical Alliance, and many smaller bodies.

To a considerable extent the later Victorian loss of momentum can be attributed to the long-term impact of past success. The conventional religiosity and moralism with which many later nineteenth- and twentieth-century evangelicals found themselves uneasy reflected the diffused influence of the evangelicalism of previous generations.[8] Inevitably, as evangelicalism became fashionable, it attracted adherents with mixed or twisted motives and gave mileage to the satirist and critic. The most memorable images of mid-century evangelical philanthropy in most people's minds are those of Charlotte Brontë's Mr Brocklehurst, harshly treating the orphans of Lowood School, and Charles Dickens's Mrs Jellyby, neglecting her own family as she labours for the welfare of the natives of Borrioboola-Gha. More subtle, but even more devastating, were the ethics of George Eliot's Mr Bulstrode, who justified his acquisition of wealth through dubious means by the conviction that he was putting it to good use in the Lord's service. Of course one only has to read the chapters by Dickey and Garnett to appreciate the elements of injustice in such literary portraits, but their very power is testimony to the manner in which early Victorian evangelicalism had become associated with the perceived hypocrisy of the socially privileged.

Although subsequent reversion to relative social marginality caused evangelicals to become more radical critics of the status quo, the late twentieth-century resurgence of social concern is an ambivalent phenomenon. To the extent that it has paralleled evangelical resurgence and the growth of the charismatic movement it can be seen as part of a process of spiritual revival. On the other hand its tendency to self-conscious theorizing, and defined projects rather than visionary initiatives, suggest that it has yet to prove itself as a potential agency of radical social transformation on the lines of eighteenth- and early nineteenth-century revivals. There is revealing paradox in the fact that, historically, the periods when the most profound social consequences have followed from evangelicalism have been those phases of revival when interest in the spiritual has been so intense that social structures have seemed fluid and negotiable. If a truly catalytic religious radicalism of this kind is to be found in contemporary Britain it is not among the white middle-class churches but among black Pentecostalists and outside Christianity altogether among ethnic minority groups and New Religious Movements. Herein lies a profound challenge for contemporary evangelicals.

In addition to pointing up the centrality of social involvement in the history of evangelicalism and providing some indications of the reasons for its ebbing and flowing, these essays also show that disagreement among themselves on social issues was the widespread experience of evangelicals. In general terms the roots of this diversity of views can be found in the fundamental characteristics of the movement, its particular expression of Protestant individualism and suspicion of ecclesiastical authority, and its emphasis on the right and duty of all to derive principles for action from private judgement of the Scriptures. More specifically, four points can be made.

First, while a general readiness to interweave the social and the spiritual was uncontroversial, at least until the twentieth century, there were significant differences when it came to establishing precise priorities and relationships. Was social improvement a necessary preliminary for evangelism or, conversely, was conversion an essential basis for social advance? Lord Shaftesbury's concern for social reform, like Wilberforce's for slave emancipation, was predicated on the assumption that this was an essential preliminary for moral and spiritual transformation in the individual – that there were occasions in which the material environment was so oppressive and dehumanizing that evangelistic efforts could make little progress. Thus in 1842 he (as Lord Ashley) concluded a speech advocating practical improvements in conditions of labour in the mines as follows:

For twenty millions of money you purchased the liberation of the negro; and it was a blessed deed. You may, this night, by a cheap and harmless vote, invigorate the hearts of thousands of your country people, enable them to walk erect in newness of life, to enter on the enjoyment of their inherited freedom, and avail themselves (if they will accept them) of the opportunities of virtue, of morality and religion.[9]

On the other hand Shaftesbury's evangelical critics – and there were many – when they did not have vested interests, were motivated by a sense that his endeavours were a dangerous distraction from real spiritual priorities. There was certainly a connection between the social and the spiritual condition of the people, but if they could only be converted to Christ this would bring a moral transformation which would inevitably enable them to improve their material conditions. In the meantime poverty and degradation were the consequence of their spiritual declension. A twentieth-century echo of this kind of divergence has been found in some evangelical unease with the emphasis of David Sheppard as Bishop of Liverpool on practical measures to improve the conditions of the poorest in society rather than on explicit evangelism.

Second, there were differing understandings about the operation of providence and the relationship of human effort to the working out of God's eschatological purposes. Were human beings essentially cogs in the great machine of divinely regulated machinery, who should merely fulfil their allotted task to the best of their energy and ability, and not seek to tamper with the mechanism? Alternatively were particular individuals agents of an interventionist God with a divine commission to bring about substantial and lasting change? Also, for much of the period under discussion, considerable evangelical attention was devoted to eschatology. Two main schools existed from the early nineteenth century, postmillennialists who held that the thousand years of Revelation 20 would be essentially a continuation of human history, reached through the gradual triumph of improvement and religion; and premillennialists who held that the thousand years would be preceded by a period of cataclysm and turmoil presaging the Second Coming of Christ. The determinative impact of eschatology in evangelical thought should not be exaggerated, but it was undoubtedly very influential. It was true that, as Dickey shows, premillennialism could be a spur to vigorous endeavours to reform society in the hope of softening the force of imminent divine judgement, but it could also, as Bebbington indicates, result in a kind of fatalistic inertia. Certainly it tended to give a theological legitimacy to extreme responses and a basis for tension with those of a post-millennial disposition who were more content to participate fully in the existing structures of society.

Third, denominational divisions were in the nineteenth century a major obstacle to united evangelical initiatives. This applied above all to the rivalry between Church and Dissent, which among evangelicals stemmed not so much from dogmatic theological difference as from profoundly held divergent convictions about the nature of the relationship between Christianity and the state. This was never more apparent than in the early history of the Evangelical Alliance, which was formed in 1846 in an atmosphere of revivalistic fervour with the object of transcending such conflicts, but in practice found its appeal limited by the mutual suspicions of Church and Dissent in England, and the Church of Scotland and the Free Church north of the Border. Among social issues, evangelical initiatives on education were particularly prone to disruption on this basis, because contact with youth seemed all-important in relation to the long-term influence of religious groups. Thus in 1843 a promising initiative for education in the factories foundered in parliament in the face of Dissenting objections, and as late as the first decade of the twentieth century much Nonconformist energy was committed to resisting the allegedly pro-Anglican (and pro-Roman Catholic) provisions of the 1902 Education Act.

Fourth, evangelicalism never existed in a vacuum and its adherents were always likely to be pushed in divergent directions by their other beliefs and attitudes. Thus in the mid-nineteenth century there were significant differences between those evangelicals whose frame of mind was still shaped by the legacy of the Enlightenment, and those who had acquired a more Romantic sensibility. Social class and locality could also contribute to very different attitudes among those subscribing to broadly similar theological positions: the inhabitant of a Highland croft was likely to see the world in a very different light from fellow-evangelicals in Lancashire cotton mills, let alone those in English country houses. In the twentieth century there have often been divisions on party-political lines, with evangelicals being found in all the three major parties.

Has the effectiveness of evangelical social involvement been limited by these internal divisions? In relation to its political impact in the nineteenth century it probably was handicapped in that way, because when parliamentary parties were fluid, by present-day standards, a united cross-party pressure group had great potential for influence. This was demonstrated over the slavery issue. On the other hand in the twentieth century it is improbable that a free-standing evangelical grouping could have enjoyed a more than marginal influence, whereas the impact of an evangelical presence across the political spectrum may have been intangible, but was by no means negligible. Such at least is the conclusion suggested by the experience of the Keep Sunday Special campaign in the 1980s, when evangelicals were the connecting link between residual Tory social traditionalism and trade union concerns over hours of work. At the local level moreover there were occasions, not least in the educational sphere in the Victorian era, when competition between evangelical groups had a salutary effect in enhancing the provision that was made. On the other hand this rivalry could go too far: some of the problems of twentieth-century evangelicalism stemmed from its cumbersome inheritance of building plant and social institutions from the Victorian era. This led to duplicated investment of human and financial resources at a period when these were no longer so lavishly available. Nevertheless, whether or not united evangelical action was desirable, the evidence of the last two centuries has been that it has seldom been attainable. It may well be that one of the most important 'lessons of history' for present-day evangelicalism is of the need to be at ease with its own internal diversity, never more evident than when social and political questions are addressed.

A long-term view also points to the dangers of giving an absolute and lasting importance to responses to circumstances which have since changed beyond recognition. For example, early nineteenth-century modes of parliamentary action are hardly appropriate in the very different political circumstances of late twentieth-century Britain. The Victorian evangelical conviction that 'a woman's place is in the home' has to be set in the context of the appalling exploitation and excessive hours to which women were subjected in the early industrial economy, and should not be regarded as a prescription automatically applicable in the working and social conditions of a later age.

There is also encouragement to be drawn from the past for those whose endeavours in the present may appear slow to bear fruit. Mid-nineteenth-century evangelical endeavour on the basis of the free market and voluntary association might have appeared something of a blind alley by the 1920s; in the 1980s and 1990s it seemed once again to have substantial contemporary relevance. At the same time in the ideological disorientation of left-of-centre politics following the collapse of communism, the Christian Socialist tradition, to which evangelicals made a substantial contribution, began to attract renewed attention. Such trends suggest considerable potential for evangelical engagement with the world; they also raise the spectre of partisan and tendentious interpretations. If there is to be a clear and viable future for evangelical social involvement in the twenty-first century, there must also be a critical engagement with the past in all its perplexing diversity and richness.

Notes

1 George Eliot, ed. David Lodge, *Scenes of Clerical Life* (Harmondsworth: Penguin, 1973), p. 320.

2 See for example Doreen Rosman, *Evangelicals and Culture* (Croom Helm, 1984); Leonore Davidoff and Catherine Hall, *Family Fortunes: Men and Women of the English Middle Class 1780–1850* (Hutchinson, 1987); Boyd Hilton, *The Age of Atonement: the Influence of Evangelicalism on Social and Economic Thought* (Oxford: Clarendon Press, 1988); D. W. Bebbington, *Evangelicalism in Modern Britain: A History from the 1730s to the 1980s* (Unwin Hyman, 1989); G. A. Rawlyk and M. A. Noll, eds, *Amazing Grace: Evangelicalism in Australia, Britain, Canada and the United States* (Grand Rapids and Montreal: Baker Books and McGill-Queen's UP, 1993); M. A. Noll, D. W. Bebbington and G. A. Rawlyk, eds, *Evangelicalism: Comparative Studies of Popular Protestantism in North America, the British Isles and Beyond, 1700–1990* (New York: Oxford UP, 1994).

3 For other important recent perspectives on evangelical identity see Derek J. Tidball, *Who are the Evangelicals? Tracing the Roots of the*

Modern   Movements (Marshall Pickering, 1994), and Alister
McGrath, *Evangelicalism and the Future of Christianity* (Hodder and
Stoughton, 1994).

4 Hilton, *Age of Atonement*, p. 3.

5 John Walsh, 'John Wesley and the Community of Goods' in K.
Robbins, ed., *Studies in Church History*, Subsidia 7 (1990), pp. 25–50.
See below, pp. 31–2.

6 For examples see David Luker, 'Revivalism in theory and practice:
the case of Cornish Methodism', *Journal of Ecclesiastical History*, 37
(1986), pp. 603–19.

7 William Wilberforce, ed. Vincent Edmunds, *Real Christianity*
(Hodder and Stoughton, 1989), pp. 148–9.

8 For variants on this argument see Davidoff and Hall, *Family Fortunes*;
Hilton, *Age of Atonement* and Ian Bradley, *The Call to Seriousness: The
Evangelical Impact on the Victorians* (Jonathan Cape, 1976).

9 Quoted Geoffrey B. A. M. Finlayson, *The Seventh Earl of Shaftesbury
1801–1885* (Eyre Methuen, 1981), p. 184.

Chapter One

Evangelicalism and Reform, c.1780–1832

DAVID HEMPTON

The generation overshadowed by the French Revolution was the most important generation in the modern history not only of English religion, but of most of the Christian world. For the Revolution altered forever the terms on which religious establishments, the chief device on which the nations of the West had relied for christianising the people, must work.[1]

This generation also witnessed the unprecedented growth of evangelical religion in the British Isles and North America which had the unintended effect of refashioning the old denominational orders in both places.[2] Indeed so dramatic was the impact of evangelicalism on the shaping of British society that historians have quite rightly tried to make connections between its growth and other major social, political and cultural changes that took place at the same time.[3]

These have often filtered down into popular evangelical interpretations of the past rehearsed in countless sermons and popular histories. As every evangelical schoolboy/girl knows, Methodism saved England from revolution; the Clapham Sect, with William Wilberforce to the fore, secured the end of the slave trade and of colonial slavery; evangelical sobriety cleaned up a dissolute nation and contributed the work discipline and moral earnestness which lay at the heart of England's 'greatness' in the Victorian period; and evangelicalism supplied the religious zeal which fought back the secularizing dynamics of

17

the eighteenth-century Enlightenment and secured the central place of religion in British society until at least the First World War. Historians, of course, take great pleasure in spoiling good stories and the precise role of evangelical religion in each of these areas has been the subject of constant revision and modification as historical techniques have become ever more sophisticated. In general this has resulted in less attention being paid to the heroic careers of evangelical leaders and rather more to the relationship between evangelicalism and other profound structural and cultural changes in early industrial Britain.[4] Nowhere has this tendency been more marked than in the rapidly changing historiography of the anti-slavery agitation.

The importance of this movement should not be under-estimated. More people signed petitions against slavery in the fifty years after 1785 than for any other single issue in British politics including the extension of the suffrage or the reform of Parliament.[5] Indeed the style and techniques of the anti-slavery agitation, from mass petitioning to the extraction of pledges from parliamentary candidates, served as models for subsequent religio-political crusades mounted by evangelical Nonconformists in the nineteenth century.[6] Historians are in general agreement that the remarkable growth of evangelicalism and the simultaneous growth of mass abolitionist sentiments in British society must be linked in some way, but the questions are how and how much?

The traditional evangelical interpretation, dating back to Thomas Clarkson's first narrative of the abolitionist movement in 1808, is based on the activities of an influential group of evangelical parliamentarians and philanthropists who overcame the vested interests of the powerful West Indian lobby and secured a great humanitarian victory.[7] More refined interpretations emphasizing the central role of evangelical religion in the abolition of slavery have still not lost their influence despite the arguments of those who prefer to locate abolitionist success within the economic framework of free market capitalism or within the political framework of advancing liberalism.[8] For example, perhaps the most distinguished historian of British abolitionism, Roger Anstey, laid great emphasis on the conjunction of the Enlightenment and the evangelical concern for

liberty, benevolence and happiness. Evangelical theology, with
its dynamic emphasis on providence, redemption and Christian
freedom, could, with equal legitimacy, be directed against the
spiritual bondage of sin *and* the physical bondage of slavery. 'In
the very warp and woof of Evangelical faith', he wrote, 'slavery,
of all social evils, stood particularly condemned, and because
slavery and freedom represented the externalization of the polar
opposites of the Evangelicals' inmost spiritual experience, they
were impelled to act in the cause of abolition with a zeal and a
perseverance which other men could rarely match.'[9] In an even
more vigorous attempt to emphasize the moral and religious
components of the anti-slavery agitation, as opposed to the
political and economic, it has been suggested that 'the "vitality"
of the Anti-Slavery Movement and its ultimate success can be
viewed in the perspective of its evangelical dynamic'.[10] For the
evangelical critics of slavery, the sins of a guilty nation could
only be expiated, and the wrath of an angry God could only
be averted, by the dedicated and unremitting actions of the
faithful.

Explaining the success of the anti-slavery agitation in terms
of its 'evangelical dynamic' is not without its problems however.
Not only were many evangelicals not abolitionists, including
the majority of those who lived in the southern states of the
USA, but it is clear that the mass mobilization of anti-slavery
sentiment in Britain extended far beyond the evangelical constituency. It was also viewed with some unease by some of the
more politically conservative evangelicals who feared popular
disorder almost as much as they hated slavery. Wilberforce was
uneasy about mass petitioning in the late 1780s, and even as
late as 1833 the Wesleyan Methodist leader, Jabez Bunting,
wrote that 'I decidedly think that the holy cause of Anti-Slavery
has already been disgraced and prejudiced in some quarters by
the system of "agitation", after the fashion of Irish Papists and
Repealers, which has been employed to promote it. The wrath
of man worketh not the righteousness of God.'[11]

Extensive research on the mobilization of public opinion
against slavery, including the ubiquitous petitions, has confirmed the importance of popular evangelicalism to the anti-
slavery agitation, but it has also shown that evangelicalism, of
itself, did not create mass mobilization; rather abolitionism

proliferated in the same ideological and political context which
was also favourable to evangelical Nonconformity.[12] In short,
abolitionism attracted the support not only of the evangelical
middle classes who had an economic as well as a religious
interest in abolition, but also appealed to the urban artisans as
part of a wider political protest against paternalism and depen-
dency in the early industrial revolution. *Both* abolitionism and
popular evangelicalism thrived in the kinds of urban communities that emerged in the early stages of industrial growth and
they shared some similar characteristics. Both were attacked
for undermining traditional authority in church and state in
the period of the French Revolution; both were based on voluntary associations and made extensive use of touring lecturers
(itinerant preachers) and popular print (religious tracts); both
led to enlarged spheres of action for women and sometimes
children; and both were capable of appealing to different social
strata and of creating communities in which moral/religious
values were treated seriously. But evangelicalism had also
something distinctive to bring to the anti-slavery movement.
The dramatic expansion of overseas missions in the first third
of the nineteenth century helped narrow the geographical and
psychological gap between social realities in Britain and the
colonies which some have argued was an essential precondition
of a genuinely popular mobilization against slavery. Problems
of mission, including the ignorance of slaves and the preaching
restrictions imposed by planters, began to occupy more space
in religious periodicals in the 1820s. Tales of imprisoned
missionaries and of persecuted slave converts added emotional
intensity to the annual meetings of the missionary societies.
Richard Watson told the anniversary gathering of the Wesleyan
Missionary Society in 1830 that overseas missions had increased 'our sympathies with the external circumstances of the
oppressed and miserable of all lands. It is impossible for men
to care for the souls of others without caring for their bodies
also. . . . We cannot care for the salvation of the negro, without
caring for his emancipation from bondage.'[13]

   Although the most important early impulses of anti-slavery
sentiment in Britain are to be located within the ranks of the
Anglican evangelicals of Clapham, the Quakers, and some of
Wesley's followers, it was not until the 1820s that the anti-

slavery movement enjoyed the mass support of an increasingly powerful evangelical Nonconformity. The fact that this support was enlarged still further by a radical libertarian strand of politics among the British working classes made the anti-slavery movement a force to be reckoned with by the early 1830s. In that sense the abolition of slavery in British colonies was neither an economic necessity whose time had come nor a disinterested political gesture from an established political élite, but was, to a considerable extent, a victory for new religious and political forces unleashed both by evangelical enthusiasm and by the structural changes in British society in the period of the industrial revolution.

The relationship between those structural changes – on a much wider canvass than mere anti-slavery sentiment – and the rise and influence of evangelical religion, is one of the most bitterly contested and largely unresolved debates in modern British history. To a remarkable extent the great French historian, Elie Halévy, set an agenda at the beginning of the twentieth century which, for good and for ill, has cast a powerful intellectual spell over the subsequent writing of the history of popular evangelicalism. According to Halévy, early industrial England, by comparison with its European neighbours, possessed an unusual and potentially volatile degree of political, economic and religious freedom. In Europe's most advanced capitalist country dynamic forces of anarchy and social revolution were moderated and re-directed by a remarkable resurgence of puritanism in the shape of the evangelical revival. Methodism was thus the antidote to the revolutionary Jacobinism that undermined the *ancien régime* in France, and 'the free organisation of the sects was the foundation of social order in England.'[14]

Halévy believed that evangelicalism, for all its popular idiosyncrasies and bourgeois hypocrisy, was the chief engine in the creation of a free and ordered society based on widely accepted notions of 'voluntary obedience'. Paradoxical though it may seem, therefore, the freest country in Europe was saved from the frightening consequences of anarchic libertarianism by the fact that its national Established Church 'left the sects outside her borders entire liberty of organization, full power to form a host of little states within the state'. Evangelicalism thus spawned a host of new religious associations, from Methodist societies to pan-evangelical charities, and worked for the reformation of society and its morals, not primarily by legal coercion, but by the power of voluntary effort and religious enthusiasm. In this way English freedoms were secured by the proliferation of communities of grace.

There is now general agreement among historians that Halévy exaggerated both the fragility of England's *ancien régime* and the power of evangelicalism to save it from its inner contradictions. There are nevertheless two things at least worth saving from Halévy's set of hypotheses. The first is the importance of evangelical religion in forging a rough harmony of values between the pragmatic and moralistic middle classes and the skilled and respectable sections of the English working classes who were notorious in Europe for their solid virtue and capacity for organization. The second is Halévy's emphasis on the relative tolerance of the Church of England and the capacity of Methodist groups to separate from the Established Church and from one another in a reasonably ordered and disciplined fashion. But the key here is not so much the libertarian sentiments of the Methodists, nor indeed their lofty principles, as any student of the bitter rivalries associated with such splits will testify, as the profound influence of *legal* frameworks in helping both to articulate religious grievances and to manage their potentially disruptive consequences.[15] What Halévy ascribed to the sole influence of evangelicalism, therefore, may, at least in part, be attributable to earlier traditions of constitutional and legal chauvinism among all sections of the English population. If popular evangelicalism did indeed stabilize early industrial society, part of the reason may be that it was able to exploit and, to benefit from, structures and values that were already in place.[16]

The important issues raised by Halévy, and subsequently expanded by a remarkably talented group of Marxist historians, have not gone away.[17] Since the Second World War a number of significant attempts have been made to construct alternative narratives of the role of popular evangelicalism in the age of the French and industrial revolutions. Although different in their presuppositions, scope and methods, many of these accounts contain some shared conclusions. One of the most influential came from the pen of Victor Kiernan in the first issue of *Past and Present* in 1952 in which he suggested that

> two conceptions of religion were living in England side by side, and the French Revolution compelled a choice between them. One was of religion as the formulary of an established society, its statement of faith in itself; the other as a catastrophic conversion of the individual, a miraculous shaking off of secret burdens. One was fixed on this world, the other on the next.[18]

Since the Established Church was 'too worm-eaten with patronage and pluralism' to meet the new challenges, Kiernan states that it was left to the evangelicals to forge the kind of changes in English society which led first of all to a greater emphasis on the individual and then eventually to a peculiarly English variety of liberalism.

A similar conclusion, via a different route, was reached twenty years later by Bernard Semmel in his book *The Methodist Revolution* in which John Wesley and the Methodists are portrayed as popular religious embodiments of Enlightenment liberalism.[19] Far from the irrational enthusiast of Anglican mythology, John Wesley was a man of the Enlightenment in his concern for religious toleration, his hatred of persecution and violence, his desire that all men should be saved (not just the Calvinist elect), his strenuous advocacy of the abolition of slavery, and his doctrines of perfection and assurance which could be seen as theological expressions of Enlightenment optimism and empiricism. Even conversion and an austere lifestyle can be given an enlightened gloss by using the more liberal concepts of freedom of choice and self-improvement through the exercise of personal discipline. In this way Methodism may be seen as England's democratic revolution in the age of democratic revolutions, because it brought to masses of men and women a new individual liberty to decide their own faith and destiny. Semmel concludes, therefore, that Methodism was an essential element of England's transition from a 'traditional' society, characterized by collective behaviour under authority, to a modern democracy based on religious toleration and individual freedom. The consequences of this were 'the most characteristic qualities of nineteenth-century England – its

relative stability, its ordered freedom, and its sense of world
mission.'

Twenty years after Semmel, Alan Gilbert, in the most recent
contribution to this old debate, takes the view that the moral
economy within evangelical chapel communities and the
moderate radicalism of many Methodist artisans helped to take
the heat out of potentially bitter class conflict and acted as 'a
political "safety valve" for the pressures of early industrial
politics'.[20] Moreover, Gilbert, whose earlier work was distinguished by its solid reliance on the statistics of religious
adherence in industrial Britain, suggests that there were in fact
sufficient numbers of Methodists and evangelical dissenters
among the urban artisan population to make a decisive difference to the characteristics of popular politics in potentially
disaffected parts of the country.

What all of these approaches have in common, therefore, is
the conviction that the growth of popular evangelicalism did
indeed make a fundamental difference to the political stability
of early industrial England and that English society was less
violent and inflexible and more ordered and disciplined than
otherwise would have been the case. Conversely, what they all
lack, it seems to me, is a convincing grasp of the social and
political milieu of chapel communities in the crucial period
1790–1850 and a sense of the eclectic prejudices and enthusiasms that shaped local religious and political conflicts. The
issues that aroused the most intense passions were not always
to do with class conflict, parliamentary reform and the extension of the suffrage.[21] Whenever chapel communities roused
themselves to political action in this period they were as much
concerned with protecting itinerant preaching, abolishing
slavery, resisting Catholic emancipation, eroding Anglican privileges, establishing elementary education and reforming morals
as they were with the 'radical' demands of working-class political leaders many of whom treated the religious enthusiasm of
the evangelical variety with the utmost contempt. Moreover,
even within the chapel communities themselves, conflicts over
who controlled the preachers, the Sunday schools, the conduct
of revivals and the style of worship occasioned as much heat as
the more familiar political problems investigated by historians.[22] Many of these issues were of course overlaid by elements

of class and cultural conflict, but the precise relationship between them is deserving of more sensitive treatment than is permitted in some studies devoted more to the history of the Halévy thesis as an historical hypothesis than to the history of evangelicalism as a popular religious movement.[23] The danger of this approach is that the religious motivation, enthusiasm and objectives of the faithful are conveniently etherized in order to move on to the 'big' questions of assessing the cultural and political impact of apparently monochrome religious movements. It is not clear to me, however, that the second stage of this analysis can be accomplished with any degree of conviction without some appreciation of the importance of religious experience in the lives of the 'revived'.[24] It is to the credit of Methodism's most controversial historian, E. P. Thompson, that although his Marxist presuppositions did not allow for a particularly insightful treatment of the nature of evangelical religious experience, he was in no doubt that the task had at least to be attempted.

The complexity of the early history of evangelicalism should nevertheless not preclude serious attempts to advance a coherent interpretation of its social and political influence. The starting point has to be a proper grasp of the sheer variety of the eighteenth-century evangelical revival, in terms of geography, theology, denomination and social class. Even within one of its most powerful traditions, that of Methodism, John Wesley's famed empiricism (perhaps the most important of all the defining non-theological elements of early evangelicalism) threw up different patterns in different places at different times. The varied sources of Wesley's inspiration and the

> very varied contexts into which Methodism found its way are crucial to the understanding of the man and his movement; for they intensified as nothing else could have done the empiricism which he absorbed from the Enlightenment. Single-model accounts of Methodism . . . ignore the breadth of its origins and the breadth of the problems it encountered.[25]

Comparative studies of Methodist growth rates in different parts of the North Atlantic world in the early nineteenth century nevertheless suggest that, however diverse the Methodist

experience might have been from region to region and from
country to country, Methodism generally made its fastest gains
in expanding societies where traditional patterns of religious
and social control were under the most serious threat.[26] This
was true of England where a fatal combination of major
structural and demographic changes on the one hand and the
profound impact of the French Revolution on the other seriously eroded the capacity of the Established Church to retain
its role as the chief instrument for Christianizing the poor.
English society being what it was, therefore, the crisis of
authority at the end of the eighteenth century occurred more
dramatically in the organization of religion than in the organization of the state. From this perspective it is possible to view
the remarkable growth of Methodism, Sunday schools, and
county associations for promoting itinerant evangelism, as
radical religious challenges to the paternalistic Anglican establishment. As against traditional Marxist interpretations of the
social impact of popular religion, therefore, evangelicalism in
early industrial England may be more appropriately interpreted
as a religious expression of radicalism than as an opiate substitute for it. Largely undenominational religious associations
eroded the religious control of the Established Church, not by
the political means which the Church had always feared, but
through the cottage prayer meetings and itinerant preaching of
an increasingly mobilized laity.[27]

The litmus test of what had been achieved in the twenty
years after the French Revolution came in 1811 when Lord
Sidmouth, under pressure from Anglican bishops, decided to
introduce a bill in the House of Lords to restrict itinerant
preaching. The aim of the bill was to limit the supply of preaching certificates by insisting that every Dissenting minister be
attached to a specific congregation, and by stating that each
preacher required written testimonials from 'substantial and
reputable householders belonging to the said congregation'.[28]
The purpose of the measure was not to cripple Dissent, but
to control the itinerant preaching of those considered too
ignorant, too young or too dangerous to be allowed to travel
the country peddling their own religious convictions. Although
designed in part merely to prevent Dissenting preachers from
claiming exemption from civil office and military service, the

bill struck at the heart of undenominational itinerant preaching and the entire Methodist connexional system. It was also
one of the last great attempts to defend the Church of England
by legislating against its rivals. Revealingly, Churchmen, not
politicians, were the driving force behind the measure.

Sidmouth's Bill was lost without a division because of the
lack of support from Spencer Perceval's government, the political inconvenience of reducing religious toleration for English
Protestant subjects while negotiating for the emancipation of
Irish Catholics, and the quite remarkable organization of
Dissenting and Methodist opposition on a scale unmatched
even by the anti-slavery campaign. The defeat of the bill was not
the end of the matter, however, because it soon became apparent that Justices of the Peace throughout the country were
behaving as if the bill had become law and were refusing to
administer oaths in accordance with the Toleration Act.
Supporters of the Church in the localities were thus achieving
in practice what had eluded Sidmouth in law.[29] The truth of the
matter was that evangelical itinerant preaching and new religious associations had driven a coach and horses through the
Clarendon Code and Toleration Act of the late seventeenth
century and a new toleration act to clear up the debris had
become imperative. With the existing laws in disarray, a new
Toleration Act was duly passed in 1812 guaranteeing the
inalienable right of every citizen to worship God according to
conscience and the right of every person to hear and to teach
religious Christian truths without restraint from the civil magistrates. In return the state was given some protection against
dangerous enthusiasts by the stipulation that no one had the
right to disturb the peace under the pretence of teaching religion. The most hated aspects of the later Stuart legislation
against Dissenters were repealed and magistrates were
required by law to grant preaching certificates on demand.
Ironically, far from restricting itinerant preaching, which had
been Sidmouth's original intention, the Toleration Act of 1812
'conferred extensive protection upon the itinerant preacher
and rendered serious opposition all but impossible'.[30]

It would be a mistake to see the events of 1811 and 1812 as
an interesting, but arcane, exercise in the technical study of
legal history. The furore over Sidmouth's Bill showed beyond

question that evangelical enthusiasm had produced a profound shift of allegiance in the nation as a whole and that the old 'fiction that the Church of England represented the people of England in their religious aspect' was probably less true in 1811–12 than at any point since the Elizabethan period.[31] Religious enthusiasm, through the pluralism it inexorably produced, was thus the unwitting beneficiary of religious toleration and greater liberalism in matters of church and state. Moreover the lessons of 1811–12 were not lost on Methodists and Dissenters. They were persuaded, not altogether accurately as it happens, that organized political pressure had brought its just reward and that English politicians had more or less accepted that a revived Dissent was now so much part of the religious landscape that its legitimate needs could not be ignored indefinitely. Finally, both the Methodist and the Dissenting leaderships, partly out of fear and partly out of self-interest, were prepared to deliver on their own propaganda by quietening, or expelling from their ranks, the politically disaffected multitudes of early industrial England. The Halévy thesis, it seems, can be approached from an almost unlimited range of directions.

There is one further twist to the events of 1811–12 which is worthy of consideration and that is the position adopted by William Wilberforce and many influential Anglican evangelicals who were well disposed neither to uncontrollable ranters (a derogatory term for populist itinerant preachers) nor to legislative restrictions on the further advance of serious religion. Caught between the endorsement of ranterism on the one hand and the possibility of unwelcome state restrictions on the whole evangelical enterprise on the other, it seems that Wilberforce was particularly concerned about the effect of Sidmouth's proposals on the various 'pastoral instructions', from unauthorized lectures to Sunday schools and prayer meetings, which many Anglican Evangelicals had already instituted in their parishes by the early nineteenth century. Wilberforce's negotiations with politicians and other religious leaders at this time show clearly how Anglican evangelicals had to take uncomfortably pragmatic positions in order to defend evangelical pastoral innovations.[32]

So far attention has been concentrated on the relationship

between the growth of popular evangelicalism and other structural changes in English society in the period of the French
and industrial revolutions. The suggestion has been that
whether one looks at the anti-slavery agitation or the growth of
religious pluralism and its relationship to the Halévy thesis,
popular evangelicalism made a powerful contribution to the
erosion of old privileges in Church and state. Some of these
reforming enthusiasms were self-conscious and purposefully
planned for, others were shared symbiotically with other great
reforming forces in early nineteenth-century society, and still
others were essentially unexpected by-products of its own
remarkable growth. But from the evangelicals' own point of
view, as Ford K. Brown's striking list of the 'ten thousand com-
passions' of evangelical philanthropy makes clear, their interest
in reform was directed not primarily to national institutions,
but to the conversion of the irreligious at home and abroad, the
diffusion of religious knowledge and the improvement of morals.
Most typically, their chosen instrument was the creation of
voluntary religious societies (often on a pan-evangelical basis)
to harness subscriptions and to promote their manifold causes.

> There were societies to improve, to enforce, to reform, to
> benefit, to prevent, to relieve, to educate, to reclaim, to en-
> courage, to propagate, to maintain, to promote, to provide
> for, to support, to effect, to better, to instruct, to protect, to
> supersede, to employ, to civilize, to visit, to preserve, to miti-
> gate, to abolish, to investigate, to publish, to aid, to extin-
> guish. Above all there were societies to suppress.[33]

Although the final comment owes as much to Ford K. Brown's
remorseless desire to discredit evangelical social concern (as a
product, in his view, of class-based social manipulation and
immense narrowness of spirit) as it does to the evidence he
presents, it does draw attention to an unattractive moral
majoritarianism in some aspects of evangelical social ethics.[34]
The over-zealous espousal of sabbatarianism among some of the
more ardent evangelicals, for example, led to all sorts of inde-
fensible ambiguities and some unpleasant cases of informing
on neighbours.[35] It was the suppressing side of evangelical
social policy, especially if it seemed that the suppressors were
both richer and less inconvenienced than the suppressed, that

was so pungently attacked by Victorian novelists such as Dickens and Trollope. Literary stereotypes notwithstanding, sabbatarianism is a good example of how evangelical approaches to an apparently straightforward issue varied over time (first generation evangelicals were generally more flexible than those who came later), among different social classes (it was a more popular cause among the middle classes than among the working classes), between Anglicans and Nonconformists (the latter were generally more uneasy about state-enforced morals than the former), and about the best tactics to employ to achieve the most satisfactory goals (between the 'principled' and the 'pragmatic').[36]

There is still one further layer of complexity, because evidence is emerging that among the army of lay visitors and evangelists sponsored by evangelical voluntary societies to convert the urban poor in industrial Britain, there were at least some who were less rigorous in the application of evangelical standards on the ground than is apparent in the official reports. First-hand experience of the sheer destitution of many urban dwellers and of how profoundly their religious opinions differed from those prescribed by evangelical orthodoxy persuaded some city missionaries either to give up altogether or to reflect more seriously on the complex causes of poverty and irreligion.[37] Compassion and self-sacrificial charity were not as absent from the evangelical mission as readers of Dickens might imagine. What is striking about the urban mission, however, is how difficult it was for evangelical missionaries to counter the inherent pelagianism of the British working classes (true religion was generally equated with 'good living' and decency) with high notions of grace, and conversely, how difficult it was for evangelicals to promote rigorous standards of discipline and sobriety (including temperance and sabbatarianism) among those who saw no harm in popular amusements.[38] With the evangelical doctrine of grace regarded as unfair (since the wicked benefited even more than the decent) and evangelical sobriety as unattractive, it is scarcely surprising that the conversion figures achieved by evangelical urban missions, though impressive by modern standards, repeatedly disappointed the aspirations of the missionaries themselves.

A similar lack of congruence between intention and result

has been amplified by the ongoing debates about the social and economic consequences of evangelical growth in the early industrial revolution. Most interpretations, such as the immensely influential book by E. P. Thompson, *The Making of the English Working Class*, have concentrated on the economic implications of Methodist belief and practice. In particular, they have drawn attention to John Wesley's emphasis on thrift and hard work. 'Without industry', he wrote, 'we are neither fit for this world, nor for the world to come.' Hence it is suggested that Methodist discipline and acquisitiveness were perfectly suited to the early development of industrial capitalism. Wesley and his followers are thus portrayed as exemplars of the Protestant ethic, and the 'transforming power of the cross', according to Thompson, is nothing more than the religious/psychological mechanism by which English labourers were 'methodized' and 'adapted to the discipline of the machine'.[39] Whatever the merits of this argument for the Methodist movement as a whole during the industrial revolution, it will not do for Wesley's own teaching, which was scarcely a model of acquisitive capitalism.[40] After providing for necessities Methodists were urged by Wesley to give away the rest otherwise they would be guilty of robbing God and the poor, corrupting their own souls, wronging the widow and the fatherless and making themselves 'accountable for all the want, affliction, and distress which they may, but do not remove'.[41] In addition, Wesley told his followers to think nothing of the future, to demand no more than a fair price and to make sure that excessive wealth was not passed on to their children.

There is yet another dimension to Wesley's economic opinions and that is his interest in the economic organization of the primitive church and its attempt to practice the community of goods. In contrast to conventional Anglican teaching, he did not think that such practices were of necessity confined to the apostolic period, though he was realistic enough to recognize that material altruism was doomed unless it was based on Christian love and fellowship of the highest quality. As with much of his economic teaching, Wesley found that persistent human acquisitiveness was against him and he was forced to retreat into the medieval solution of voluntary poverty for a self-denying spiritual élite. Even so his sermons never lost their

anti-materialistic bite – at times close to desperation – as he
viewed with dismay the first fruits of Methodism's upward
social mobility.[42]

Wesley's rigorous teaching to his followers on the spiritual
dangers of acquisitiveness and conspicuous consumption was
carried over into his more general attitudes to economy and
society in later eighteenth-century England. In his *Thoughts on
the Present Discontents*, for example, Wesley blamed the country's economic ills on luxury, waste, engrossing, distilling and
unnecessary taxes. With opinions based more on biblical insights
and empirical observations than on a coherent economic theory, Wesley's pamphlet is a thinly-veiled attack on what Edward
Thompson has himself called the 'theatrical materialism' of the
rich. Horses and carriages, useless pensions, extravagant waste
and an insatiable thirst for luxury are all condemned at a time
when 'thousands of people throughout the land are perishing
for want of food'.[43] Wesley also repudiated Adam Smith's view
that surplus accumulation was the basis for economic well-
being. Wesley's intensely ethical and biblicist stance, combined
with a settled conviction that all great spiritual movements
surged from the poor, left little room for complacency among
his followers, but obedience to his wishes inexorably gave way
to evasion and then to accommodation.

E. P. Thompson, whose recent death has robbed us of one of
Britain's greatest ever social historians, has been criticized for
assuming that the social groups he deals with have 'a unanim-
ity of conceptualization' which has the effect of underplaying
their internal diversity and complexity.[44] This is certainly evident in his treatment of Methodism during the industrial
revolution. A dynamic and socially diverse movement cannot
be reduced to a single cohesive theory about religion and the
emergence of industrial capitalism without diminishing the
complexity of human motivation on the one hand and the sheer
variety of popular evangelicalism (including its rural expressions) on the other. As with the other issues we have investigated, from the anti-slavery agitation to the Halévy thesis, and
from the rise of religious pluralism to the growth of toleration,
evangelical social and economic influence often flowed in
unexpected tributaries to unpredictable destinations. A movement which emphasized both the supremacy of grace and the

need for self-improvement and which numbered aristocrats and labourers within its ranks, is not amenable to single-model analyses, however sophisticated they may be in conception. What one can say with certainty, however, is that the conversionist zeal, moral discipline and social concern of countless thousands of evangelicals of all social ranks made early industrial British society more stable, more humane and more religious than it otherwise would have been. What religious establishments by their very nature could not secure unaided was therefore partly achieved by an unparalleled upsurge in evangelical religious associations. There was of course a price to be paid in terms of the sheer vulgarity, arrogance and hypocrisy of some evangelical religion which was ruthlessly and unforgettably exposed by some of England's finest Victorian novelists.[45] But the price that might have been paid without the manifold fruits of evangelical enthusiasm in early industrial England, as is the way with all counter-factual propositions, may only be conjectured.[46]

Notes

1 W. R. Ward, *Religion and Society in England 1790–1850* (Batsford, 1972), p. 1.
2 See for example Mark A. Noll, *A History of Christianity in the United States and Canada* (Grand Rapids: Eerdmans, 1992); R. Currie, A. Gilbert and L. Horsley, *Churches and Churchgoers: Patterns of Church Growth in the British Isles since 1700* (Oxford: Clarendon Press, 1977); and the essays in M. A. Noll, D. W. Bebbington and G. Rawlyk eds, *Evangelicalism* (Oxford UP, 1994).
3 E. P. Thompson, *The Making of the English Working Class*, (Harmondsworth: Penguin, 1968); G. W. Olsen, *Religion and Revolution in Early Industrial England* (Lanham, MD: University Press of America, 1990).
4 A. D. Gilbert, *Religion and Society in Industrial England: Church, Chapel and Social Change 1740–1914* (Longman, 1976).
5 Seymour Drescher, 'Public opinion and the destruction of British colonial slavery', in James Walvin, ed., *Slavery and British Society 1776–1846* (Macmillan, 1982), pp. 22–48.
6 D. A. Hamer, *The Politics of Electoral Pressure* (Hassocks, Sussex: Harvester Press, 1977); D. W. Bebbington, *The Nonconformist Conscience* (George Allen & Unwin, 1982).

7 Thomas Clarkson, *The History of the Rise, Progress and Accomplishment of the Abolition of the African Slave Trade by the British Parliament* (2 vols, London, 1808).

8 The various historiographical traditions are well described by Seymour Drescher, *Capitalism and Anti-Slavery: British Mobilization in Comparative Perspective* (Oxford UP, 1987), pp. 1–24.

9 Roger Anstey, *The Atlantic Slave Trade and British Abolition 1760–1810* (Atlantic Highlands, NJ: Humanities Press, 1975), p. 406.

10 Edith F. Hurwitz, *Politics and the Public Conscience: Slave Emancipation and the Abolitionist Movement in Britain* (George Allen & Unwin, 1973), p. 15.

11 W. R. Ward, *Early Victorian Methodism: the Correspondence of Jabez Bunting, 1830–58* (Oxford UP, 1976), p. 29.

12 Drescher, *Capitalism and Anti-Slavery*.

13 Quoted by Roger Anstey in 'Religion and British slave emancipation', David Eltis and James Walvin, eds, *The Abolition of the Atlantic Slave Trade* (Madison, Wisconsin, 1981), p. 47. For a wider interpretation of Methodism and anti-slavery see David Hempton, *Methodism and Politics in British Society 1750–1850* (Hutchinson, 1984), pp. 208–16.

14 See Elie Halévy, *The Birth of Methodism in England*, trans. B. Semmel (University of Chicago Press, 1971) and *England in 1815*, vol. 1 of his *A History of the English People in the Nineteenth Century* (Ernest Benn, 1961).

15 Hempton, *Methodism and Politics*, ch. 2.

16 What this brief discussion of the Halévy thesis has done is to confirm the validity of David Bebbington's clearly expressed view that evangelicalism, as one would expect, both shaped and was shaped by the culture in which it took root (D. W. Bebbington, *Evangelicalism in Modern Britain* (Unwin Hyman, 1989)). Separating cause from effect, if it must be done at all, is however a difficult business for the historian, especially perhaps for the historian of religion, and ought to signal the amber light of caution to those who feel drawn to the sublime convenience of grand theories. Nowhere has this difficulty been more clearly drawn out than in the controversies surrounding Boyd Hilton's immensely erudite attempt to show the importance of evangelical theology in helping to disseminate ideas of free trade in early nineteenth-century Britain (*The Age of Atonement*, Oxford: Clarendon Press, 1988). While Hilton himself is genuinely unsure if religious changes preceded social ones or vice versa, some of his most stringent critics remain unconvinced that evangelicalism influenced economic thought more than economic thought influenced evangelicalism. See the review by Norman Gash in *The English Historical Review* (January, 1989), pp. 136–40; and D. W. Bebbington, 'Religion and society in the nineteenth century', *The Historical Journal*, 32 no. 4 (1989), pp. 997–1004.

17 See E. P. Thompson, *The Making of the English Working Class* and
    Eric Hobsbawm, 'Methodism and the Threat of Revolution in
    Britain', *History Today* (1957).
18 V. Kiernan, 'Evangelicalism and the French Revolution', *Past and
    Present*, no. 1, pp. 44–56.
19 Bernard Semmel, *The Methodist Revolution* (New York: Basic Books,
    1973).
20 Alan D. Gilbert, 'Religion and political stability in early industrial
    England', in Patrick O'Brien and Roland Quinault, eds, *The
    Industrial Revolution and British Society* (Cambridge UP, 1993), pp.
    79–99.
21 J. C. D. Clark, *English Society 1688–1832* (Cambridge UP, 1985).
22 W. R. Ward, 'The religion of the people and the problem of control,
    1790–1850', *Studies in Church History*, 8 (1972), pp. 237–57.
23 For good examples see D. A. Gowland, *Methodist Secessions: The
    Origins of Free Methodism in Three Lancashire Towns* (Manchester UP,
    1979) and David Colin Dews, 'Methodism in Leeds from 1791 to
    1861', 2 vols (unpublished M.Phil. thesis, University of Bradford,
    1984).
24 An important exception is J. S. Werner, *The Primitive Methodist
    Connexion* (Madison: University of Wisconsin Press, 1984).
25 W. R. Ward, 'The Evangelical Revival in eighteenth-century Britain',
    in Sheridan Gilley and W. J. Sheils, eds, *A History of Religion in
    Britain* (Oxford: Blackwell, 1994), pp. 252–72.
26 See for example Richard Carwardine, *Trans-Atlantic Revivalism:
    Popular Evangelicalism in Britain and America 1790–1865* (Westport,
    CT: Greenwood Press, 1978) and Mark A. Noll, 'Revolution and
    the rise of Evangelical social influence in North Atlantic societies',
    in Noll, Bebbington and Rawlyk, eds, *Evangelicalism*, pp. 113–36.
27 See W. R. Ward, 'Revival and class conflict in early nineteenth-centu-
    ry Britain', in Ulrich Gäbler and Peter Schram, eds, *Erweckung am
    Beginn des 19. Jahrhunderts* (Free University of Amsterdam, 1986),
    pp. 87–104; Deborah Valenze, *Prophetic Sons and Daughters: Female
    Preaching and Popular Religion in Industrial England* (Princeton UP,
    1985); and Julia Stewart Werner, *The Primitive Methodist Connexion:
    Its Background and Early History* (Madison: University of Wisconsin
    Press, 1984).
28 For the complex negotiations surrounding Sidmouth's Bill see
    Deryck W. Lovegrove, *Established Church, Sectarian People: Itinerancy
    and the Transformation of English Dissent 1780–1830* (Cambridge UP,
    1988); and David Hempton, 'Thomas Allan and Methodist politics
    1790–1840', *History*, 67 no. 219 (1982), pp. 13–31.
29 David Hempton, 'Methodism and the law, 1740–1820', *Bulletin of
    the John Rylands University Library of Manchester*, 70 no. 3 (1988),
    pp. 93–107.
30 Lovegrove, *Established Church, Sectarian People*, p. 141.

31 Norman Gash, 'The crisis of the Anglican Establishment in the early
    nineteenth century' in his *Pillars of Government* (Edward Arnold,
    1986), p. 19.
32 Ford K. Brown, *Fathers of the Victorians* (Cambridge UP, 1961), pp.
    285–8.
33 Brown, *Fathers*, p.328.
34 For rather more favourable accounts of evangelical social concern in
    this period see E. M. Howse, *Saints in Politics* (University of Toronto
    Press, 1952); Kathleen Heasman, *Evangelicals in Action* (Geoffrey
    Bles, 1962); and Kenneth Hylson-Smith, *Evangelicals in the Church
    of England 1734–1984* (Edinburgh: T. & T. Clark, 1988).
35 See for example P. D. Stubley, 'Serious religion and the improvement
    of public manners: the scope and limitations of Evangelicalism in
    Hull 1770–1914' (unpublished Ph.D thesis, University of Durham,
    1991).
36 John Wigley, *The Rise and Fall of the Victorian Sunday* (Manchester
    UP, 1980).
37 See J. A. Burdett, 'A Study of the Relationship between Evangelical
    Urban Missionaries and the Working Class Poor in Birmingham,
    Norwich and Edinburgh, c.1830–1860', (M.Phil. thesis, University
    of Birmingham, 1994); and Donald Lewis, *Lighten their Darkness:
    The Evangelical Mission to Working-Class London, 1828–1860* (West-
    port Connecticut: Greenwood Press, 1986).
38 For the content of the popular religion of the urban poor see David
    Hempton, 'Popular Religion 1800–1986' in T. Thomas, ed., *The
    British: Their Religious Beliefs and Practices 1800–1986* (Routledge,
    1988). For a more recent, and in some respects a more sophisticat-
    ed treatment, see S. C. Williams, 'Religious Belief and Popular
    Culture: A Study of the South London Borough of Southwark c.
    1880–1939', (unpublished D.Phil. thesis, University of Oxford,
    1993).
39 Thompson, *The Making of the English Working Class*, pp. 397–8. I deal
    with this issue more comprehensively in 'Motives, methods and mar-
    gins in Methodism's Age of Expansion', *Proceedings of the Wesley
    Historical Society*, 49 (October, 1994), pp. 189–207.
40 Wellman J. Warner, *The Wesleyan Movement in the Industrial Revolution*
    (Longmans, 1930), pp. 136–245; and John Walsh, 'John Wesley and
    the community of goods', in Keith Robbins, ed., *Studies in Church
    History*, Subsidia 7 (Oxford: Blackwell, 1990), pp. 25–50.
41 Warner, *The Wesleyan Movement*, p. 210.
42 A. C. Outler, ed., *The Works of John Wesley*, vols. 1–4 *Sermons*
    (Nashville: Abingdon Press, 1984–5). See especially Sermon on the
    Mount VIII and numbers 50, 87, 108 and 131.
43 John Wesley, *Thoughts on the Present Scarcity of Provisions* (1777),
    Works XI, p. 57.
44 Suzanne Desan, 'Crowds, community and ritual in the work of E. P.

Thompson and Natalie Davis', in Lynn Hunt, ed., *The New Cultural History* (Berkeley: University of California Press, 1989), pp. 47–71.

45 David Hempton, 'Popular religion and irreligion in Victorian fiction' in Tom Dunne, ed., *The Writer as Witness: Literature as Historical Evidence* (Cork UP, 1987), pp. 177–96.

46 See for example the concluding paragraph in Sheridan Gilley '"Official Religion"', in Terence Thomas, ed., *The British: Their Religious Beliefs and Practices 1800–1986* (Routledge, 1988), pp. 19–47.

Chapter Two

'Going about and doing good' Evangelicals and Poverty c.1815–1870

BRIAN DICKEY

Conventional wisdom among historians has long lauded the welfare state. Most scholars reach back to explore its beginnings in the nineteenth century.[1] But, as José Harris has recently argued, this is an idealist liberal interpretation of reality.[2] The later-nineteenth-century theorists, and their scholarly admirers who observed 'the evolution of the British welfare state', wrote with feeling and confidence of the power of the state to promote the common and the individual good. They therefore looked with scorn on that previous generation of the post-Napoleonic war years which had emphasized individuality and the virtues of voluntary group action. Much of that welfare state triumphalism has been linked with Anglican self-congratulation rooted in an incarnationist theology that fitted well with idealist liberalism.[3] A major victim of this powerful combination of intellectual and moral forces has been nineteenth-century evangelicalism. It has been condemned outright for lacking confidence in the state, for lacking social theory of any sort, for relying on mere emotionalism,[4] for unfeeling individualism, and even worse. In particular, R. H. Tawney poured scorn on evangelical trust in market economics and asserted that a corporatist, 'Christian socialism' was the only correct Christian response to economic questions. His hostile assessment is, however, now being contested.[5]

38

This chapter will proceed upon the premise that while
nineteenth-century evangelicals could indeed separate social
action from spiritual religion, they were well aware of the many
connections. What is more, their responses in the field of social
action were intelligently based upon relevant understandings
of social issues and feasible responses. Despite Tawney's claims
that the church had 'stopped thinking', evangelicals *did* have
some worked-out social theories. They *did* have some deliberate
methods. These theories and methods were revealed in a complex range of particular applications. Evangelicals, more than
most other social theorists and practitioners, addressed people
in their individual circumstances. Their faith emphasized personal salvation and the vulnerability of elaborate social organizations to the consequences of human sinfulness. Modern
scholars, deeply influenced by that idealist thinking which so
discounted the directness, pragmatism and particularity of
evangelical philanthropy, have generally failed to appreciate the
importance of their contribution.

As Britain recovered from the twenty-five-year apocalyptic
struggle against the French Revolutionaries and their apotheo-
sis, Napoleon Bonaparte, evangelicals in large numbers continued to go about doing good. But now the justifications and
the methods they would use were clearer, and the benefits of
industrial expansion greatly extended the means available. The
work of the previous generation of philanthropists could now
be taken up and applied with renewed vigour.

In the 1780s, at the close of the first generation of the evangelical revival, John Wesley had urged his followers to establish
'strangers' friend and benevolent societies'. The first was in
London in 1785; by 1789 one was operating in Leeds, another
in Manchester by 1791,[6] and soon in other cities where Wesley's
followers were numerous and respectable. These Wesleyan
societies were evidence of evangelicals responding to poverty,
especially in the growing new towns of the early industrial
revolution. They focused on the outpeople, those in the growing cities lacking direct claims on the basis of settlement to the
statutory benefits of the Poor Laws. They defined their target
group in quite direct biblical terms, drawn from the Old
Testament prophets and Christ's teaching, and they found
their membership base from within the fellowship of
Methodism.

Late Georgian social theory prompted efforts to promote good behaviour among the lower orders. These included William Wilberforce's 'Proclamation Society' (1787), Thomas Bernard's Society for Bettering the Condition and Increasing the Comforts of the Poor, the 'Betterment Society' (1798), followed by the Society for the Suppression of Vice (1802).[7] This campaign for the reformation of manners drew on a wide range of anxious social engineers, by no means all of them evangelical. More obviously evangelical were the new missionary societies. It was in part a response by evangelicals to the outbreak of the war against the French, which prompted some Christians to believe there was but a short time left to evangelize the world before the final armageddon was upon them. A string of societies centred on London were established to promote that evangelistic cause: the Baptist Missionary Society, the London Missionary Society, the British and Foreign Bible Society, the Church Missionary Society, the Religious Tract Society. This surge of associational effort to promote agreed evangelical causes and to manage the threats to established order, laid out an enduring pattern of techniques by which social endeavours among evangelicals would be promoted throughout the nineteenth century.

One inspiration for the form of the public philanthropic society was the eighteenth-century joint stock company, that great engine for corporate economic risk-taking. Other models were the chapel and the local pub as venues for communal action.[8] The public philanthropic society, unlike the charitable trust, meant communal accountability measured each year at the annual meeting. Combined with that was a reliance on the expert labours of secretary and treasurer, and, as often as not, a search for especially prestigious representatives of the ruling class to serve even nominally. The annual reports listed not only the names of the subscriber members (the shareholders), but also gave statistics of throughput, returns of reformed, healed or otherwise saved cases, bringing joy to the subscriber-shareholders in lieu of cash dividends. As the century wore on, the societies became the dominant mode by which philanthropy was expressed. The greatest symbol was Exeter Hall, where from the 1830s so many London-based evangelical charities held their annual meetings before audiences of several thousand respectable supporters. It was as 'chair' of so many of these that the Earl of Shaftesbury confirmed his public reputation in the 1850s and 1860s as the very embodiment of evangelical charitability.[9] What is also noticeable in the field of charity, if not in the area of evangelism, is that these societies generally came to focus not on an exclusive denominational membership, but on an inclusive model. The definitive focus was upon the chosen object of care. The clearest example of this was the transformation of the initially Wesleyan Strangers' Friend Societies. By the 1830s they had become open in their membership to all respectable people who could afford the subscription. In the nineteenth-century phase of evangelicalism, sectarianism was not applied to acts of charity.

This associational model posed an important and well-remembered problem, symbolized forever in that powerfully imagined character, Mrs Jellyby in Charles Dickens's *Bleak House*. Dickens was no friend to evangelicals and his attack on their purported philanthropic hypocrisy lives on in many newspaper articles today. The issue was that a permissive voice and an associational mode required publicity: the great meetings at Exeter Hall were exercises in self-advertisement and fund-raising, using all the prejudices and susceptibilities of mid-nineteenth-century society. Yet surely the Lord taught secrecy in alms-giving? 'Let not your right hand ...' How could these evangelicals be so blatant? What right had they to be so successful in their fund raising! It was an easy and an obvious point for journalists such as Dickens to make. The real alternative, however, was not an increase of private goodness: it was to be the rise of the bureaucratic state in compulsory mode and expensive style. Meanwhile evangelicals pressed on busily, going about and doing good.[10]

Moreover, these good works of charity went forward with increasingly less concern for denominational identity. It was the shared concern to care which itself united the participants, together with the possession of the time and resources necessary, which they might then deploy upon the chosen objects of care, whether these were sick poor in the town, disadvantaged children, those with some specific form of medical need, or whatever. It is important to notice that in this period there is little evidence of a desire to create specifically evangelical forms of corporate philanthropic action. The degree of self-conscious activity signalled by the earlier Wesleyan societies was increasingly believed to be self-defeating, if only because it was more and more obvious that only by combination would the necessary resources be available and action be facilitated in the local community. If the object of care defined the identity of a society, then all who were willing to respond could join in.

There is something of a spectrum here. Those societies which addressed specifically evangelistic causes such as the conversion of Jews or Catholics attracted a predominantly evangelical list of subscribers. When it came to the Ragged School Union, most but not all supporters of this reformative and evangelistic work among children in the slums were evangelicals. But by the time the target group was, for example, the sick poor people of a city, a much wider range of people of good will could agree to work together. Evangelicals focused on the practical task, and so revealed once more their commitment to action.

If method was being refined from the late eighteenth century, motive was becoming more complex in the Victorian era. Wesley's exhortations of the 1780s to care for the stranger were direct and positive. So were William Wilberforce's remarks in his *Practical View* at the end of the century. Hannah More writing from the 1770s onwards conveyed the same assumption that charity was a Christian obligation inherent in serious religion. 'To neglect works of charity, not to be so largely liberal in the performance of them according to our ability, is an infallible evidence that our professions of piety mean nothing.'[11] Any Bible-reading person would find exhortations to 'charity' and to 'doing good' in the New Testament. In the 1830s Michael Thomas Sadler, the Tory evangelical factory reformer, could still assert bluntly that 'We are now called upon strictly to observe the command of the Divine Author of our religion to relieve those who have none to help them.'[12]

Sometimes, however, it was not merely a matter of being helpful in the way Sadler implied. There were also those who spoke of a duty to subordinates with the firm expectation that a reciprocal response of gratified thankfulness would be evoked, thus preventing secular disaster such as had overtaken the French.[13] More generally, the tradition of paternal responsibility, especially among landowners and rural clergy, was strong. It was central to Lord Shaftesbury's engagement in good works. It was not an especially evangelical concept, but one which evangelicals found easy to accept. After all, evangelicals were also likely to possess a firm trust in the present order of society, especially if they were already sharers in its benefits.[14] Here for them was a major cement in society's functioning. Interacting with this expectation that charity had a beneficent impact on social relations were the implications of Parson Malthus's argument that population was growing faster than the capacity of the British economy to produce food and other resources. Unless a more reasonable and restrained pattern of sexual behaviour was adopted by the poor, disaster loomed.

It was through the labours of John Bird Sumner, Bishop of Chester 1828–48, and Archbishop of Canterbury 1848–62, that the postwar generation of evangelicals was instructed in the mysteries of the wealth of nations and the problem of an ever-rising population. This gentle polemicist has received considerable scholarly attention recently as the crucial translator of the arguments of Adam Smith and Thomas Malthus into terms which evangelicals could understand and act upon.[15] Such evangelicals looked to a set of stable moral laws, ordained by divine providence and generating rewards and punishments by which human behaviour might be shaped consistently. The inferences Sumner drew included relying on existing state structures for the management of the problems posed by poverty, together with the sanctions of the market which came upon the immoral and the unthinking as they wasted their money and produced more children. Scarcity was a gift, a challenge, divinely ordained. Inequalities challenged human ingenuity, evoked industry, promoted civilization and discouraged idleness. Sumner had turned the bleak pessimism of Malthus into a celebration of divine wisdom which evangelicals could understand and from which they could draw confidence.

Sumner's thought can be traced through a series of important statements: from his major *Treatise On the Records of Creation* (1816) through to his *Christian Charity: Its Obligations and Objects* (1841). A pattern of developing thought emerges in the writing of this hopeful postmillennialist who saw himself co-operating with God in managing society according to the moral law. His 1816 *Treatise* emphasized the role of the laws of good economic management promoted by Adam Smith. The problem was to avoid a dependent state of indigence while accepting the necessity of wealth differentials and coping with the recklessness of the labouring classes.[16] As a member of the Poor Law Royal Commission of 1832–3, he went so far as to propose the abolition of the Poor Laws altogether as beyond the proper degree of economic intervention allowable for the state. This was Smithian liberalism carried to a very large distance indeed. In the end, however, he accepted the confident bureaucratic assertions of Edwin Chadwick that administrative action could transform the system without producing economic disruption. It was an important concession which permitted the creation of the new order of the Poor Laws of the nineteenth century and moved away from the morally based order that evangelicals sought to promote. The focus in the 'New' Poor Law on rule, on supervision and on economic meaning all went to create a separate system of state-controlled bureaucratically managed aid, increasingly out of the reach of philanthropy.[17]

From the time of the 1833 Poor Law Report, Sumner became more willing to contemplate charitable intervention to resist or at least ameliorate the worst effects of the economy, and even of the Poor Laws, upon the poor. He called in the later 1830s and the 1840s for intelligent but not indiscriminate charity, which could lead the way for new legislation, but continued to emphasize the need for a recognition of 'the divine root from which [benevolent] conduct springs'. Christian charity was born, not of the rules of economic theory or the regulations of the Poor Laws, but of an experience of God's grace and love to a forgiven sinner.[18] Public communal charity was certainly appropriate, indeed still necessary. Sumner participated in any number of charitable activities, both national and local, and it is important to emphasize his increasing willingness to act in practical, philanthropic ways. However, for him the primary task of the church itself remained the provision of increased facilities for worship and spiritual instruction. Christian conversion was the most reliable means of securing a lasting improvement in the social as well as spiritual condition of the individual. He did not, on the other hand, contemplate fundamental change in the structure of society as a whole. Sumner's approach was to set the tone of moderate evangelical responses to poverty for more than a century.[19]

Even more widely acclaimed than Sumner as an evangelical spokesman was Thomas Chalmers, Scottish divine and church statesman. Almost single-handedly he set out by precept and practice to transform the Scottish system of poor relief. He brought from rural Scotland, first to Glasgow and then late in life to Edinburgh, that same suspicion of centralized, compulsory state action – especially the poor rate – which Sumner had imbibed from Adam Smith. For Chalmers the way forward was a somewhat nostalgic recreation of a fully-orbed parish system of preaching and care which engaged the rich and the poor alike. His experiment at St John's, Glasgow, between 1819 and 1823 drew from the rural parish the concepts of regular visitation, day and sabbath schools, and parish poor relief based on voluntary church-door collections and private gifts. Neither a poor rate nor even public charitable societies would serve as well, Chalmers believed, as the face-to-face ministrations of the visitors and deacons whom he deployed.[20]

Neither the Glasgow experiment, nor Chalmers's subsequent efforts to abolish the Scottish Poor Law system, nor his campaign for an increase in parish schools, nor his final effort at West Port in Edinburgh, succeeded. Neither poverty nor pauperism was reduced. The romantic rural vision and the reliance on spontaneous philanthropy found little resonance in either Glasgow or Edinburgh. Worse, his last campaign in the Scottish capital was overtaken by the Disruption of 1843; his energies were then absorbed in denominational survival, swamping the national campaign of social regeneration.[21] Chalmers thus failed to validate an alternative social theory and practice upon which to base the link between faith and society. Nevertheless his proposals virtually became received doctrine among evangelicals in England as well as Scotland. Like Sumner, he reinforced the evangelical preference for voluntary, face-to-face action, a distaste for state intervention, and above all the key necessity for preaching the gospel. The Chalmers experiments were therefore important in fixing many nineteenth-century evangelicals into a social policy option based on a rurally-derived, paternalistic model of pre-industrial social relations, a confidence in the rational workings

of the market and the power of associational effort. It was not
that they failed to move from practice to theory but that they
chose a theory which, as the nineteenth century wore on, was
less and less able to cope with the dynamic and unstable realities of an industrializing nation. Rural parochialism just would
not work in an urban environment. Nor, as we shall see, would
the persistent emphasis on voluntarism alone address those
urban problems without an acknowledgement of the possibility
of a role for the state in raising and distributing aid for the poor.

But not all evangelicals in this era were moderate in their
views of the nature of the times. Whereas many perceived the
providential moral order as working in predictable fashion
alongside the economic order, others looked for the special
intervention of God in the affairs of the world. These latter
paid much attention to the question of what the millennium
meant, and increasingly believed that the present times were
declining into total disaster before the wonderful thousand-
year reign of Christ was unfolded. About the timing of that
revelation they could do nothing, but meanwhile much needed
to be done, aided by God's special interventionist acts, to
achieve the salvation of the nations. It was more likely to be
people of this persuasion who energetically took up the opportunities for social reform, as long as it fitted with the meaning
of the times. Later in the century an even more extreme and
dispensationalist account of the times promoted an even more
pessimistic withdrawal from all social activity save a simple
urgent gospel preaching. But in the 'Age of Improvement' the
premillennialists, most notably Lord Ashley, seventh Earl of
Shaftesbury from 1851, emphasized the urgency of action.
Action was going to produce results: problems such as child
abuse in factories, or the exploitation of youthful chimney
sweeps, could – indeed must – be addressed by public and even
state intervention. On this view voluntary societies had great
power not just to ameliorate the needs of the respectable poor,
but to address the burdens of the downtrodden. It might even
be the case that factors outside the control of the poor, such as
rapacious landlords or killing drains, were the cause of their
distress. By the 1850s there are hints in Shaftesbury's thinking
of increasing willingness to address environmental problems,

which might even involve state action, such as by the Board of Health where he served energetically as President (1848–1854), during the years of the terrible cholera outbreaks. Shaftesbury's career is an important corrective to any impression that all evangelicals trusted blindly to providence or to market forces. Certainly, in an optimistic age much amelioration, much dutiful obedience to the word of God, could be undertaken.

Although rural poverty still exercised evangelicals, it was on the cities, and above all on London, that their preoccupations were centred. It is in the application of the attitudes which have been sketched above in the arena of the rapidly expanding cities that the lists of organizations become bewildering, the titles of the societies so distant from the post-modernist 1990s.

> There was no actual Infant Bonds of Joy, but there was a Forlorn Females Fund of Mercy. There was an Institution for the Protection of Young Country Girls, and a Maritime Female Penitent Refuge for Poor, Degraded Females. There was a Friendly Female Society for the Relief of Poor, Infirm, Aged Widows, and Single Women, of Good Character, Who Have Seen Better Days. There was an Aged Pilgrims Friend Society, and a Ladies Association for the Benefit of Gentlewomen of Good Family, Reduced in Fortune Below the State of Comfort To Which They Have Been Accustomed. Above all, perhaps, there was a Society for Returning Young Women To Their Friends in the Country.[22]

The range and virtuosity of the charities of the capital constantly attracted comment and, eventually, systematic listing as well as the accusations of hypocrisy and the execrations of the power of 'Exeter Hall' which have already been discussed.[23] Hospitals spread across the capital, both general-purpose and particular (especially for women); numerous efforts to rescue women from prostitution were established; child rescue became popular by mid-century, especially with Shaftesbury's patronage.

For some in London after the French wars the central problem was begging.[24] The Mendicity Society, established in 1818, was the most self-conscious assault on that social problem which increasingly came to affront the rising tide of prosperous and respectable citizens of the capital. Many of the later techniques of organized charity were here foreshadowed – tickets for subscribers to issue, lists of applicants, formal and demeaning consultations. This society was pragmatic, utilitarian and hostile to unthinking acts of charity. Potentially it was an attack on the emotionalism of the evangelical style. So concerned, however, were some of the leaders of evangelicalism, and so attracted were they to the rational workings of moral and economic laws, that it gained the open support of William Wilberforce. For a generation the Mendicity Society was an influential force in attacking begging and exercising some control over the poor of the capital, gaining about £5,000 annually in donations, and plainly supported by evangelicals among others until it stumbled into harsh judgementalism in the face of popular unrest in 1848.

On the other hand, many evangelicals swung their efforts behind the specifically evangelistic societies, especially the London City Mission (established 1835).[25] This society was one in which the premillennialist anxiety about the times could combine with the postmillennialist belief in the active providence of God. But even this fine example of the association focused upon a crucial task began to sensitize evangelicals about the structure of social problems in the east end of London, as its publicity turned to pleading for action to remove the causes of social distress, which would demonstrate practical solutions to social problems.

All over Britain in the growing towns, whether ancient or new, similar concerns were expressed in similar societies, with evangelicals much involved.[26] The emphases of scholars vary. There remains the significance of the state structure, the Poor Laws, within which all philanthropic effort was conducted. In some cities, notably York, the accumulated benevolence of the centuries remained a significant resource in coping with the poor (although evangelicals there were busy in establishing a quite typical range of new voluntary charities). In the newer cities steps had to be taken to start up philanthropic effort virtually from nothing, preferably with the support of the great landowners such as the Butes in Cardiff or the Fitzwilliams in Leeds. But above all, most depended upon the philanthropic energies of the city dwellers themselves, organizing to address the problems reckoned in their city to be the most pressing and seeking support from whatever sources proved feasible.

In many of these cities evangelicals could be found active, concerned, generous. It was the local problem, not a shared evangelicalism, which drew the locals out to help. Indeed, the case of Preston makes the point. There, evangelicals failed to make much impact on the religious institutions of the town, yet the range, organization and character of the town's philanthropies mirrored those of towns such as Leeds where evangelicals were much stronger. Denominational exclusivism was everywhere rejected, except by Roman Catholics, concerned for the faith of their vulnerable fellow-believers.[27] Hospitals, refuges for women and children, outdoor relief agencies, aged homes, and a growing myriad of specialist helping societies, spread across Britain, supported by special crisis funds – for the victims of winter, of dearth, of cholera, of the American Civil War and many other such occurrences.

Much of the enquiry about provincial philanthropy looks closely at the motives observable in these activities. As in the capital, it is not difficult to discern a calculating concern for the maintenance of the existing social order, even a fear that it would break down amidst the rapid changes economic expansion brought. R. J. Morris writes of the Leeds case:

> If there was a dominant strand of ideology it was evangelical religion. This acted not so much as a basis of religious belief but as a vehicle for transmitting certain powerful views of social structure and social responsibility . . . The search for order and stability was the most important imperative of all . . . [The funds and the societies] sought a hierarchical relationship in which duty and benevolence of the wealthy found obedience, deference and trust from the poor . . . to counter the instabilities created by the market economy . . . [The societies were] the basis of orderly social and cultural bargaining in conditions favorable to the élite. The ideology which emerged contained an open acceptance of inequality.[28]

Morris is both right and wrong. There can be no doubt many of the rising urban middle classes were evangelicals. But to argue a merely instrumental intent or even outcome for evangelical faith among these increasingly confident new middle-class

urban élites is unduly reductionist. True, the newly prosperous
sought to manage society in ways which maintained its existing
order and balance. But faith, and evangelical faith more than
most, possessed an inner dynamism which could call men and
women to philanthropic good works, whatever the cost or the
circumstances. That their good works did not generate a more
egalitarian society is not enough of a reason to denigrate their
validity. And, as Jane Garnett shows in her chapter in this
volume, there was a great deal of conscious evangelical self-
examination and exhortation which pressed on the consciences
of the urban élite and which reminded them urgently that the
forces of the market did not always produce worthy outcomes.

Kidd, in discussing the case of Manchester, develops a similar argument to that of Morris. But he reminds us that the
complex range of agencies which emerged in the 1830s did not
only provide social management of the poor people being
helped. He shows that among the Manchester voluntary societies there was also an observable degree of tolerance and
flexibility which often mitigated the harshest constraints of
the major provider, the Poor Law, especially through their
continued focus on specific needy groups of people. It is that
ready response to specific needs which makes the evangelical
approach to urban philanthropy so admirable. They were by no
means merely 'other worldly', nor did they evade their responsibilities to offer help to the needy.

The methods these societies used were consonant with
the evangelical preference for particular and personal action.
Applicants had to apply in person, their particular needs were
assessed, the aid appropriate was decided upon. The rhythm of
this process, whether at the admission desk of a hospital, the
office of a benevolent society, or the matron's room of a refuge,
was unmistakably similar to the penitent's progress from sin to
salvation – admitting need, looking to the all-powerful provider
of hope, and proceeding, now equipped with resources, to a
new life with fear and trembling. It was a rhythm that made a
great deal of sense, and one which avoided the pitfalls of the
bureaucratic state, the unrestrained juggernaut of rights-based
claims to universal benefits which has all but bankrupted the
optimism of the 'welfare state' in the generations since the
Second World War. To emphasize the individual meant a focus

on specific need and desert, sometimes supported by investigation in the field. It also meant a preference for aid in kind over
cash in hand, a resort to the institutional models of industrial
growth, where the factory and the warehouse became the hospital, the refuge, the asylum, the 'home'. The cultural forms of
the early industrial revolution and the dominant ideologies
which went with it plainly set the scene and gave shape to the
opportunities for evangelical philanthropists, as for others, in
these years. Subsequent changes to those dominant forms and
ideologies produced the great transformations of the twentieth
century and the apparent disappearance of a distinctively evangelical approach to poverty.

Women, just as much as men, found ready confirmation for
the duty of charity, and they exercised their love in a myriad of
ways.[29] For many, their engagement with charity sat centrally
within the evangelical account of Christian living; indeed, it
may be that evangelical teaching developed the notion of
women as especially caring *beyond* its proper reference points
in Christian doctrine. F. K. Prochaska argues that 'benevolence
was not simply, as evangelical doctrine would have it, the result
of conversion, a product of a true acceptance of the Gospel
covenant. It was often a product of that anxiety of soul which
asks, "am I saved?"'[30] For some women, perhaps more powerfully than for men, he suggests, the terrifying implications of
Matthew 25.41–3 which follow the teaching about giving a
glass of water to 'the least of these' was profoundly unsettling:
'depart from me, ye cursed, into eternal fire'. It may well have
engaged them in a potentially frenzied round of doing good.
Others, Prochaska suggests, were also driven by the notion of
Christ as the martyr of love.[31] The potential for overwrought
endeavour and for utter dejection at the outcome in failure
drawn back on the donor is obvious in these extensions of
Christian teaching. While relevant in understanding the breadth
of female involvement in philanthropy, it is important to insist
that such self-doubt was not the experience of most evangelicals, for whom the doctrine of assurance of salvation was
central.

The most controversial context for women's philanthropic
endeavours was the effort to reclaim and reform prostitutes.
The experimental intensity with which both men and women,

almost always of deep evangelical faith, attacked this problem
is remarkable.[32] There is no question that prostitution was
widely recognized as a social problem. But solutions, whether
legislative, moral or social, were not easy to come by, and the
concerned activists came to know that reality. The Guardian
Society sought stronger police powers, though the police were
for long unwilling to exercise them. There were refuges (often
called Magdalen homes); there were many societies for the
Protection of Young Females, which sought to suppress
brothels; and there was the Vice Society. The Society for the
Suppression of Vice had been founded in 1802, and its origins
lay in a distinctly Georgian discourse about vice that possessed
differences from what followed in the period with which this
chapter is concerned.[33] It began by attending to vice as indis-
cipline, but by mid-century the intense moral meaning of the
term 'vice' had come to dominate its lobbying. Thus Ashley
called with feeling in the House of Commons in 1838 for
legislation 'to protect women . . . from fraudulent practices to
procure their defilement'.[34] Subsequently rescue stories proliferated, especially in London, trawling the streets, searching for
signs of reformation among the women, offering accommodation on strict conditions. It was indeed a powerful expression
of evangelical concern, however limited the gains.[35]

The philanthropic endeavours of evangelical ladies were
constrained by the doctrine of the separate spheres for men
and women in which to labour.[36] The men did the public things
and ran the finances, the women addressed the housekeeping,
interviewed female applicants, and sometimes contributed
directly to the subscriber lists in their own names. A striking
example was Mary Jane Kinnaird, daughter of William Henry
Hoare of the banking family, and niece of Baptist Noel. Her
husband Arthur Kinnaird was on the children's hospital committee along with many other evangelicals. The Kinnairds were
both active in supporting ragged schools, in promoting the
evangelical revivals of 1859–60, and the Moody and Sankey
mission. Among Mary Jane's philanthropies were Mrs Ranyard's
Biblewomen's Mission, the Christian Colportage Association,
several foreign missions, the Prayer Union and the YWCA.
She was the 'leading evangelical lady philanthropist of her
generation'.[37]

Such philanthropic ladies also began to conduct societies on their own for especially female objects, notably children (schools, orphans and so on) and most of the residences for prostitutes. There was sometimes clamour resisting public efforts to shift the boundaries of those gendered spheres. Some women asked, as did Eliza Conder at the 'vulgar clamour' at the International Anti-Slavery Convention in London in 1840 (when there was an attempt to introduce female delegates as part of the representation from the United States): 'If we are thus to start out of our sphere, who is to take our place? Who as "keepers of the home" are to "guide the house", and train up children? Are gentlemen kindly to officiate for us?' But there were still thousands of women 'engaged in stretching and shifting those boundaries by dint of their philanthropic work, while providing thousands of hours of unpaid social work. Women might not have been exerting real social power and engineering major social change through their associations, but nor were they simply taking as given the boundaries of female social action.'[38] This is an important reminder of the dangers of a simple characterization of female evangelicalism in the mid-nineteenth century.[39]

The issues relating to poverty in the years from 1815 to the 1860s with which this chapter has been concerned began to attract particular attention after slavery had been transformed into an evangelical crusade.[40] In a similar way the emergent later nineteenth-century crusade for temperance sits at the other end of this review.[41] It was not an especially or exclusively evangelical cause when it was taken up by the churches. Certainly temperance attracted evangelical attention, but many others turned to this problem as the next way forward for social improvement. By contrast, the Young Men's Christian Association was in its origins very different from its late twentieth-century guise as an almost secular liberal agency providing cheap hostel accommodation.[42] George Williams, its founder, came from Congregational and Anglican traditions, shaped by moderate Calvinism in the 1820s and 1830s. It was their evangelical faith that Williams and Samuel Morley expressed in the mid-century as they set about providing a structure of Christian fellowship in London and then elsewhere for respectable clerks and other such white-collar young men. The goal was to win these young men to Christ and form their minds in the best evangelical tradition as they prepared for their careers in business. That is what attracted Lord Shaftesbury to the movement and why evangelicals lauded it so lavishly. Launched in the 1840s, it had become a world-wide movement by 1900. By that stage though, it was subject to new attitudes and new conceptions of membership.

The themes of this study of evangelicals and poverty in the high Victorian period have been clear enough. There were lines of policy which evangelicals sought to apply as they addressed the rapidly changing social landscape around them. Confidence in the working of beneficent providence was to be expressed by action consonant with that providence. Much turned on the question of moral cause, and the consequent allocation of blame. But this did not hold back evangelicals from vigorous participation in the sphere of public philanthropy. Nor would those moral issues ever be allowed to displace the task of evangelism. Both charity and gospel focused on the individual, whose reclamation, whose salvation, was so anxiously desired. Cases had to be considered on their merits, not as great unwieldy classes of claims to undifferentiated rights. In addition, there were major social issues to be addressed, such as slavery, prostitution or drink. There were opportunities for associated action through public societies rather than the compulsory voice of the state. In those societies a wide degree of tolerant participation was achieved. These were generous and optimistic virtues which many in the next two or three generations worked hard to overturn and even to denigrate as they promoted the virtues of the power of the state and the significance of universal rights. Others built on the evangelical tradition of charity in the search for an organized and more scientific methodology, but not necessarily informed by that central evangelical dynamic of love. By the 1950s, the balance had shifted decisively to the proponents of the welfare state, to the detriment of the voluntarist tradition, especially in its evangelical form. But by the 1990s many had come to believe that neither state action, nor voluntary associationism nor face-to-face solutions like those promoted by Thomas Chalmers would alone be enough. All and more must be integrated into a viable social policy for Britain in the twenty-first century. In this new debate, the

virtues and wisdom of that nineteenth-century evangelical view
of poverty and philanthropy were once more being examined
with sympathetic attention.[43]

Notes

1 Derek Fraser, *The Evolution of the British Welfare State* (Macmillan,
   1984, 2nd edn) is the standard account, though nineteenth-century
   philanthropy and religious motivation in particular is all but
   ignored.
2 José Harris, 'Political thought and the welfare state 1870–1940: an
   intellectual framework for British social policy', *Past and Present*, 132
   (1992), pp. 116–41.
3 Boyd Hilton, *The Age of Atonement: the Influence of Evangelicalism on
   Social and Economic Thought, 1795–1865* (Oxford: Clarendon Press,
   1988), pp. 298–339.
4 Even Ian Bradley, *The Call to Seriousness: The Evangelical Impact on
   the Victorians* (Jonathan Cape, 1976), esp. ch. 6, 'Philanthropy and
   paternalism', written with sympathy and an evident understanding of
   evangelicalism, asserts that 'The basis of the Evangelicals' response
   to poverty and suffering was emotional rather than ideological'
   (p. 120).
5 Malc Anderson, 'Historiography and nineteenth century social concern in Britain', *Lucas: an Evangelical History Review*, 2 (1988), pp.
   7–29; A. M. C. Waterman, *Revolution, Economics and Religion:
   Christian Political Economy, 1798–1833* (Cambridge UP, 1991).
6 R. J. Morris, *Class, Sect and Party: the Making of the British Middle
   Class, Leeds 1820–1850* (Manchester UP, 1990), p. 205; G. B.
   Hindle, *Provision for the Relief of the Poor in Manchester 1784–1826*
   (Manchester UP, 1975).
7 M. J. D. Roberts, 'The Society for the Suppression of Vice and its
   early critics, 1802–1812', *Historical Journal*, 26 (1983), pp. 159–76;
   Joanna Innes, 'Politics and morals: The reformation of manners
   movement in later eighteenth-century England' in Eckhart
   Hellmuth, ed., *The Transformation of Political Culture: England and
   Germany in the Late Eighteenth Century* (Oxford UP, 1990), pp.
   58–118.
8 R. J. Morris, 'Voluntary societies and British urban elites,
   1780–1850: an analysis', *Historical Journal*, 26 (1983), pp. 95–118.
9 G. B. A. M. Finlayson, *The Seventh Earl of Shaftesbury 1801–1885*
   (Eyre Methuen, 1981), pp. 153–4, 249–53, 417–18, 483–5.
10 Valentine Cunningham, *Everywhere Spoken Against: Dissent in the
   Victorian Novel* (Oxford UP, 1975) has a perceptive discussion of
   Dickens' flippant treatment of Dissent and evangelical Anglicanism,

and of the fictional tradition from which he drew (ch. 8).

11 See, e.g. Hannah More, *Moral Sketches of Prevailing Opinions and Manners Foreign and Domestic: with reflections on prayer* (1819, 2nd edn), pp. 190ff, quote at p. 199.

12 Quoted by Morris, *Class, Sect and Party*, p. 216.

13 Morris (*Class, Sect and Party*) cites T. W. Tottie, the agent for Earl Fitzwilliam in the Leeds district making that point.

14 J. Douglas Holladay, 'English evangelicalism, 1820–1850: diversity and unity in "vital religion"', *Historical Magazine of the Protestant Episcopal Church*, 51 (1982), pp. 147–57, notes, however, that working-class evangelicals were more likely to find in their faith both a consolation for the hardships they endured and an inspiration for their struggles for social justice (p. 157). On paternalism see David Roberts, *Paternalism in Early Victorian England* (Croom Helm, 1979) and F. M. L. Thompson in G. E. Mingay, ed., *The Victorian Countryside* (2 vols, Routledge and Kegan Paul, 1981), vol. 2, pp. 457–74.

15 R. A. Soloway, *Prelates and People: Ecclesiastical Social Thought 1783–1852* (Routledge and Kegan Paul, 1969), pp. 96–101; *Age of Atonement*, p. 77; Waterman, *Revolution, Economics and Religion*, pp. 150–70.

16 Soloway, *Prelates and People*, pp. 109–12.

17 K. D. Snell, *Annals of the Labouring Poor, Social Change and Agrarian England, 1660–1900* (Cambridge UP, 1985) most powerfully argues the case for the commercialization and bureaucratization of the Poor Laws after 1834. Soloway (p. 184) suggests that Sumner may have later come to regret agreeing with the over-confident Chadwick in the wording of the Report.

18 Don Anderson, 'The Bishop's Society: the Anglican Home Mission Society in the Diocese of Sydney' (unpublished Ph.D. thesis, University of Wollongong, 1990), p. 99.

19 Anderson, 'The Bishop's Society', p. 101.

20 Stewart J. Brown, 'The disruption of urban poverty: Thomas Chalmers and the West Port Operation in Edinburgh 1844–47', *Records of the Scottish Church History Society* 20 (1978), pp. 65–89, quotation at pp. 65–6; see also his *Thomas Chalmers and the Godly Commonwealth in Scotland* (Oxford UP, 1982). Chalmers's own principal exposition of the views discussed here was *The Christian and Civic Economy of Large Towns* (3 vols, Glasgow, 1821–6).

21 For a review of nineteenth-century Scottish philanthropy generally, see Olive Checkland, *Philanthropy in Victorian Scotland: Social Welfare and the Voluntary Principle* (Edinburgh: John Donald, 1980).

22 F. K. Brown, *Fathers of the Victorians: The Age of Wilberforce* (Cambridge UP, 1961), pp. 325–41, quoted at pp. 323–4.

23 S. Low, *The Charities of London* (1850).

24 M. J. D. Roberts, 'Reshaping the gift relationship: the London Mendicity Society and the Suppression of Begging in England,

k and the Victorians: The Temperance Question in
Faber and Faber, 1971); L. L. Shiman, *Crusade*
rian England (Basingstoke: Macmillan, 1988).
ve been efforts put in train to re-establish a
thin the YMCA in the 1990s.
rochaska, *The Voluntary Impulse*; see also Anne
Policy: Workhouse to Workforce (Faber, 1989).

1818–
201–3
25 Donal
Workin
1986)
26 David
A. Jov
Digby
cies',
1981)
philar
Histo
Manc
1860
Studi
(Mar
Relie
1988
Histo
27 Marg
of Cl
Ph.D
28 Mor
29 F. K
Engl
Phila
30 Proc
31 Proc
32 Edw
1700
33 Rob
34 Quo
35 Bris
36 Best
Fort
(Hu
37 Nor
Eng
(un
anal
wro
lem:
Dic
part
38 Dav
39 For
this

40 See above, pp. 17–2
41 Brian Harrison, Dr
England 1815–1872
Against Drink in Vic
42 To be fair, there H
Christian ministry
43 Most eloquently in
Digby, British Welfa

Chapter Three

Evangelicalism and Business in Mid-Victorian Britain

JANE GARNETT

In a memorandum to the Royal Commission on the Mercantile Laws of 1854, it was stressed that Britain's position as the greatest manufacturing and trading nation was due not just to material success, but to the 'admixture of moral elements'.[1] In many of the debates of the 1830s and 1840s about free trade, such moral elements had been held to be implicit in the often complacent identification of Protestantism and commercial progress. Yet free trade in this sense implied integrity and confidence in transactions, otherwise there could be no freedom, and by the 1850s it was becoming clear to many observers that Britain had traded on her status as a Protestant nation, without thinking through the moral assumptions that might imply. As a result her commercial reputation abroad was suffering: in 1855, for example, the Spanish government was reported to have found so many adulterated drugs and other goods coming into the country from Great Britain, that they had to appoint inspectors at every port.[2] 'An Englishman's word was his bond'; but the business failures of 1847–8 and the revelations of commercial practice to which they led were held by contemporaries to have marked the first point at which the credit of English merchants generally came under suspicion in foreign countries.

This apparent crisis of confidence struck at home as well as abroad. The economy throughout the 1850s was dynamic, but essentially unstable. The cost of growth was high, and individual enterprises repeatedly suffered from excess capacity, careless

investment and consequent failure. The subsequent commercial
crisis of 1857–8 was preceded by a new wave of speculation.
There was a persistent awareness of the increasing number of
ways in which stability could be undermined, as indeed it was
again in 1866–68.[3] The publicized failure of large enterprises
involving men of supposedly high character meant that, in the
words of one commentator, 'all the received tests of respectability seemed to be of no avail, and people literally could not
tell who they might trust.' The same commentator felt keenly
the scale of fraud. As he said, 'From time immemorial clerks
have embezzled, but only the nineteenth century could produce
Walter Watts, who opened two theatres with money surrep-
titiously obtained from the Globe Insurance Company.'[4] Yet
the big scandals did not stand alone. The ramifications were
widespread. This was a time when an immense number of new
companies was formed; capital accumulation was encouraged
by the repeal of the usury laws, partly in 1832, fully in 1855;
and new trades had arisen as a result of the Municipal Corpo-
rations Act of 1835, which gave a legal right to all to set up
shop. The removal of commercial restrictions widened the
scope for enterprise, and created new opportunities which both
demanded risk and could stimulate fraud. Moreover the contrast between overall national growth and apparently greater
swings for particular sectors of the whole, aroused acute
anxiety. Throughout the period, intensifying competition led to
trading expedients such as adulteration, misleading advertise-
ments and abuse of credit. Abuses seemed too seldom to be
checked by law or even by convention.

There was a number of possible responses to these perceived
threats to commercial confidence, which in turn related to the
broader question of the self-confidence and ambition of the
middle-class commercial and industrial community, and how
it saw itself in relation to the nation as a whole. It was evident
that commercial law lagged behind commercial practice.
Chambers of Commerce in the major commercial cities were
consolidated in the early to mid-century to press for legal
reform, and overlapped with other bodies such as the National
Association for the Promotion of Social Science and the
Financial and Administrative Reform Associations.[5] The principal issues raised in the period from the 1850s to the 1880s

were those of compulsory registration of members of a partnership, the extension of the principle of limited liability, the
amendment of the bankruptcy laws and the laws relating to
debt, the improvement of the law of copyright and the law
relating to adulteration. In each of these areas, legal reform was
slow, and never systematic. At the same time, by far the greater
part of the daily dishonesties of trade and finance was too
subtle to be caught in the meshes of legislation. Moreover, legal
structures were not necessarily sufficient to promote the active
trust which was fundamental to business life. As one evangelical commentator put it: 'A man may be able to say "I have
committed neither theft nor fraud", and yet he may have been
a reckless debtor, an unfaithful servant, an inattentive agent, an
extravagant partner, or a negligent consignee.'[6] The onus was
felt to be on the commercial community to examine the ethical
assumptions which lay behind its activity and to reformulate
them in such a way that their continued relevance could be
perceived.

The most influential group to undertake this task came from
within the evangelical churches. By the 1850s, many evangelical ministers – Anglican and Nonconformist – were joining
together in a concern to promote the common elements of their
faith, and were also reasserting its ethical trust. The foundation
of the Evangelical Alliance in 1845–6 represented, even more
than a negative anti-Catholicism, a commitment to a positive
Protestantism. In promoting this, it encouraged the increased
involvement of the laity, which itself helped to break down
barriers between the religious and the secular.[7] In matters of
theology and eschatology distinctions remained, although
extreme Calvinism, for example, had diminished. On issues of
economic ethics especially there was a growing interdenominational consensus of approach.[8] The ministers who shaped
this debate usually came from commercial areas, had often had
direct experience of commerce themselves,[9] and preached to a
variety of middle-class communities. Indeed, evangelicals were
so identified with these groups that they were tainted with the
slur of commercialism by their critics. In 1855 Sir John Dean
Paul, a prominent evangelical Anglican layman, and partner in
the firm of Strahan, Paul and Bates, whose bankruptcy case
was going through the criminal courts, was used by the press

as a focus for attack on the hypocrisy of evangelicals, who were discussed as if they were coterminous with the commercial middle classes. *The Times* felt that:

> We must, however reluctantly, resign ourselves to the belief that men of business look to the religious spirit of the public as a useful aid in their operations. Religion is to them as an advertising van, or a gaudy shopfront, or a poetic effusion from MOSES and SONS. They trade upon the Bible as BARNUM did upon the Fejee mermaid or the woolly horse.[10]

The evangelical press not surprisingly reacted sharply, arguing that *The Times* would have done better to recognize how far religion was directly or indirectly responsible for the level of public morality and private honesty which *did* exist. They did, however, take the point that English clergy and ministers had until recently not paid detailed enough attention to the issue of Christian principles in trade. They had tended either to ignore the commercial world, or to confine themselves to platitudes. It was necessary to get through to different groups within the broad stratum of the middle class, by challenging them on specific issues relevant to their own experience.[11] There was no sense in denouncing petty larceny to a congregation of cotton masters; nor could smaller manufacturers or traders be let off the hook by detached contemplation of crimes on the grand scale.[12] This period marked the increasing sophistication of an attempt to counter the allegation that there was a distinction between personal morality and the ethical code of the commercial world – indeed between the religious and secular spheres.

In examining the pattern of commercial crises, evangelical ministers were at one with other commentators in recognizing that dishonesty and recklessness were evidently chargeable not just to individuals, but to certain widely prevalent methods of conducting business. Yet equally they stressed that it would not do to write off the commercial world as intrinsically corrupt. Nor would it do to regard crises as acts of God inaccessible to the individual's comprehension. 'If you believe simply in the working of laws . . . and leave all to Providence, you will end up in trouble and take others with you.'[13] Those optimistic free traders who systematically equated religious criteria and the criteria of political economy were in danger in this respect: potential conflicts were obscured and the need for a point of contact in morality neglected. The pursuit of atomized individualism under the broad umbrella of self-acting laws was actually a denial of responsibility, and was ethically and psychologically ineffective. Without a conviction of the importance of personality and individual responsibility, no real moral energy was possible. Many evangelicals recognized that Protestant pride in Britain's economic progress could become detached from genuine religious values.[14] This had serious implications, both for the individual Christian involved in business life, and also for the long-term health and social stability of the nation.

For evangelical clergy and ministers, the positive corollary of the popular identification of evangelicalism with commerce was that there was real scope in this context for influence to be exerted and for good examples to be presented. In this sense evangelicals promoted themselves as particular guardians of the morality of the business world. As the Baptist Jackson Goadby stressed, a religious commitment was obviously not an inevitable element in commercial life:[15] there could be successful businessmen who were not Christian, and Christians who were neither upright nor successful businessmen. But these evangelicals preached to those amongst their number who did wish to carry their religious principles into their business life, and who could then in turn provide models to inspire a wider evangelical enterprise. The Birmingham Congregationalist R. W. Dale argued in 1866 that if those who professed Christianity were also to manifest exemplary trustworthiness in business, the churches would soon fill up.[16] The hypocrisy of some middle-class churchgoers was certainly one of the elements conducing to working-class scepticism about the value of religious observance. Moreover, exemplary businessmen and industrialists whose religious commitment actively propelled their business activities could give real substance to the identification of Protestantism and commercial progress, and raise the general tone of economic ethics. In his exemplary life of Frank Crossley, the Manchester engine manufacturer, James Rendel Harris stressed that 'such men revitalise the Christian creed, and prevent its leading formulae from falling into disuse or decay'.

The publication of the life in 1899 was intended to spread this example more widely, and continued a tradition of exemplary lives of evangelical businessmen which had begun to proliferate in the 1850s.[17]

Some evangelicals, like Crossley, were powerfully affected by the revival of the late 1850s, which passed particularly through commercial areas of Scotland, Ireland, and the North and West of England. A spirit of revival was welcomed, and was renewed in the 1870s, but it was one which put down roots in day-to-day experience and growth and which was maintained by consistent evangelical energy across the period.[18] Others, like Crossley, had been struck in the 1850s and 1860s by the writings of F. D. Maurice and Thomas Erskine, and other liberal writers who confronted some of the narrownesses of the 'old evangelicalism'.[19] But the common thrust of the literature which addressed itself to the ethical foundations of commercial life was firmly the challenge to sustained and systematic evangelical mission. Although individual emphases differed, fundamental was the necessary tension between sin and grace, which gave an ethical impetus to evangelicalism. To move too far down the liberal path seemed to run the risk of upsetting this balance and weakening the dynamic thrust. As the Congregationalist Samuel Pearson put it:

> To preach morals without mercy, ethics without Atonement, progress without pardon; that is to create a dreamland out of present-day fancies . . . sin must first be recognised; and then, and only then, will God be seen as redeeming us through His son.[20]

Such was the distinctiveness of evangelical ethics, which could give positive *guidance*, not simply act as a negative restraint. Evangelicals would be called positively to account for their stewardship. The Golden Rule on its own was neither sufficient, nor self-sustaining.[21] By the same token, the simplified pieties of political economy, as it was popularly understood and incorporated in conventional morality, were inadequate to underpin a truly evangelical responsibility.

The issues raised by this responsibility were addressed in sermons, in lectures, in public meetings, in tracts, in biographies, in the evangelical press. Evangelical organizations like the YMCA were crucially important in providing a focus of community. This was particularly important for young men coming as individuals to work in towns and cities, who were often disorientated and vulnerable to temptation. The organization could also, like churches and chapels themselves, provide reputable business contacts. Ministers of all denominations saw the immense influence which the YMCA could have, and flocked to give lectures at public halls, recognizing that many who would not in the first instance go to church would go to these.[22] Lectures and biographies were written which focused on individual businessmen. The Wesleyan William Arthur's *The Successful Merchant* (1852) had gone into forty-three editions by 1855, was translated into Welsh, Dutch, French and German, and had sold over eighty-four thousand copies by the end of the century.[23] Such biographies were intended to cut across the secular success literature, especially the popular writings of Smiles and Carlyle, which came close to a simplified religious position, but which offered little specific guidance through the complexities of ordinary business life – and indeed the ever-present possibility of failure. These lives represented a sustained attempt to make appealing and stimulating *in its own right* the idea of commercial life as an ethical battlefield. The tone was critical. The heroes were not flawless, and failure was emphasized as well as success. The rhetoric thus elevated the heroism required to preserve an individual's integrity amidst all the pressures of commercial life, while keeping it within reach as an aim. The advocacy of a this-worldly mundane piety was characteristically Protestant and evangelical.[24] The literature was intended to appeal to a cross-section of the middle class: to those who were – or might feel that they could be – in a position to make choices. For many, promotion to a managerial position was not an unreal aspiration. B. G. Orchard, writing in 1871, reckoned that half the partnership firms in Liverpool which were twenty years old had a partner who had once been a clerk. More generally, the white-collar world encouraged the idea of a social order in which achievement and self-esteem depended on individual resolve and the maintenance of a conscious sense of direction.[25] For considerable numbers of Christians in business, the moral dilemmas of their working lives encouraged an increasing self-examination and a heightened search for the guidance which this sort of literature offered.

Within this debate there were various broad areas of focus.

Fraudulent practices were itemized and the problems of extended layers of responsibility spelled out. The relationship between the scope of legislation and the scope of morality was confronted. The proper relationship for an evangelical between business life and the rest of Christian life was fundamental, and raised questions of the amount of energy to be devoted to different occupations; of the managerial style of employers and policy towards employees generally; and of appropriate levels of investment or reinvestment in business *vis-à-vis* philanthropic expenditure.

In the first place, stress was laid on the responsibility of everyone engaged in commerce to be *aware* of the dangers and the moral dilemmas, and of the possible consequences of particular actions. Moral restraint varied according to the degree to which evil consequences were perceived.[26] Many evangelical commentators focused on the role of overtrading in causing crisis (although attention was also paid to the possibility of over-production, to the ways in which demand could fluctuate, and to the impact of foreign competition). Overtrading was obviously an elastic concept: it could imply downright sharp practice or simply the genuine commercial misjudgement perhaps inevitable if the entrepreneur was to fulfil his function of risk-bearing.[27] Evangelicals did not make it a simple category. They recognized the necessity of taking risks, but equally argued that it was necessary to be aware as far as possible what risks it was one was taking and how justifiable they were. At this point they were clear in their ruling: no man who could not afford to lose had the right to speculate. Even if this might hamper the odd commercial genius, it was felt that benefits to the community at large in the generally improved tone of commercial transactions would far outweigh this. An atmosphere of mutual distrust would make people less confident about taking initiatives.[28] This approach was particularly pertinent to the middling and lower strata of tradespeople, who were precisely those whose honest profits were most likely to be squeezed and who were most vulnerable to failure. They were also those who were most likely to have their confidence shattered and to retire from business, thus diminishing employment opportunities.[29] These people in turn formed the core of the evangelical community in the major cities. Some evangelicals extended the discussion on this issue into a more general critique of the language of political economy, and indeed of the concept of free competition. The Methodist Benjamin Gregory, author of an exemplary biography of a Wesleyan commodity merchant, defined overtrading as the sinking of money faster than it could find its level, even in valuable undertakings which were almost sure to be remunerative *in the long run*. Here one might be dealing not with fraud, but conceivably with carelessness. Similarly, although perfectly free competition might *ultimately* be the best guarantee of excellence, it was all too easy to lose sight of the qualifications contained in the word 'ultimately'. Economists often forgot that life was too short, for example, for fraud to be properly exposed.[30]

In the retail sector, traders were asked to consider carefully the question of giving credit on goods purchased for consumption. The problem of tradesmen luring people to exceed their limits was seen to be a serious one, especially when the trader was much more experienced than the customer. One Oxford student was said to have been visited in his first week by fifty tradesmen – wine-merchants, tailors, bootmakers, cigar sellers – all offering credit without bothering to find out what the man's personal circumstances were.[31] The practice of offering what was known as 'leading articles' (i.e. loss leaders) was held to be unfair competition. The exemplary Christian grocer Samuel Budgett was criticized for this by his biographer William Arthur, who stressed that Budgett's own motivation might have been honourable, but that there was scope for the unscrupulous to advertise a few articles at tempting prices to catch the unwary, and then fleece them by selling poor goods at great profits.[32] It was revealed that some employees were being trained to operate a system of 'double prices' – one price for the customer who would pay what was asked and another for the customer who demanded cheapness; or indeed were being rewarded for success in selling off old stock. This was held not only to be a breach of trust towards the employee, who was thereby faced with an intolerable moral dilemma, but also to be setting a bad example for the way in which business would be conducted in the future by those very same employees who might one day in fact be competing with their former employers.[33]

The problem of adulteration was one of the most central for relations between traders and consumers. A series of articles was commissioned by the *Lancet* on this subject in the early 1850s, and the findings were disturbing:

> Everywhere shams abound. Coffee is chicory; chicory itself has its cheaper substitute . . . pickles are seasoned with salts of copper, and even our children may be reckoned happy if their sugar-plums have no affinity with sugar of lead.[34]

Competition stimulated ingenuity and items could be adulterated innumerable times at every stage. Pepper, flour, bread, beer – all were affected. A Select Committee set up in 1855 recommended legislation, which was embodied in an Act of 1860, but adulteration continued at a serious level for another twenty years. Penalties were inadequate, and the legislation did not, for example, extend to drugs. There was no adequate coverage of wholesalers as opposed to retailers. Most significantly, in evangelical eyes, the legislature left adulteration a venial offence. A distinction was made between pecuniary frauds and the injury to public health, and only the strictly dangerous adulterations were unequivocally vetoed. Otherwise it was reckoned that the public were protected by competition, and that they would prefer to benefit from increasing cheapness, whatever the quality. Evangelicals launched into a campaign to condemn this emphasis, and to point out the logical extension of this type of reasoning. As the *Record* newspaper said:

> Even if most of the adulterations are harmless . . . what must be the condition of the TRADE CONSCIENCE . . . when these practices are so widely established that they carry no shame? Men will take false courage from it, and trade will become more corrupt.[35]

The evangelical press also followed closely the debates on bankruptcy legislation, and made clear where it felt the wood was being missed for the trees. Much public attention seemed wrongly to be focused on the actual and immediate processes of bankruptcy, rather than on the long-term background, and the rules of the credit trade itself. This was a necessary point to make. At the 1852 Select Committee, only one person argued for a greater emphasis on the morality of the bankrupt's trading, not just on the immediate cause of bankruptcy.[36] One of the most important practical ways to enable an individual businessman to keep a check on the level of his involvements was by proper accounting procedures. The principle of regularity, care in keeping accounts, and the ability to estimate average income over several years, had an interlocking religious and economic significance. Such care would not only encourage responsibility, but would also enable bankruptcy investigations to proceed more fairly; gradations of moral guilt could be established more readily, and there would be greater incentive to proceed with integrity. This was certainly the approach adopted by Nonconformist churches in their own internal disciplinary hearings of cases of bankruptcy.[37] The examination of the business practice of the creditors was just as important: creditors often kept debtors floating for a time, so that they could get paid in full, at the expense of others who unwittingly executed new orders. Again, in this sort of case direct fraud might not be an issue, although there were celebrated cases such as that of the brokers Overend, Gurney and Co., one of whose acting partners actually detected fraud but kept quiet about it for eight months in order to preserve the credit of the firm.[38] In general, the essential point to be put across was that the remoter consequences of an apparently well-motivated action could not only harm a much wider circle, but also prejudice the circumstances in which business was done. In the case of credit relationships between businesses, it was held that each trader should as far as possible keep a check on the credentials of those with whom he had dealings. This was increasingly difficult, as the ramifications of business spread more widely. But the burgeoning commodity dealers, James Budgett and Co., in this generation at least living up to the strict Wesleyan inheritance of James's father Samuel, the firm's founder, kept complex records on credit-worthiness, and maintained a tight and effective credit policy.[39]

The historical trend towards the enlargement of scale of business operations necessarily threatened the scope for independent action, and this might be taken to limit the relevance of the sort of approach so far described. In fact the stage had not been reached when companies were financed solely by remote investors, interested only in the dividends, but otherwise unconcerned with the running of the business, although obviously once companies could be formed with limited liability (after 1855) this development could be foreseen.[40] Yet this did not lead evangelicals either to oppose such changes in company law, nor to reduce their concern for individual responsibility. Indeed many evangelicals regarded such changes as beneficial in principle from the point of view of enabling small capitalists to enter into commercial investments.[41] Several evangelical manufacturers converted their companies to limited liability in the 1870s and 1880s, with the specific aim of bringing their employees into part-ownership and increasing their interest and responsibility in the firm.[42] The emphasis of evangelical writers was on the one hand to stress the scope for responsibility and on the other to point out the need for great prudence on the part of the investing public, especially if they were investing in a firm with which they had no personal contact. The fate of the first five thousand limited companies, formed between 1856 and 1865 (over half of which lasted for less than ten years) demonstrated both the inherent risks and the ignorance of the public. Potential investors were urged not to be won over by a superficially attractive prospectus, but to look carefully at the rates of interest offered, and be aware that high interest often meant low security.[43] Evangelicals did not argue unrealistically that shareholders could exercise effective control over all the details of company management. More important seemed to be to publicize the limits to their active control, so that illusions could less easily be perpetuated about where responsibility lay. There did remain points at which shareholders could and should exercise their responsibility. An illustration of the collective moral power of evangelical shareholders came in the celebrated controversy over the Sunday opening of the Crystal Palace. Here shareholders' votes did count, and several votes were necessary before a decision could be reached. In 1858 a Captain Young stood out at a meeting of the Brighton Railway Company, to try to prevent them from running excursion trains on Sundays. The directors replied that they were only supposed to consider the strictly financial interests of the company, and that a religious obligation was out of place in a business meeting. This brought into sharp focus the broader issue of the relationship between the individual and the corporate conscience and the degree to which distinctions *could* be made between private and public realms of behaviour.[44] The logic of mid-Victorian evangelicalism naturally lay in integration of these realms.

Some issues, like Sunday excursion trains, caused particular crises of conscience for evangelicals who held strong principles, for example on temperance. The engineer Frank Crossley, an ardent teetotaller, discussed a specific case with the Revd Alexander Maclaren: whether he should sell his engines to brewers, given that some of them might be used directly in the manufacture of alcohol. Maclaren confirmed that the principle 'I sell to anybody; the use made is the buyer's affair, not mine' would not do. 'What would be said of a cutler who sold a knife to a man who said "Sell me a sharp knife to cut my mother-in-law's throat with"?' But the opposite extreme, that one is bound to take into account all the possible evil uses which could be made of an article, was unworkable, because they could not conceivably be traced. Maclaren felt the particular question under discussion to be a very delicate one, but in the end advised that since the specific use of the engines was not certainly known, Crossley was not at fault in selling. In fact Crossley compromised, in part because his brother, with whom he was in partnership, did not feel so strongly as he did, and nor did other members of the firm. It was decided that commercial travellers for the company should not call on brewers, nor should the firm advertise in brewing papers. The share of the profits from any sale of engines to brewers accruing personally to Frank Crossley would be sent directly to charity.[45] This case touched on questions which troubled other evangelicals, and raised real dilemmas in determining how far a tender conscience could extend, especially when a decision was not in the hands of a single individual.

Some evangelical manufacturers felt that they were contributing towards the abolition of particular abuses by only using supplies from certain sources. George Hitchcock, the London draper, sold only 'free grown' (i.e. Indian as opposed to American) cotton goods.[46] Cadburys in the early 1900s investigated reports that their cocoa supplies were cultivated by slave labour and, after years of investigation at their own cost, in 1909 promoted a cocoa manufacturers' boycott of growers who used contract (i.e. effectively slave) labour.[47] The Quaker chocolate manufacturers were an obvious example of evangelicals who were specifically committed to their particular trade and promoted it as part of their broader evangelical purpose. Edmund Charles Tisdall (1824–92), London milk retailer and wholesaler, who had grown up in Nonconformist and temperance circles, similarly devoted himself passionately to the goal of pure milk at low prices, and pushed for improved legislation and inspection.[48] Thomas Cook's successful travel business grew directly out of his calling as a Baptist preacher and promoter of the temperance movement.[49]

In most cases, however, the precise form of industry or trade was not so significant. What was important for the evangelical was to assess what a proper stewardship entailed. The Revd William Braden, speaking in King's Weigh House in 1876, argued that business relationships should be lawful (not just by secular law), lawfully fulfilled and should develop the highest character. An employer should have regard both to his own moral position, and to justice in his treatment of employees. 'No large charitable contributions can make up for lack of charity in your own business.' Even in terms of efficient running of the business, lack of charity would be damaging: envy, distrust, censoriousness would result: 'Often as little as possible will be done, and that little thought too much, and without any gladness or satisfaction in the work'.[50] Certainly, fair treatment of employees, which involved rewarding talent, maintaining high standards, as well as providing good working conditions and terms of employment, had both temporal and spiritual advantages. There were many examples of evangelical employers whose integrity of dealing and generous treatment of employees won them a loyal workforce.[51] Morale and energy in such businesses was high. The Revd W. Kirkman's biography of T. C. Hincksman stressed that the latter was highly esteemed by his workforce as

> they beheld from day to day, all year round, the same quiet, consistent, well-ordered life, his spirit and conduct offering no contradiction to his professions and prayers in the sanctuary . . . The way in which he conducts his business will tell in favour of or against Primitive Methodism.[52]

Such a managerial stance served an important integrative function, but one which was effective precisely because it could be seen not to be simply calculating or instrumental. Not all Christian businessmen were good employers. But they were the more open to scrutiny if they purported to trade under a Christian flag. Some employers exercised an authoritarian paternalism which was invoked to justify resistance to independent working-class action, but this was not general, nor was it advocated or approbated in the advisory literature.[53]

The question of degrees of commitment to business as opposed to other areas of life was especially acute when it related to church activities. Many evangelical businessmen fulfilled roles as class leaders or Sunday school teachers in their local churches, and served on local and national committees dedicated to missionary or philanthropic enterprise, as well as supporting these causes financially. It was – and is – a real question whether the primary commitment of a Christian businessman is not to promote the economic efficiency of his business.[54] This was something of which mid-Victorian evangelical commentators took due account. Investment of capital in a well-run business was a fundamental good. Evangelical moderation, even if inspired by scrupulous religious motives, did not necessarily represent good stewardship of a business. The puritanism of Henry Wilson, of the Sheffield Smelting Company, led him to fear expansion and refuse to plough back profits into the firm, thus ultimately seriously checking its development.[55] But evangelicals were more often concerned that the need for capital accumulation could be used as a pretext for avarice. In the widespread campaign for systematic beneficence, the injunction to set aside a tenth related to *clear* income and thus could not be held to conflict with reinvestment in business.[56] A similar rule applied to stewardship of time: an evangelical businessman – at whatever level – was expected to give his primary commitment to his work, and in so doing would serve the religious cause best. But again warnings were given about overwork, which could in fact be narrowing of horizons and of creativity. Just as it was deemed both more 'charitable' and more efficient to reduce hours for employees,[57] so it was more efficient in the broadest sense for an employer to spend some time in recreation (which could include work for the church). This was a question of systematic organization. Many evangelicals were able to promote highly successful businesses, whilst also taking on other roles. Thomas Hudson Bainbridge (1841–1912), the Newcastle department store proprietor, having been a local preacher in his youth, conducted a class for forty years at Brunswick Wesleyan Chapel – in his words, 'the weekly hour of self-scrutiny and spiritual stocktaking'. He then took a lead in founding Jesmond Wesleyan Church, where for twenty years he superintended the children's service. He acted as secretary to Moody in his mission to the North East, and later supported Hugh Price Hughes' Forward Mission. These activities were integrated with, and were integral to, his successful business life.[58] Sir George White (1840–1912), Baptist shoe manufacturer and liberal paternalist employer, was for many years a deacon, active Sunday school worker, and for a long period ran an adult school attended by about two hundred and fifty workers.[59] On the other hand Samuel Morley and J. J. Colman rejected invitations to become deacons of their respective churches, because they did not feel that they could do justice to such a responsible job in the church as well as to their own businesses.[60] Some did withdraw to some extent in later life from such active participation in business in order to make time for church activities. It seems that Frank Crossley, having moved to live in and run a mission hall in Ancoats, may have delegated some of the daily running of the business to his brother (he certainly left to him the running of the mission which they had built together alongside their works).[61] But this was a question of responsible delegation, not neglect of business, or rejection of the pursuit of maximum legitimate profitability. As John Young, a Wesleyan chemist, said: 'While we are at work, we should work . . . think deeply and seriously by what means one's business may be extended so as to yield the greatest possible return'.[62]

This survey of the areas of debate on economic ethics engaged in by mid-Victorian evangelical writers, and at least in some cases practised by members of the evangelical business community, has argued for the centrality of their contribution. Far from maintaining the division of life into religious and secular spheres and focusing their attention on issues of individual conversion narrowly conceived, by the 1850s evangelicals

were increasingly concerned with the practical working out of
that conversion in the increasingly complex commercial world.
This preoccupation and its significance have until recently
been neglected, partly through continued concern either with
a few major 'enlightened entrepreneurs' or with the special
contribution of the Christian socialists. Matthew Arnold's and
George Eliot's characterizations of Nonconformist narrowness
and hypocrisy have died hard, and evangelicalism as a whole in
the mid-Victorian period has been distorted through the lens
both of contemporary rivals – Tractarians and liberal churchmen – and of subsequent generations. In no respect has this
been more the case than in the sphere of economic ethics. The
Christian socialists of the 1840s and 1850s are still often seen
as unique in their time in attempting to bridge the gulf between
the church and the world and to develop a social theology.[63]
The self-conscious revival of concern with the social mission of
the churches in the late nineteenth and early twentieth centuries tended for its own purposes to underplay some previous
initiatives. From an early twentieth-century Christian socialist
perspective R. H. Tawney painted a vivid picture of the development of post-Reformation capitalist society in which religion
became a private, individual matter, no longer concerned with
the regulation of social institutions and economic activity. The
gulf between religion and commerce, reinforced in theoretical
terms in the late eighteenth century by Adam Smith's invisible
hand of the market, had, in Tawney's view, persisted ever
since.[64] Certainly mid-Victorian evangelical critics were keen
to reform the capitalist system, not to overturn it, but this did
not imply a lack of commitment to challenging the ways in
which social good and individual self-interest had been glibly
elided. Evangelicals appealed to the individual conscience, but
this was recognized as operating in a complex structure of
social ethics. The appeal to an individually felt sense of duty
and responsibility was held to have real pertinence in the world
of business in which legal structures could never be sufficient.
What Tawney was calling for in the 1920s was for industry to
operate according to a code of professional ethics.[65] This dem-
and for an emphasis on duties rather than rights had been
precisely the preoccupation of many mid-Victorian evangelicals. Such evangelical attention was focused on the broad

spectrum of the middle classes. They recognized the importance of their role in such communities and sought to build up middle-class self-confidence, at the same time as they saw themselves providing a stimulus to behaviour which would regenerate both the Protestant nation and the evangelical community within it. In this sense the debate constituted a more broadly based contemporary counterpart to the critique of industrial and commercial society offered by first-generation Christian socialists, and helped to pave the way for the later nineteenth-century debate on social ethics, and the wider recognition of the role of ethical factors in the construction of economic theory.[66]

Notes

1   *Parl. Papers* 1854, xxvii (1791), Royal Commission on the Mercantile Laws; Memorandum of Henry Ashworth, p. 195.
2   J. Postgate, *A Few Words on Adulteration* (Birmingham, 1857), p. 3.
3   See D. M. Evans, *Facts, Failures and Frauds: Revelations, Financial, Mercantile, Criminal* (1859; repr. New York and Newton Abbot: David and Charles, 1968), p. 3; idem, *The History of the Commercial Crisis 1857–8 and the Stock Exchange Panic of 1859* (1859; repr. New York and Newton Abbot: David and Charles, 1969), pp. 10–11; S. G. Checkland, *The Rise of Industrial Society in England* (Longmans, 1964), pp. 37–8; J. R. T. Hughes, *Fluctuations in Trade, Industry and Finance* (Oxford: Clarendon Press, 1960), pp. 10–30; R. A. Church, *The Great Victorian Boom 1850–73* (Macmillan, 1975), p. 43.
4   Evans, *Facts, Failures and Frauds*; cf. *Baptist Magazine* 44 (1856), pp. 690–1.
5   See G. H. Wright, *Chronicles of the Birmingham Commercial Society and Chamber of Commerce*; T. S. Ashton, *Economic and Social Investigations in Manchester 1833–1933. A Centenary History of the Manchester Statistical Society* (repr. Hassocks: Harvester, 1977); O. R. McGregor, 'The Contribution to Law Reform of the National Association for the Promotion of Social Science' in his *Social History and Law Reform*, The Hamlyn Lectures, 31st series (1981), pp. 17–26.
6   J. Hinton, 'On the elements supplied by the Holy Scriptures for the formation of an industrial character, individual and national' in S. Martin ed., *The Useful Arts* (1851), p. 270.
7   *Record*, 29 Oct. 1860.
8   For further elucidation of this and other themes, see E. J. Garnett, 'Aspects of the Relationship between Protestant Ethics and

Economic Activity in mid-Victorian England' (D.Phil. thesis, University of Oxford, 1986), forthcoming as an Oxford Historical Monograph.

9 e.g. the Congregationalist Thomas Binney of King's Weigh House; the Wesleyans William Arthur and John Rattenbury; the Baptists W. L. Giles of Birmingham and Hugh Stowell Brown of Liverpool; the Manchester Anglican James Bardsley.

10 *The Times*, 13 Sept. 1855, p. 6.

11 *Record*, 17 Sept. 1855, p. 2.

12 *Record*, 30 Dec. 1859, p. 2.

13 E. Freedley, *Money* (1853), p. 61.

14 H. Stowell, 'The Christian Man in the Business of Life' in *Manchester Lectures: Christianity in the Business of Life* (1858), p. 95; R. S. Hardy, *Commerce and Christianity: Memorials of Jonas Sugden* (1858), p. 192.

15 J. Goadby, *The Influence of Business on the Christian Life* (1870), p. 5.

16 R. W. Dale, *Discourses delivered on Special Occasions* (1866), p. 50.

17 J. Rendel Harris ed., *The Life of Francis William Crossley* (2nd edn, 1899), pp. 149, 218, vi.

18 Harris, *Crossley*, p. 52; C. Finney, *C. G. Finney: An Autobiography* (1882), p. 388; J. F. Findlay, *Dwight L. Moody. American Evangelist 1837–1899* (University of Chicago Press, 1969); G. France, ed., *Reminiscences. Thomas Hudson Bainbridge* (1913), pp. 60–7; R. Carwardine, *Transatlantic Revivalism* (Westport CT: Greenwood Press, 1978); L. S. Hunter, *John Hunter, D.D. A Life* (1921), p. 49; cf. C. Brown, *A Social History of Religion in Scotland since 1730* (Methuen, 1987), pp. 138–41.

19 Harris, *Crossley*, p. vii; Hunter, *John Hunter*, pp. 20, 29; R. W. Dale, *The Old Evangelicalism and the New* (1889), *passim*.

20 S. Pearson, *Service in Three Cities. Twenty-five Years Ministry* (1891), pp. 106, 15.

21 W. Braden, *Our Social Relationships and Life in London* (1876), p. 97; Harris, *Crossley*, pp. 165–6; D. Davies, *Owen Owen. Victorian Draper* (Aberystwyth: Gwasg Cambria, 1984), pp. 20–1.

22 J. Symons, *The History and Advantages of Young Men's Associations* (1856); C. Binfield, *George Williams and the YMCA* (Heinemann, 1973); W. E. Shipton, *The YMCA in London. Its History, Objects and Development* (n.d., c.1855), p. 11; F. M. Holmes, *Exeter Hall and its Associations* (1881).

23 W. Arthur, *The Successful Merchant; sketches of the Life of Mr Samuel Budgett, late of Kingswood Hill* (1852).

24 See Garnett, thesis, cap. 4.

25 B. G. Orchard, *The Clerks of Liverpool* (1871), p. 5; B. Harrison, *Peaceable Kingdom. Stablity and Change in Modern Britain* (Oxford: Clarendon Press, 1982), p. 173; H. Corke, *In our Infancy. An Autobiography Part I: 1882–1912* (Cambridge UP, 1975), p. 2.

26 W. H. Lyttelton, *Sins of Trade and Business. A Sermon; and The Morals of Trade by Herbert Spencer* (1874), p. 72.

27 See C. N. Ward-Perkins, 'The Commercial Crisis of 1847', *Oxford Economic Papers*, n.s. 2 (1950), p. 83.

28 H. Kemp, *The Same Rule for the Merchant and the Private Man* (Hull, 1858), p. 11.

29 *The Economist*, 31 Jan. 1857; R.W. Church, *The Dynamics of Victorian Business* (George Allen and Unwin, 1980), p. 38.

30 B. Gregory, *The Thorough Business Man* (1871), p. 322.

31 *Record*, 6 Jan. 1848.

32 Arthur, *The Successful Merchant*, p. 85.

33 H. M. Villiers, 'Gold and Gold Seekers', *Lectures delivered before the YMCA in Exeter Hall 1852–3* (1853), p. 156; R.W. Dale, 'The Use of the Understanding in keeping God's Law', *Weekday Sermons* (1867), p. 17; J.Todd, 'Men of Business: their position, influence and duties', *The Man of Business* (Edinburgh, 1864), p. 78.

34 Discussion in *Record*, 23 July 1855, p. 2.

35 J. Postgate, *A Few Words on Adulteration*; *Parl. Papers* 1856 viii (379), Select Committee on the Adulteration of Food, Drink and Drugs, I, pp. 3, iv; J. Aubrey Rees, *The Grocery Trade; its History and Romance*, 2 vols. (1910), ii, p. 186; *Record*, 25 Aug. 1856, p. 3.

36 *Record*, 22 May 1861, p. 2; *Congregational Sermons* (1861), p. 78; Freedley, *Money*, pp. 186–99; *Parl. Papers* 1852–3, xxii, p. 112.

37 *Methodist New Connexion Magazine* 55 (1852), pp. 82–3; for disciplinary procedures, see, e.g., City of Birmingham Archive and Library, Carr's Lane Discipline Committee (Congregationalist), Book II, pp. 65–7: the case of Philip Levin (1869), whose failure was treated sympathetically as his books had been very correctly kept; contrast Manchester Central Library Archives, Hardshaw East Monthly Meeting Minutes (Quaker), vol. vii, pp. 6–7: the case of Robert Levitt (1870), whose books had been very irregularly kept and who was disowned.

38 Evans, *Facts, Failures and Frauds*, pp. 651–52.

39 London, Guildhall Library: Budgett MSS, 20: 364, 363, 362/1.

40 Until the last quarter of the nineteenth century well over 90 per cent of firms in GB were family-based partnerships. Cf. D. Jeremy ed., *Religion and Business in Britain* (Aldershot: Gower, 1988), p. 6. See also H. Shannon, 'The Limited Companies of 1866–1883', *Economic History Review* iv (1932), pp. 290–316, for a discussion of the growth from c.1875 of what was effectively the private limited company (although there was no such formal legal category at that time), which was defined by the lack of appeal to the general public for funds, and by a fair amount of personal acquaintance amongst members. Such companies constituted a fifth of effective formations in the period 1875–83.

41 *Pace* B. Hilton, *The Age of Atonement* (Oxford: Clarendon Press, 1988), esp. pp. 276–97. The link between legal limitation of liability and limitation of sin was not generally made by evangelicals. At this point the *Record*, for example, maintained a tough line on eternal

punishment, but did not reject limited liability (although it was critical of some of the *ways* in which the law operated), regarding a heightened sense of responsibility as a prerequisite if the law was to operate effectively. This was particularly necessary, given the radical nature of Lowe's bill, which made, for example, no statutory regulation to keep any specific books. See P. Cottrell, *Industrial Finance 1830–1914* (Methuen, 1983), pp. 52–6. *Record*, 10 Aug. 1855; *Record*, 19 Feb. 1864.

42 *In Memoriam John Rylands* (Manchester, 1889), p. 30: the Manchester textile manufacturer John Rylands (1801–88) formed a limited company in 1873. Directors were chosen from those who had long held positions of high responsibility in the firm, and of the first issue of 75,000 shares, 25,000 were allotted to employees of the firm. Cf. Sir Henry Mitchell (1824–98), *Dictionary of Business Biography* (hereafter *DBB*) ed. D. Jeremy, C. Shaw, 5 vols (Butterworth, 1984–6), iv, 262–5 (entry by D. Jenkins).

43 H. Shannon, 'The first five thousand limited companies and their duration', *Economic History* 2 (1931), p. 399; *Record*, 30 May 1866, p. 2. See also J. B. Jefferys, 'The Denomination and Character of Shares, 1855–1885', *Economic History Review* 16 (1946), pp. 45–55, for a discussion of the trend (which began after the 1866 panic) towards the issuing of shares of a lower denomination, of which a larger proportion was called up.

44 *Record*, 10 Nov. 1858, p. 2; W. McCombie, *Modern Civilisation in relation to Christianity* (Edinburgh, 1864), p. 75ff.

45 Harris, *Crossley*, pp. 82–6.

46 *DBB*, v, p. 828, entry for George Williams by C. Binfield.

47 D. Jeremy, *Capitalists and Christians. Business Leaders and the Churches in Britain, 1900–60* (Oxford: Clarendon Press, 1990), pp. 145–9.

48 *DBB*, v, pp. 534–5 (entry by P. J. Atkins).

49 *DBB*, i, pp. 766–9 (entry by J. Simmons); cf. Simmons, 'Thomas Cook of Leicester', *Trans. Leics. Arch. and Hist. Soc.* 49 (1973–4), pp. 18–32.

50 W. Braden, *Our Social Relationships and Life in London* (1876), pp. 105–13, 117–36.

51 See, for example, entries under Allcroft, Higgs, Balfour, J. J. Colman, F. Crossley, B. Hingley, H. Lee in *DBB*.

52 W. Kirkman, *T. C. Hincksman of Lytham (1799–1883)* (n.d. ? 1885).

53 Examples in *DBB* include Stevenson Arthur Blackwood, Arthur Chamberlain, Richard Longden Hattersley. The Congregationalist Masseys of Openshaw were even-handed in resisting both trade unions and employers' organizations. See C. Binfield, 'Business Paternalism and the Congregational Ideal: a preliminary reconnoitre' in Jeremy ed., *Religion and Business*, pp. 118–41, at p. 127.

54 R. Campbell, 'A critique of the Christian Businessman and his paternalism', Jeremy, ed., *Religion and Business*, pp. 27–46, at p. 42.

55 Binfield, 'Business Paternalism', p. 129.

56 J. Garnett, '"Gold and the Gospel": Systematic Beneficence in mid-nineteenth-century England', in W. J. Sheils and D. Wood, eds, *Studies in Church History*, 24 (1987), pp. 347–58, at pp. 354–5.

57 *Record*, 28 Aug. 1851, p. 3; 27 April 1859, p. 2; *Christian Observer* 55 (1855), pp. 81–3; 61 (1861), p. 403ff. See Garnett thesis, cap. 3, esp. pp. 144–6; cf. Braden, *Social Relationships*, pp. 112–13.

58 G. France ed., *Reminiscences. Thomas Hudson Bainbridge* (1913), pp. 10–12 and *passim*.

59 *DBB*, v, pp. 776–9.

60 Binfield, 'Business Paternalism', p. 125.

61 Harris, *Crossley*, pp. 127–8ff.

62 G. Milburn ed., 'The Diary of John Young. Sunderland Chemist and Methodist Lay Preacher covering the years 1841–43', *Surtees Society* 195 (1983), p. 135.

63 See, for example, R. H. Preston, *Religion and the Ambiguities of Capitalism* (SCM Press, 1991), pp. 11, 40. Torben Christensen's work was important in modifying the heroic view of the Christian socialists, although he felt that the division of life into a religious and a secular sphere against which the Christian socialists protested was 'deeply rooted in Evangelicals and Tractarians alike'. *The Origin and History of Christian Socialism 1848–54* (Aarhus: Universitetsforlaget, 1962), p. 218. His later important but subsequently neglected article, 'F. D. Maurice and the Contemporary Religious World', in G. J. Cuming ed., *Studies in Church History* 3 (1966), pp. 69–90, stripped away more of the mythology surrounding the ways in which Maurice's ideas were treated in his lifetime, and deplored twentieth-century neglect of mid-Victorian evangelicalism. David Thompson has recently emphasized the contribution of evangelicals to the emergence of the social gospel in the later nineteenth century, and sees Dale's role as important; but he does not give any account of the breadth of evangelical activity from the 1840s. D. M. Thompson, 'The Emergence of the Nonconformist Social Gospel in England' in K. Robbins ed., *Studies in Church History*, Subsidia 7 (1990), pp. 255–80; idem, 'The Christian Socialist Revival in Britain: A Reappraisal' in J. Garnett and C. Matthew eds, *Revival and Religion since 1700. Essays for John Walsh* (Hambledon Press, 1993), pp. 273–95.

64 R. H. Tawney, *The Acquisitive Society* (1921; repr. Brighton: Wheatsheaf Books, 1982), pp. 17–30, 176–84.

65 Tawney, *Acquisitive Society*, pp. 88–9.

66 See further on this last point J. Garnett and A. C. Howe, 'Churchmen and Cotton Masters in Victorian England' in D. Jeremy ed., *Religion and Business*, pp. 72–94, at p. 74.

Chapter Four

British Evangelicals and Overseas Concerns, 1833–1970

BRIAN STANLEY

On 1 June 1840 the inaugural meeting of the African Civilization Society took place in Exeter Hall on the Strand in London. The chair was taken by the young Prince Albert. A distinguished audience of four thousand packed the hall to hear Sir Thomas Fowell Buxton, successor to William Wilberforce as the champion of the anti-slavery cause, outline his scheme for the redemption of Africa from the curse of the slave trade. He proposed a recipe of British naval power, Western civilization, legitimate commerce, and, above all, Christianity. Although the audience comprised most shades of ecclesiastical opinion, the meeting symbolized the extent to which the distinctively evangelical imperative to regenerate the globe through Christian missionary enterprise had secured the endorsement, not merely of the churches, but also of large sections of the British political establishment.[1] Whereas, as recently as 1813, evangelical arguments that the British role in India carried with it inescapable spiritual obligations towards the indigenous inhabitants had met with general derision, by 1840 the evangelical contention that providence had marked out for Britain a humanitarian and salvific role in the world was widely accepted. The anti-slavery campaign that culminated in the abolition of slavery in the British colonies in 1833–4 had transformed the missionary impulse from the preoccupation of a despised sectarian minority into a developing public enthusiasm which would eventually issue in the popular imperialism of the late

81

Victorian period. Although Buxton's Niger expedition was a disaster, his project was the inspiration for a major and sustained British missionary advance into West Africa, and hence placed the African continent firmly in the centre of the British Christian and humanitarian conscience, where it remained into the age of Livingstone (in the third quarter of the century) and beyond. More broadly, the union, symbolized in Exeter Hall in 1840, between humanitarian concern for the oppressed, the evangelical imperative to spread the gospel, and a willingness to employ British power to promote these objectives, was to characterize much evangelical thinking on international questions for the remainder of the nineteenth century.

Evangelicals are Christians for whom, almost by definition, the spread of the gospel is a passion and priority. To that extent their outlook on the world has consistently been a missionary perspective, even though the geographical limitations on their evangelistic enthusiasm have sometimes been quite severe. What was distinctive about the outlook of British (and also, to a large extent, American) evangelicals on the world in the period from 1833 to the 1920s was their insistence that the priority of world mission demanded a certain set of agreed policies, or at least a certain set of agreed principles determining policy, from government.

Admittedly, evangelical views on overseas issues were not monochrome. The divergences in the 1820s and 1830s between the moderate evangelicals who believed that society worked best if natural law and free trade were given free rein, and the radical Tory premillenarians who called for state intervention to curb the oppressive influence of evil men were partially, and paradoxically, reflected in attitudes to overseas questions. Whereas anti-slavery was a passionate commitment of the moderates (because slavery contravened the natural law of freedom), some radicals, such as Edward Irving and Henry Drummond, defended slavery as part of the providential order.[2] However, in Britain, in contrast to America, evangelical apologists for slavery remained a small and non-vocal minority. Much of the dynamic of the radical Tories who campaigned for factory legislation in Britain in fact derived from their identification of working conditions in the mills and factories as 'white slavery'.[3]

A more fundamental and enduring division within the evangelical community was over the question of the appropriate relationship between Church and state. Anglicans and Nonconformists differed on how far it was appropriate to look to the state to provide material assistance to missionary endeavour. Nonconformists originally resisted any funding of mission schools by colonial governments. Evangelical Anglicans, on the other hand, saw state aid for Christian education as a necessary expression of the mutuality of Church and state in the preservation of the social fabric. These two conceptions came into regular conflict, most notably in India in the aftermath of the Mutiny or Rebellion of 1857–8. The revolt of the Indian sepoys appeared for a time to threaten the very continuance of British rule in India. All evangelicals responded to these events by demanding that British policy should forswear compromise with Hindu 'idolatry', but Nonconformists and Anglicans disagreed over the terms under which Christian teaching should be introduced into government schools.[4] It was also true that Nonconformist missionaries were generally more prepared than Anglican ones to adopt stances that were openly critical of government policy. For example, when India missionaries at the end of the 1880s rather belatedly began to agitate about the fact that a substantial proportion of the revenues of British India derived from the opium trade, a high percentage of Congregationalist and Baptist missionaries joined the campaign, whereas Methodists were less prominent, and Anglicans less enthusiastic still. There is some evidence that those who hung back were influenced by fears that the government grants-in-aid on which their schools work depended might be jeopardized.[5]

Nevertheless, despite the existence of this major fault-line within evangelicalism, there was a considerable measure of agreement amongst evangelicals over the principles which ought to govern British global policy. The first of these principles was that British influence in the world should be employed on the side of the victims of oppression rather than on the side of the oppressors. In particular, those who were the victims of the slave trade or who were in a state of actual or virtual slavery remained a concern of evangelical opinion long after the abolition of British colonial slavery in 1834.

The second principle which evangelicals looked to see reflected in British foreign policy was that British influence should never be responsible for hindering the global progress of the gospel. They felt that, sadly, the reverse was too often the case, notably in India in the first half of the nineteenth century, where the policy of the East India Company, through which India was ruled until 1859, appeared to be directed towards the support, rather than the subversion, of Hinduism. Most Nonconformists would have declared themselves content if the policy of East India Company or Colonial Office had been palpably directed to ensuring a level playing field between the forces of evangelical Christianity and its religious competitors. Evangelical Anglicans, with their conception of Church and state as complementary aspects of the same Christian polity, tended to go further in asking the state to throw its weight decidedly on the side of the gospel. It was frequently the case, as in late nineteenth-century India, that evangelical concern to see the advance of the gospel transformed missionaries whose theology appeared to lay little stress on issues of social justice into radical campaigners against inhumane social practices that hindered missionary work.[6]

A third principle, undergirding the other two, took the form of an insistence that government ought to be swayed more by the absolute claims of 'duty' than by narrow considerations of short-term self-interest. Britain's global influence and imperial power were given to her by God in trust for moral and eternal purposes. In the long term, if she opted for duty and virtue she would find that she had also chosen the path of blessing and prosperity. In the short term, however, there would be occasions when Britain's Christian duty to protect the oppressed or dissociate herself from religious error or moral evil would demand material sacrifice. Thus missionary journals consistently denounced the involvement of the nation in immoral trades such as the opium trade in China or, somewhat later, the liquor trade in southern Nigeria, and called for morality to take precedence over profit. Yet in both cases evangelicals persuaded themselves that ultimately the repudiation of immoral trading activity would prove to the benefit of legitimate commerce.[7] Their underlying confidence that the path of virtue would prove to be the path of happiness revealed the continuing influence on evangelicalism of characteristically eighteenth-century patterns of thought.

Beneath each of these three principles lay a set of Enlightenment assumptions about the division of the world into civilized Christian nations and uncivilized non-Christian or 'heathen' nations. Oppression, it was readily recognized, was not the exclusive preserve of the heathen. Indeed, much evangelical energy was expended in protest against the exploitation of 'native' peoples by those who bore the name of 'Christian' yet showed none of the fruits of Christianity. It was precisely the 'primitive' and unenlightened condition of heathen societies that made their inhabitants peculiarly vulnerable to exploitation by unscrupulous representatives of higher civilizations. Nevertheless, it remained an axiom of missionary literature well into the twentieth century that the heathen world was to a unique degree itself a place of cruelty and dark oppression, and that conversely it was the responsibility of those nations that had been enlightened by Christian influence to point to a more humane and civilized scale of values. Viewed in its broadest perspective, the goal of the missionary enterprise was to move primitive societies along that scale towards Christian civilization, even though leading missionary thinkers recognized that civilization could not simply take the form of duplicating Western models.[8]

The insistence, second, that British governments should not give encouragement to alien and idolatrous religious systems rested ultimately on the premise that Britain was a Christian nation peculiarly accountable to God in a not dissimilar way to Old Testament Israel. Even Nonconformists, whose ecclesiology, when strictly applied, ruled out the concept of Christian nations, tended in practice to think in these terms.

Third, the assertion that the choices facing governments could, at least on occasion, be presented in terms of a stark juxtaposition of right and wrong reflected a confidence that the historical process had a meaningful and discernible direction under the hand of God; providence, though admittedly mysterious, was not totally obscure.

The remainder of this chapter will examine firstly how these three interlocking principles shaped evangelical responses to global issues in the nineteenth and early twentieth centuries. It will then be argued that, from the 1920s onwards, some of the foundations on which these assumptions were based were progressively undermined, with the result that, as the twentieth century proceeded, evangelical thinking on global issues began to lose the substantial degree of coherence and consensus that it had hitherto displayed.

The evangelical global conscience had been forged in the late eighteenth and early nineteenth centuries in particular relation to West Indian slavery. The West Indies, and notably Jamaica, continued to hold a special place in the awareness of Nonconformists, who had strong missionary interests in the Caribbean. When in 1865 blacks at Morant Bay in Jamaica rose in revolt against continuing exploitation by their erstwhile owners, and were savagely punished by Governor Eyre, most evangelicals ranged themselves with the liberal and radical voices calling for Eyre's recall and prosecution. The secretary of the Baptist Missionary Society, E. B. Underhill, whose public representations on behalf of the Jamaican peasantry were blamed by Eyre for stirring up the rising, played a prominent role in the ensuing controversy in Britain. Baptists and Congregationalists strongly supported him. Wesleyan Methodists and evangelical Anglicans, always more anxious about the dangers of revolt against established authority, were, however, less clear-cut in their attitudes.[9]

Evangelical anti-slavery sentiment after 1834 was, however, focused more consistently on the African continent than on the Caribbean. Buxton's Niger expedition alerted evangelicals to the continuing vitality of the slave trade across the Atlantic and ingrained in Christian public dogma the principle that the introduction of the gospel to the heart of Africa was the only lasting remedy for the running sore of the slave traffic. David Livingstone, returning to Britain in 1856 after his epic trans-African journey, was able to utilize this tradition to gather support for a new government-sponsored expedition to bring civilization, lawful commerce and Christianity to Africa, this time to its Eastern shores, via the river Zambezi. Although the Zambezi expedition of 1858–64 was no more successful than its West African predecessor,[10] it ultimately fulfilled the same function for East and Central Africa as the Niger expedition had done for West Africa. Missionary strategists turned their attention to the east of the continent, and after the death of

Livingstone in 1873, to the penetration of the African interior, to the exploration of which Livingstone had devoted his last years.

As a result, during the last quarter of the century, while British secular imperialism was drawn to tropical Africa for both strategic and economic reasons, the British missionary conscience fastened magnetically on the same region, both because of the intrinsic compulsion of the vision of winning 'Africa for Christ',[11] and because this was the stage on which the next act of the dramatic conflict between gospel freedom and oppressive slavery was being played out. For here the forces of evangelical missions were ranged not merely against Arab slave-traders and a militant Islamic expansionism orchestrated from Zanzibar, but also against a now resurgent Roman Catholic missionary enterprise that sheltered under the umbrella of the imperial designs of France or Portugal. It was in this context that evangelical concern for the oppressed and commitment to the advance of the gospel combined to make many evangelicals into advocates of imperial expansion to a degree that their present-day descendants find intensely embarrassing. Nonconformists, traditionally committed to principles of peace and non-intervention in overseas affairs, could now appear on occasion almost as pro-imperial as Anglicans.[12]

Thus, at the Berlin conference on West Africa in 1884–5, the Baptist Missionary Society strongly supported the Belgian King Leopold II's Association Internationale du Congo, and subsequently supported its offspring, the Congo Free State. The Society believed, with some justice, that Leopold's promise to keep the Congo open for free trade and Christianity was much to be preferred to the prospect either of Portuguese annexation, with its attendant consequences of an extension of slave trading and a Roman Catholic monopoly of missionary activity, or of Islamic control of the upper Congo river.[13] Similarly, from 1887 to 1889 the General Assemblies of both the Church of Scotland and the Free Church of Scotland applied pressure on Lord Salisbury's government to declare Nyasaland a British sphere of influence in order to forestall control either by Arabs from the north or Portuguese from the south. The eventual consequence was that Nyasaland became a British protectorate and was kept safe for Presbyterian missionary expansion.[14] Most notorious of all from a modern Christian perspective, a determined campaign by evangelical Anglican opinion in 1892 to persuade the Liberal government not to 'abandon' Uganda to French Catholic missions or, supremely, to Muslim slave-traders, eventually secured the declaration of a British protectorate over Uganda in 1894.[15]

Similar trends are observable in relation to other parts of the globe. Wesleyan Methodists, who had a strong missionary presence in Fiji, campaigned successfully from 1872 to 1874 in favour of British annexation of Fiji on the grounds that it was necessary to curb the 'Pacific slave trade' – the traffic in cheap labour that had been developed to service the settler-run plantations of the islands.[16] In 1906 Congregationalist missionaries and supporters of the London Missionary Society expressed fears that the imminent transfer of Papua New Guinea from Colonial Office control to the Australian government would lead to widespread exploitation of the native population by white settlers.[17]

Evangelical concern for native peoples at the mercy of exploitative commercial or political interests did not lead invariably to demands for British annexation, but some form of government action or protest to remedy the situation was almost always called for. When the Baptist missionary J. S. Bowskill was imprisoned by the Portuguese colonial authorities in northern Angola in 1914, falsely accused of stirring up a native rising and agitating for British annexation, the Baptist Missionary Society was quick to make representations to the Foreign Office and mobilize protest in press and parliament. In reality, the Portuguese fear that British Baptist opinion might agitate for British intervention had little substance, but the momentum of the Baptist campaign derived from the familiar juxtaposition of an evangelical missionary defending native interests against forced labour and a Portuguese state that appeared to have the backing of Roman Catholic missions.[18]

In the years after the First World War, the theological assumptions which had undergirded evangelical responses to humanitarian and religious crises in the non-Western world were progressively undermined. The process was uneven and protracted, and evangelicals were slower than others to abandon the intellectual framework inherited from the nineteenth century. At the same time, evangelicalism itself lost its cohesion, as the movement increasingly bifurcated into liberal and conservative or fundamentalist wings.

Evangelical commitment to the cause of the oppressed overseas did not disappear in the twentieth century, but it was displayed mainly by those at the liberal end of the evangelical theological spectrum, and particularly by those who held influential metropolitan positions within the missionary movement. Pre-eminent among such in the inter-war period was J. H. Oldham, secretary of the International Missionary Council. Oldham was a consistent thorn in the side of the Colonial Office, urging indigenous interests against European settler demands, especially in Kenya, where a system of virtual forced labour was applied by the landowners of the 'White Highlands'. Oldham, however, could count on the unqualified support of neither evangelical opinion in the churches nor of all evangelical missionaries on the field. In 1920–3, when Oldham's campaign against forced labour was at its height, conservative evangelical missionary thinking was preoccupied with the theological battle against creeping liberalism within the evangelical camp. In East Africa itself, the chief opponent of forced labour was the Anglo-Catholic Bishop of Zanzibar, Frank Weston; evangelical missionary leaders were less clear-cut in their opposition.[19]

The retreat among conservative evangelicals from the 'social gospel' in the 1920s had the effect of distancing them from the campaigns waged on behalf of native interests by such as J. H. Oldham. Their political thinking on global questions was rarely articulated, and, when it was, it tended to be more heavily influenced than before by prevailing racist and imperial sentiments. Evangelical thinking lost much of its distinctiveness, and now mirrored more closely the divisions within public opinion as a whole. In August 1935 the General Secretary of the Baptist Union, M. E. Aubrey, surveying the range of denominational opinion on the Abyssinian crisis, had to confess that he had never known such a variety of opinion amongst Baptists on such an issue. Many Baptists deplored the Italian invasion of Abyssinia and wished to uphold the flouted authority of the League of Nations. Others, however, clearly sympathized with the widely expressed view that a slave-holding African nation should never have been admitted to the League of Nations, and that the needs of Italy as a white 'civilized' nation for an outlet for its surplus population should be respected.[20] On the other hand, the magazine of the Bible Churchmen's Missionary Society, which had work in Ethiopia, was forthright in its support for Emperor Haile Selassie and condemnation of Italy's 'lust of conquest'.[21] However, the response of the Society to the crisis was more theological than political in nature: its annual report for 1935 called on evangelical Anglicans not to mount a political protest against Italian aggression, but rather to reflect with thanksgiving that 'Amidst the chaos and the darkness, amidst the impotence and failure of Christian Europe, there is one little ray of light which fills one's soul with praise – at any rate B.C.M.S. has done her bit for Righteousness and for Truth.'[22] In marked contrast to the buoyant mood of the Victorian age, evangelicals were now increasingly conscious of their status as a beleaguered minority within the churches. As a result, political crises on the global stage came to be seen primarily as confirming evidence of the need for true believers to hold ever more firmly to the light of gospel truth amidst the surrounding darkness. Campaigns for the victims of oppression overseas were no longer high on the agenda.

Evangelicals in the twentieth century were no less committed than their nineteenth-century predecessors to the view that British foreign policy should never be responsible for hindering the progress of missionary work. However, under the more settled imperial conditions of twentieth-century India or Africa, instances of British imperial influence being exerted contrary to missionary interests were much less common. With occasional exceptions, the *pax Britannica* seemed to favour Christian concerns and to be a reassuring bulwark against the unknown quantity of nascent nationalism. In India above all, missionary and imperial objectives now converged with alarming ease. Some new missionaries arriving in India, such as Lesslie Newbigin in 1936, were horrified by the extent to which missionaries had assumed the outlook and lifestyle of the *sahibs*.[23]

Nineteenth-century Christian attitudes to global affairs were founded on a belief in the active providence of God and of the unique calling of Christian nations, and of Britain in particular, within that providential order. Perhaps the most telling

contrast between nineteenth- and twentieth-century Christian
mentalities is provided by the weakening (and, in places, complete disintegration) of this providentialist framework. The
progressive distancing of God in the public mind from the
detail of historical events is a clear index of the inroads of
secularization.[24] Within evangelicalism, however, the weakening of the providentialist view of history was more gradual and
less marked than in other sections of the churches. Admittedly
some evangelicals now adopted a pessimistic premillennial
eschatology which held that no improvement in the spiritual
condition of the world could be expected until Christ returned
to establish his millennial reign, and hence were much less
inclined to see the world as the arena of divine sovereignty.
However, there was no necessary connection between a premillennial stance and a loss of confidence in providence.
Henry Grattan Guinness's *The Approaching End of the Age*, first
published in 1878 but re-issued significantly in 1918, was in no
doubt that missionary progress in China, Japan and the African
interior, or the decline of Turkish power in the Middle East,
were among the hopeful signs that the end was approaching.[25]
Evangelicalism as a whole retained the fundamentals of a belief
in the direct divine control of the historical process for longer
than any other group within the church. Indeed, considerable
numbers of evangelicals between the wars took their belief
in the unique calling of Britain to the extreme of British
Israelitism, in which the identification between the Anglo-
Saxon race and God's covenant people was made explicit.[26]
    Neither can it be asserted that those evangelicals who were
of more liberal theological disposition abandoned all sense of the
hand of God in the historical process. Max Warren, General
Secretary of the Church Missionary Society from 1942 to 1963,
possessed an acute awareness of the controlling hand of God in
contemporary history.[27] To that extent, Warren stood squarely
in the tradition of his forebears. Yet Max Warren's providentialist landscape displayed very different contours from that of
the Victorians: for him, the hand of God was to be seen just as
clearly in the forces of Chinese Communism or Indian nationalism as in the power of the British empire. With a vision
shaped particularly by the Old Testament prophets, Warren
drew much sharper distinctions than had his evangelical

predecessors between that which God used and that of which he approved.[28] In place of the stark nineteenth-century juxtapositions between Christian and heathen, enlightened and benighted, Warren emphasized ambiguity and complexity. In so far as the current nationalist resurgence in Asia and Africa fostered aggression and self-centredness, it was indeed to be deplored, but to the extent that nationalism promoted diversity and respect for vernacular cultures it was to be welcomed by Christians as an expression of God's creative preference for harmony over drab uniformity.[29]

Although confidence in God's working within the historical process remained broadly intact, Warren led the more liberal sections of evangelicalism towards a perspective on global affairs in which Britain and the other sending countries of the historic missionary movement no longer occupied centre stage in the divine purpose. The new outlook was reinforced above all by the impact of the enforced missionary exodus from Communist China between 1949 and 1953. The China débâcle, more than any other episode, was the primary reason for what Warren described as an 'orgy of self-criticism' that seized the missionary movement in the early 1950s.[30] The CMS missionary David Paton took the lead in urging Christians to apply their theology of providence to the Communist take-over. Like Warren, he suggested an analogy between the Communists and the Assyrians in Isaiah 10 or Cyrus in Isaiah 45: a godless people were being raised up by God to be the instruments of his judgement on his own people. The missionary movement, far from being able to claim the automatic endorsement of divine purpose, in fact stood under divine judgement for its pride and complicity with Western imperial aggression.[31] Similar views were enunciated by Victor Hayward, General Foreign Secretary of the Baptist Missionary Society from 1951 to 1959. Hayward, well in advance in the 1950s of majority opinion within his own largely evangelical denomination, was later even prepared to suggest that the Maoist revolution, rather than Christian missions, might be God's chosen instrument to deliver China's millions from oppression and despair.[32]

Those, such as Hayward, who by the end of our period were willing to contemplate the possibility that Marxism rather than Christianity might be God's providential vehicle for the

liberation of non-Western peoples, had placed themselves outside the arena of evangelicalism, with its historic insistence that
the communication of the gospel of Christ's redemption in
order to lead people to conversion constituted the first priority
of the church. Nevertheless, many evangelicals who did not
share Hayward's theological liberalism were affected in different ways by the new climate of self-doubt which began to
erode the confidence of the British missionary movement from
the 1950s onwards. Even some of those whose theological
framework remained strongly conservative now recognized
that the nationalist backlash had profound implications for the
future of Christian missions. Cecil Bewes, a missionary for
twenty years in Kenya before becoming Africa Secretary of the
CMS in 1949, interpreted the Mau Mau rebellion which took
hold among the Kikuyu people in 1952, both as a sign that 'the
most advanced tribe in Africa' had 'reverted to pagan bar-
barism', but also as a warning to missionaries that they could
never 'go back to the old days of easily-assumed leadership,
the old superior days of life on a pedestal'.[33] The old categories
had not been abandoned, but they no longer led automatically
to assumptions of the priority of the West in the purposes of
God.

The concept of Britain's imperial trusteeship that had been
so foundational to nineteenth-century Christian thinking on
global issues could not survive these fundamental transformations in the evangelical understanding of history. Max Warren
saw it as one of his primary tasks after the end of the Second
World War to help his missionaries to perceive that the days of
trusteeship were numbered:

> A few might realise that an England whose resources, mate-
> rial and psychological, had been strained to the limit, was in
> no condition to maintain an empire, even if it wished to do
> so. Yet it had been under the umbrella of that empire's pro-
> tection and its fundamental, if sometimes muddle-headed,
> liberalism that the missionary had worked. He might, and
> often did, disagree with the local District Commissioner as
> to ways and means and timing. But the missionary had no
> doubt as to the genuineness of that District Commissioner's
> concern for the people in his charge. Insensibly, the missionary

absorbed and shared the benevolent paternalism of the Raj. Rarely did the missionary or the District Commissioner sense the mounting resentment of the governed at the whole concept of 'trusteeship', at a pupillage apparently to continue indefinitely, at the humiliation of being under alien rule.[34]

The old missionary conscience in relation to humanitarian issues overseas did survive in attenuated form into the 1960s, but it could no longer mobilize the degree of support in the British churches that it had once been able to command. In 1961 the Portuguese colonial government savagely repressed a revolt by the Bakongo people of northern Angola among whom the Baptist Missionary Society had long worked. Up to 50,000 Africans were killed. Prompted by Clifford Parsons, the Associate Foreign Secretary of the BMS, three Baptist ministers from Southend set up an Angola Action group to campaign against Portugal's colonial policy. Within the Baptist denomination the campaign took off, and, with the assistance of the *Guardian* newspaper, entered the national political arena. Possibly for the last time, the House of Commons in July 1961 heard a Leader of the Opposition, Hugh Gaitskell, using the testimony of British evangelical missionaries to impugn the policy of the British government (the Macmillan government supported Portugal) on an issue of 'native welfare'. Yet even amongst Baptists there were considerable reservations about the Action Group's campaign, especially from the conservative heartland of the denomination.[35] Those who were most strongly evangelical in their theology had lost their forebears' sensitivity to moral and humanitarian issues on the global stage. Their missionary concerns were more strictly evangelistic. Conversely, those who had slipped their evangelical moorings in favour of more liberal theological anchorages were less and less interested in global evangelization. It was the latter who would dominate debate and agitation in the British churches on world issues in the 1970s and 1980s, but these questions were no longer closely yoked to the context of missionary activity.

Notes

1   On the Exeter Hall meeting and the Niger expedition see Howard
    Temperley, *White Dreams, Black Africa; The Antislavery Expedition to
    the Niger, 1841–1842* (New Haven and London: Yale UP, 1991).

2   Boyd Hilton, *The Age of Atonement: The Influence of Evangelicalism on
    Social and Economic Thought, 1795–1865* (Oxford: Clarendon Press,
    1988), pp. 16–17, 98, 211.

3   J. C. Gill, *Parson Bull of Byerley* (SPCK, 1963), pp. 63–9.

4   David W. Savage, 'Evangelical Educational Policy in Britain and
    India, 1857–60', *Journal of Imperial and Commonwealth History* 22
    (1994), pp. 432–61.

5   G. A. Oddie, *Social Protest in India: British Protestant Missionaries and
    Social Reforms 1850–1900* (New Delhi: Manohar, 1979), pp. 231–43.

6   Oddie, *Social Protest*, pp. 18–22, 245–6.

7   See B. Stanley, *The Bible and the Flag: Protestant Missions and British
    Imperialism in the Nineteenth and Twentieth Centuries* (Leicester:
    Apollos, 1990), p. 108; J. H. Boer, *Missionary Messengers of Liberation
    in a Colonial Context: A Case Study of the Sudan United Mission*
    (Amsterdam: Editions Rodopi, 1979), pp. 187–8.

8   See W. R. Hutchison, *Errand to the World: American Protestant Thought
    and Foreign Missions* (Chicago UP, 1987), pp. 77–90.

9   D. A. Lorimer, *Colour, Class and the Victorians* (Leicester UP, 1978),
    pp. 178–200; B. Semmel, *The Governor Eyre Controversy* (Mac-
    Gibbon and. Kee: 1962); B. Stanley, *The History of the Baptist
    Missionary Society, 1792–1992* (Edinburgh: T. & T. Clark, 1992), pp.
    97–9.

10 See Owen Chadwick, *Mackenzie's Grave* (Hodder & Stoughton,
    1959); B. Pachai, ed., *Livingstone: Man of Africa* (Longman, 1973),
    pp. 29–60.

11 'Africa for Christ' was the slogan with which the Baptist Missionary
    Society launched its Congo mission in 1877; see Stanley, *History of
    the BMS*, pp. 117–18.

12 D. W. Bebbington, *The Nonconformist Conscience: Chapel and Politics
    1870–1914* (Allen & Unwin, 1982), ch. 6.

13 Stanley, *History of the BMS*, pp. 124, 135–9; D. Lagergren, *Mission
    and State in the Congo: A Study of the Relations between Protestant
    Missions and the Congo Independent State Authorities with Special
    Reference to the Equator District, 1885–1903* (Uppsala: Gleerup,
    1970), pp. 66–75.

14 Roland Oliver, *The Missionary Factor in East Africa* (2nd edn.,
    Longman, 1965), pp. 119–28; J. McCracken, *Politics and Christianity
    in Malawi 1875–1940* (Cambridge UP, 1977), pp. 157–9.

15 D. A. Low, *Buganda in Modern History* (Weidenfeld & Nicolson,
    1971), pp. 55–83; Stanley, *The Bible and the Flag*, pp. 127–32.

16 Stanley, *The Bible and the Flag*, pp. 115–16.

17 N. Goodall, *A History of the London Missionary Society 1895–1945*
    (Oxford UP, 1954), pp. 414–15.

18 Stanley, *History of the BMS*, pp. 336–41.
19 Stanley, *The Bible and the Flag*, pp. 147–9; H. Maynard Smith, *Frank Bishop of Zanzibar* (1926), pp. 246–53.
20 *The Baptist Times*, 29 Aug. 1935, p. 631; cf. Daniel Waley, *British Public Opinion and the Abyssinian War 1935–6* (Maurice Temple Smith, Ltd., 1975), pp. 22–4.
21 *The Missionary Messenger* 13 (Oct. 1935), p. 127.
22 *Bible Churchmen's Missionary Society: Annual Report* (1935), p. 34.
23 Lesslie Newbigin, *Unfinished Agenda: An Autobiography* (SPCK, 1985), pp. 40–2.
24 Owen Chadwick, *The Secularization of the European Mind in the Nineteenth Century* (Cambridge UP, 1975), pp. 250–63.
25 Henry Grattan Guinness, *The Approaching End of the Age* revised edn (1918), pp. 348–9.
26 D. W. Bebbington, *Evangelicalism in Modern Britain: A History from the 1730s to the 1980s* (Unwin Hyman, 1989), p. 225; Gerald Studdert-Kennedy, *British Christians, Indian Nationalists and the Raj* (Delhi: Oxford UP, 1991), pp. 190–8.
27 F. W. Dillistone, *Into All the World: A Biography of Max Warren* (Hodder & Stoughton, 1980), pp. 80–1, 147–9.
28 Dillistone, *Into All the World*, pp. 148–9.
29 M. A. C. Warren, 'The Missionary Obligation of the Church in the Present Historical Situation', *International Review of Missions* 39 (Oct. 1950), pp. 396–7.
30 Max Warren, The Christian Mission and the Cross' in Norman Goodall, ed., *Missions Under the Cross* (Edinburgh House Press, 1953), p. 27; cited in A. N. Porter, 'War, colonialism and the British experience: the redefinition of Christian missionary policy, 1938–1952', *Kirchliche Zeitgeschichte* 5 (1992), p. 287.
31 David M. Paton, *Christian Missions and the Judgment of God* (SCM Press, 1953), pp. 18–20; see George Hood, *Neither Bang Nor Whimper: The End of a Missionary Era in China* (Singapore: Presbyterian Church in Singapore, 1991), pp. 198–215.
32 V. Hayward, *Christians and China* (Belfast: Christian Journals Ltd., 1974), pp. 106–7; see Stanley, *History of the BMS*, pp. 396–400.
33 T. F. C. Bewes, *Kikuyu Conflict: Mau Mau and the Christian Witness* (Highway Press, 1953), p. 73.
34 Max Warren, *Crowded Canvas: Some Experiences of a Life-Time* (Hodder & Stoughton, 1974), p. 174.
35 Stanley, *History of the BMS*, pp. 450–6.

Chapter Five

Gender Attitudes and the Contribution of Women to Evangelism and Ministry in the Nineteenth Century

JOCELYN MURRAY

Nineteenth-century Evangelical women undoubtedly made a leading contribution to social improvement.[1] This activity, however, was relatively uncontroversial, because it was seen as an extension of domestic roles as mothers and caregivers. Accordingly, with a view to gaining insights into the gender attitudes operating at the heart of evangelical concerns, I shall in this paper concentrate rather on the involvement of women in evangelism and ministry. This was a very different matter which is still, in the 1990s, a matter of controversy among evangelicals, women as well as men. During the course of the nineteenth century it came to be accepted that women might be used overseas as missionaries in direct evangelism, as well as in indirect evangelism through teaching and nursing. Yet denominations and societies which accepted this, allowing women missionaries to preach and instruct, banished them from the pulpit and platform when they stepped back on to British soil, confining their deputation work to drawing-room meetings for ladies.

I want therefore to look at instances where women, despite difficulties, did involve themselves in evangelism within Britain. What kind of women were they? How did they surmount the obstacles put in their paths? Were they supported by men? Did opponents change their views?

At the beginning of the nineteenth century all women who could afford it, whether single, married, or widows, spent their lives at home. They had limited civil and legal rights, and were in fact legal minors throughout their lives. Gifted individual women contributed to art, literature and drama, but often with difficulty and at great personal cost. A female child's opportunities of education were limited; if it were necessary for a 'lady' to support herself, her options were few. By the end of the nineteenth century the legal and civil position of women had substantially changed, although their right to vote was still two decades away. Higher education was available to some at least, and a few women had entered most of the professions. Yet, in the churches of Britain, with one or two minor exceptions, their official position was scarcely different from what it had been a century earlier.

Why was change within the churches so slow?

Three clusters of facts, beliefs and opinions can be identified which restricted women in regard to evangelism and ministry, and made change very slow. First, there were specific biblical passages, in particular teachings found in Paul's epistles, which appeared to forbid the public ministry of women. These negative interpretations prevailed in almost all denominations and among all theological groups whether Roman Catholic, Anglican or Free Church, whether high, low or broad church. Second, there was more general biblical teaching on women, largely derived from the creation accounts in the early chapters of Genesis. This teaching suggested that women had been inferior from their creation, were unfit to exercise leadership, and were designed by God to be subordinate to men.[2] Third, there were ecclesiastical and traditional factors: the teachings of the church from the earliest times that deacons, priests and bishops should be male, together with an emphasis on the leadership of clergy and a low value attached to lay participation. These traditions held particular weight among Roman Catholics and High Anglicans, but ordained male leaders of all churches were jealous of their own positions.

In the nineteenth century women increasingly received greater respect in society, and were allowed new roles. The Methodist revival and the extension of evangelical influence had led, by the beginning of the Victorian period, to an ideal for women very different to what it had been a few decades earlier. The tone of the court around the young girl-queen reinforced this ideal. There was an emphasis on sexual morality, on the family, on the mother's God-given role in bringing up her children, which was increasingly accepted. Likewise there was an emphasis on the obligation of the wealthier women to engage in charitable acts towards their inferiors. The tone of upper-middle-class and upper-class society was, if not Christian, at least Christianized.

But this development, for which evangelicals were largely responsible, also implied an image of 'woman' into which she and her works had to fit if she was to be acceptable. Important parts of this image involved (and involve) 'femininity', as seen by men. She needed to be attractive in appearance, with a pleasing voice, and a suitably subservient carriage. If she was unfortunate enough to be plain, or large and ungainly; if she was unmarried; if she had a loud voice or an imperious manner, she was suspect. If she engaged in work which required her to exercise direct control, rather than subtle manipulation, she was doubly suspect.

Stated biblical interpretations, legitimizing the inferiority of women, and their exclusion from public ministry, propounded and defended by churchmen on exegetical grounds, were accepted by many churchwomen. There is no evidence that evangelicals, whether from the Anglican or Free Churches, were less swayed by these arguments than were other Christians. Dr John Angell James was the highly respected pastor of Carr's Lane Congregational Chapel, Birmingham, from 1805 until his death in 1859, and an important figure in the founding of the Evangelical Alliance. In his very popular handbook, *Female Piety*,[3] he wrote, '[t]hat woman is intended to occupy a position of subordination and dependence, is clear enough from every part of the word of God.'[4] After stating that 'woman' is the 'cause of death and sin to our world', and then expounding on her position of subordination and dependence, he later encourages her by adding that '[woman] generally knows her place, and feels it her happiness as well as her duty to keep it.' Such views were shared by pious and well-educated Christian women of a variety of theological persuasions. The High Church Charlotte M. Yonge summarized the argument from Genesis thus: 'I have no hesitation in declaring my full belief in the inferiority of woman, nor that she brought it upon herself. . . . It was the woman who was the first to fall and to draw her husband into the same transgression. Thence her punishment of physical weakness and subordination. . . .'[5] A prominent evangelical, Charlotte Elizabeth Tonna, expressed a similar view. She had evidently been a tomboy and, in her memoirs, discussing her childhood relationship with her brother, she wrote, 'I never was considered unfeminine, and the only peculiarity resulting from this constant companionship with one of the superior sex, was to give me a high sense of that superiority, with a habit of deference to man's judgement and submission to man's authority, which I am quite sure God intended the woman to yield.'[6] Thus there was agreement between leading Christian men, and laywomen whose ministry, because it was exercised in writing, was acceptable. Men are superior; women are inferior, and radical or blue-stocking Christian women who aspired to leadership would harm the cause of Christ.

Women in evangelism and ministry: the first phase

The religious ferment around 1800 turned accepted practice upside-down, and spiritual gifting became more important than tradition.[7] The circumstances of this revival, as of others, were favourable to the ministry of women. John Wesley, although somewhat reluctantly, had allowed women to preach.[8] Some had come into prominence even before his death in 1791. Mary Fletcher,[9] who began preaching and teaching at Leytonstone, Essex, where she organized schools and an orphanage, later itinerated and preached in the Leeds area. She was far from being the only one; many women, like Mary Taft, travelled and preached with or without husbands.[10] Among other women was Elizabeth Tomlinson, better known by her married name of Evans – Betsy Evans, wife of Samuel – who, as Dinah Morris, entered literature in the pages of George Eliot's *Adam Bede*.[11]

Such participation by women was justified, or at least tolerated, in the early stages; but it was less likely to be acceptable as
the movement became institutionalized and moved towards the
status of being a denomination. In 1803 the Methodist Conference, the central stream of the emerging Methodist churches,
called the preaching of women into question, without actually
forbidding it. Conference pronounced it 'both unnecessary and
generally undesirable' but proceeded to formulate conditions
under which it might be allowed 'in extraordinary circumstances'.[12]

Revivalism continued, however, and the Methodist New
Connexion, the Bible Christian Methodists of Cornwall, and
the Primitive Methodists, all contained a significant number
of preaching and evangelizing women, some of whom attain-
ed fame or, depending on one's view, notoriety.[13] The Bible
Christians of Devon and Cornwall persisted the longest with
women preachers, announcing them publicly on their list of
circuit preachers. Catherine, the wife of their leader, William
O'Bryan, was a preacher, and in 1814 there were fourteen
women named in their circuits. In 1825–27 the number had
risen to twenty-seven, but thereafter it declined, and the last
woman still active was named in 1863. Among the Primitive
Methodists a tradition of woman preachers also continued.[14]
They held a vital place in the work of Bible Christians and
Primitive Methodists, and no scriptural objections were
raised.[15]

The Bible Christians and the Primitive Methodists were
especially active in rural areas, and as long as preaching took
place in the open air or in barns, and class meetings were held
in cottages, the contribution of women, often ministering to
other women in a semi-domestic setting, was valued. New
Testament Scriptures were not called on to prevent them, and
the traditions of the church and the leadership of ordained
men had little influence in a movement where preaching was
in any case the work of the laity. But as an institution arose,
marked by the building of chapels, and the formerly persecuted
sect became a respected denomination, and as men were
trained and set aside for ministry, the participation of women
in leadership came to seem no longer desirable.[16]

In 1832 the Primitive Methodists still listed thirteen women preachers, but in 1835 both the Methodist Conference and the Methodist New Connexion 'expressed strong disapproval of female preaching *not so much for its own sake as because of certain concomitants*'.[17] It seems that, while the Bible and church tradition could not hinder them, the desire to appear respectable in the eyes of other churches was able to bring about a change. The result was that 'female preaching almost ceased to exist for a protracted period'.[18]

George Eliot, in *Adam Bede* (1859), left us with an appealing picture of an early Methodist woman preacher – feminine and attractive. But the descriptions we have of the living women do not match up, and probably assisted the case against women preachers. Later writers have described them as 'ranters'; 'Praying Nanny' was said to have been bold and loud; Ann Carr of Lincolnshire was described as stout and broad, with a 'powerful voice' and an unfeminine degree of boldness in her manner.[19] Such women did not fit the image which a later generation of Methodists wished to project.

But in the new industrial cities as well as in poor isolated rural cottages, women had a very real ministry to their sisters. If that ministry required preaching and teaching, there were women who would do it. Ann Carr, with female assistants, extended her ministry to the Midlands and, in 1821, to Leeds, where she built up a group of women. They separated themselves from the Primitive Methodists and were called 'Female Revivalists'.[20] They ministered to domestic female workers in the textile industries. At least two chapels were built (in the Leylands, 1825; in Brewery Field Holbeck 1826); schoolrooms were opened; a Friendly Society was organized. In 1824 a hymnbook was published; the second edition of 1838 contains 476 hymns. Many are standard Wesleyan hymns but some appear to have been written especially for women.[21] Ann Carr died in 1841; the group continued, although in decline, until 1853, but then, like many other small Methodist-related groups, disappeared.

The overseas missionary movement, which effectively began in the last decade of the eighteenth century,[22] also came to involve many Christian women across all the denominations. The first missionaries to go overseas were, of course, men, but those from British societies were expected to be married, and their wives participated in their husbands' work, giving women a new field of ministry. The first single women sent out were the sisters of male missionaries, but by the 1820s a few were going in their own right. The first important 'field' for women was India, where it was early recognized by missionaries in Calcutta that females were needed to reach high-caste Indian women and girls secluded in the *zenana*. Miss Mary Ann Cooke, later Mrs Wilson, reached Calcutta in 1820. She was a central figure in the Society for Promoting Female Education in the East (SPFEE), and influential in attracting other women into missionary work. A number of the pioneers were women who went out independently, without the support of a missionary society. We should also note the important role of missionary widows – women who, unnoticed during their husbands' lives, were 'taken up' as widows and continued acknowledged work. Maturity and widowhood were, if anything, an advantage.

The missionary calling became increasingly attractive, because, despite many physical hardships, it offered women a freedom that they could not yet find in their own country. But missionary women were, by definition, still lay workers, and, like laymen, were generally second-class missionaries, in contrast to clergy. A layman might, after study, achieve ordained status; this a lay woman could never do. Mrs Wilson, writing in 1835 and giving advice on how single women could settle and work in India, recognizes this situation. 'There never was a period more inviting than the present for the labours of a host of pious humble-minded Christian Females: in short, they are as much required as missionaries and may be as useful in evangelising these pagan countries.'[23] The woman herself could not change her sex, or her status.

Women in charitable and deaconess work

Meanwhile in Britain, social and industrial changes were causing church leaders to make parallel changes in attitudes to the use of laymen and laywomen. As the urban population grew, the parochial church system – as well as what little was provided in the way of amenities, education and health care – simply broke down. Ordained clergy could not cope; lay volunteers were needed. So we see the beginnings of 'City Missions', co-operation between 'Church' and 'chapel' in the massive tasks, and also church initiatives in social work.[24]

Such activity provided outlets for women at a number of levels.[25] Upper-middle-class and middle-class women (and a considerable number of titled women also) were patrons, fundraisers and supervisors; respectable working-class women were the hands and feet who carried out the day-to-day work. William Pennefather's Mildmay Mission contributed particularly to the more formal *training* of women and the Ranyard Mission, founded by Mrs Ellen Ranyard, provided complex and successful informal training and used local working-class women as Bible women and eventually as district visitors.[26] The women who visited door-to-door were not seen primarily as 'social workers' by their organizations; they were intended to be evangelists, selling Bibles, giving away tracts, witnessing by word and deeds in order to bring their contacts to conversion. There was, however, a constant stress on the fact that they were never to usurp the place of the parish minister.[27]

William Pennefather[28] inaugurated his first annual conference, later known as the Mildmay Meetings, in 1856, when he was incumbent at Christ Church, Barnet. These meetings aimed at bringing together evangelicals of different denominations. His wife founded the Association of Female Workers in 1857. After he moved to Mildmay, in east London, the conferences continued there. Pennefather likewise founded the 'Training Home for Female Missionaries' (later the Missionary Training Home for Young Women) in 1860, while at Barnet, having the model of German deaconess orders in mind.[29] First at Barnet, and later in east London, it took women for a preliminary period and then sent them on for further training at 'The Willows' (for missionaries), the Deaconess House or in the Nursing Home. The deaconess went into parish work; many of the missionary candidates went on to work with the Church Missionary Society or the Church of England Zenana Missionary Society.

In terms of a church-related career for women, the Pennefathers and Mildmay achieved a great deal, but the ministry of the deaconesses, as envisaged by William Pennefather, was largely practical service, and the aspect of evangelistic 'ministry' was carefully circumscribed.

He loved the name [deaconess] as he found it in Romans xvi.i, and he was most anxious that it was possible to develop women's power in practical service, in a happy combination of love and labour, without any approach to the evils of conventual life. But he had also a strong conviction that woman's work ought to be as simple and natural and unofficial as possible, and shrank from anything that might make it too formal or self-asserting.[30]

In other words, women had to stay in their place.

Women in the Second Evangelical Awakening

John Angell James wrote in *Female Piety*, 'Neither reason nor Christianity invites woman to the professor's chair, nor conducts her to the bar, nor makes her welcome in the pulpit, nor admits her to the place of ordinary magistracy.'[31] Even apparent proponents of women's ministry held such views, and women who sought to challenge the *status quo* faced an uphill struggle. In 1853, however, a young woman, Catherine Mumford, member of a Primitive Methodist Chapel in Brixton, South London, wrote a letter to her pastor after she heard him preach a sermon on the inferiority of women.[32] Already she was using Old Testament and New Testament Scriptures to support her argument. Several years later, now married and living in the north of England with her husband William Booth, the later founder of the Salvation Army, but then a minister of the Methodist New Connexion, she was upset to read a pamphlet, based on a sermon by a local minister, Arthur Augustus Rees, violently attacking the right of women to preach.[33] The occasion of the attack was the visit to Newcastle of the American evangelists, Walter Palmer of New York and his wife Phoebe, author of the popular book, *The Way of Holiness*.[34] Mrs Palmer was the leading personality of the two and the better speaker.

Catherine Booth's response was published in 1859.[35] It is interesting to compare her spirited defence of female preaching with a pamphlet by an Anglican clergyman, W. R. Collett, dated 1863. Both discuss the same New Testament passages, chiefly from Paul's epistles and the Acts. Collett finds that all Paul's references point to the woman's role as one of servanthood and hospitality. Her 'teaching' must be limited to children and other women, and even then must be carefully guarded from becoming 'preaching'. Any prophesying [by women] 'must have been private' – 'it is likely that [Philip's daughters] did not exercise their gifts publicly'.[36] He asserted, 'Woman is supposed to work in a parish . . . she is helper [to the ordained minister]; she is working in aid, not in the place of, the parish priest.' And he, like others, emphasizes the importance of woman's feminine qualities. 'Not the least part of every woman's work in the church is to make religion attractive by the grateful warmth of a loving heart and the pure light of a lovely life.'[37]

Catherine Booth made incisive and well-judged comments on the same passages, often using the Greek. Collett described Phoebe (Romans 16.1) as 'a succourer of many', Booth emphasized that she was a *diaconon*, a minister; 'the word is only translated servant because she was a woman'. To the argument that female preaching is unnecessary, because there is plenty of scope for women to work in private, she responded, 'we cannot be blind to the supreme selfishness of making her so welcome to the hidden toil and self-sacrifice . . . without allowing her a tittle of the honour which He has attached to the ministration of His gospel.'[38] Her conclusion is, 'what we sincerely believe, that woman has a *right* to teach. Here the whole question hinges. If she has the *right*, she has it independently of any man-made restriction which does not equally refer to the opposite sex.'[39]

It is no coincidence that the question of women's preaching – 'female ministry' – was taken up in the 1860s, as it was just at this time that the effects of the Second Evangelical Awakening were beginning to be felt in England.[40] Palmer and his wife had already been travelling, teaching and preaching in Britain for several years.[41] The Palmers and another evangelistic couple, Robert and Hannah (Pearsall) Whitall Smith, also from the USA, made a remarkable contribution to religious life in Britain in this period; the Palmers in the early stages of the Great Awakening; the Smiths in the 1870s. Both couples had been influenced by the American revivalist, Charles Grandison Finney, who also visited Britain.[42]

Phoebe Palmer and Hannah Pearsall Smith both became well-known in Britain for their writings on holiness as well as from their speaking tours. Hannah Pearsall Smith's *The*

Christian's Secret of a Happy Life (1886), was an instant best-seller, like Phoebe Palmer's earlier *The Way of Holiness*. Palmer was a Wesleyan, and her teaching on holiness, which drew on Wesleyan perfectionism, influenced Charles Finney himself.[43] She placed much emphasis on the will, saying often, 'God *wills* that you should be holy.' She is important for the example she modelled of a wife and mother preaching and teaching. In particular, like Finney, she emphasized that those who have been converted had an obligation to testify to their faith – mainly by their lives but also by their words. Indeed, failure to testify meant risking the loss of the blessing. So she openly and strongly criticized churches which inhibited women from public prayer, speaking and testifying.[44] Charles Finney's own (second) wife Elizabeth became prominent in Britain as a speaker at Ladies' Meetings. From his earliest campaigns Finney had been criticized by some because he allowed – even encouraged – women to testify in 'promiscuous assemblies'.[45]

Prayer meetings for revival had been organized in many centres before the advent of overseas speakers; men like William Booth were speaking at revival meetings. By 1859 enough was happening for the Christian publisher, R. C. Morgan,[46] to commence a weekly paper, *The Revival*. From the beginning – and this one would never guess from reading only J. Edwin Orr's account[47] – women are noted in *The Revival* as participants in revival preaching. The first so noted is Mrs Palmer; the second Mrs Finney, who addressed Ladies' Meetings during her husband's campaign in Bolton (March 1860). In 1864 issue after issue carries news of 'Mrs Col Bell of Bristol' who, with an assistant, Mr Sutherland, sold Bibles and preached in the open air in Wales, Shrewsbury, and Derby. In August the pair were arrested for obstruction and fined.[48] Meanwhile other women's ministries were noted: Mrs [Fanny] Grattan Guinness; Mrs Booth, Miss McFarlane of Edinburgh; Mrs Poole, working with her husband, 'Fiddler Josh'; Miss Graham; Miss Armstrong; Mrs Thistlethwaite; Miss Octavia Jary.

In 1866 comes the first mention of Miss Hooper of Bath. Geraldine Hooper,[49] from a landed Somerset family, elegant and ladylike, became an exceedingly popular speaker. When she died in 1872 it was reported that 10,000 attended her funeral. Her friend, Fanny Guinness, defended 'women's ministry in the Gospel' as something to which 'a few, *very few* [women] are called; . . . the *rule* is men – the *exception only*, women. . . . Nature, revelation and experience alike indicate men as the proper occupants of public spheres, and women of private ones.'[50]

Another single woman who quickly became a well-known revival preacher was Miss Jessie McFarlane of Edinburgh. She is first mentioned in *The Revival* in August 1864. Like Geraldine Hooper, she was attractive and easy to listen to; a newspaper report describes her as 'somewhat tall and prepossessing in appearance, and her elocution is graceful and cogent.'[51]

Female ministry of this kind could hardly continue without stirring up controversy. Both Mrs Guinness and Gordon Furlong (who wrote Miss McFarlane's obituary), refer to 'antagonism' and 'criticism'. In November 1862 R. C. Morgan had dealt directly with the topic of 'women's ministry'. He referred to the Garden of Eden, and to Paul's directions, which he connects to 'that which is fit and seemly in the nature of things'. However, since in the old as well as the new dispensation 'holy women as well as men of old spoke, moved by the Holy Ghost', a gifted woman cannot be forbidden to minister. Nevertheless women should not be allowed to rule, as this would lead to 'confusion'. They should also, Morgan maintained, be 'obediently silent' in the Assembly of the Saints.[52] In other words, while women may preach evangelistic sermons in halls, schoolrooms, or in the open air, they may not presume to do so in church.

Not surprisingly, this editorial statement led to a good deal of discussion, some of it in later issues of *The Revival*. R. C. Morgan continued to report on the ministry of women, usually with commendation. By 1865, under the heading, 'Female preaching and preaching in general', he commented on Mrs Booth's meetings in Islington, after noting that in Scotland there was a strong feeling against women's preaching. He wrote, 'It is very long since any man or woman made in our hearing a more searching and experimental, though winning, declaration of the truth of the Gospel.'[53]

From statements in the biography by Morgan's son it seems

that the publisher maintained his open attitude to the ministry
of women to the end of his life.

So also in regard to the Gospel ministry of women: my
father held that none could lawfully hinder in the proclamation of their message such as were moved by the Divine
Spirit: and he supported his contention by reference to
Deborah, the Samaritan woman, Priscilla and other Bible
characters; and urged with reason that consecrated woman
had a sphere which no man could effectively share. Of
course, this brought him into conflict with some good and
earnest people who, with equal tenacity, opposed his conclusions; but while respecting their convictions, he had gone
through too much of criticism and antagonism of various
kinds . . . to be greatly troubled as to the result.[54]

In February 1870 *The Revival* was renamed *The Christian*; it
continued as a weekly paper. It still mentioned meetings
addressed by women, but one gets the impression that this
ministry was becoming less common. Mrs Brodie (Miss
McFarlane) died in 1871; Mrs Dening (Miss Hooper) in 1872.
By the 1870s Christians converted in the revival were being
incorporated into churches, old and new, and, as in the case of
Wesley's revival, such a period of incorporation was much less
favourable to the preaching ministry of women. Many who
were willing to accept women as 'prophets', preachers and
evangelists were not willing to accept them as pastors and
teachers within the churches.[55] Numerous charitable organizations continued and expanded, taking up the time and energy
of thousands of Christian women. Evangelistic campaigns
continued, both through British evangelists and through the
visits of the American preacher Dwight L. Moody. But in the
remaining years of the nineteenth century there was little
evidence that women preachers continued their ministry.[56]

Women's ministry in preaching and evangelism continued,
however, in the Salvation Army and in the overseas missionary
movement, which expanded and developed as a direct result of
the revival of the 1860s. From its beginning the Salvation Army
used men and women in equal roles in its work. This is not surprising in view of Mrs Booth's long-held convictions, and her
own very successful ministry. That ministry, incidentally, began

in and continued through the 1860s while she herself must have been much occupied with her growing family. Between 1856 and 1867 she gave birth to three sons and five daughters, all of whom grew up to become active in the Army. Women, including those of the General's own family, took their place in the leadership succession.

By the 1860s it was becoming commonplace for single women to serve as overseas missionaries, and many of those who did so had received specialist training as teachers, nurses, or deaconesses. An important result of the revival was the founding of a large number of new interdenominational societies, operating on the 'faith' principle. The largest and most influential of these was the China Inland Mission (CIM) (1865), founded by James Hudson Taylor. Between 1860 and 1865 Taylor and his family were living in London, after their first period in China. When he returned to China in 1865 he took with him a party of sixteen missionary recruits, including nine single women. He showed himself unusually open to the ministry of women, and from the beginning used them as pioneer evangelists and not only as teachers and nurses, like some of the older societies. Among the factors which contributed to Taylor's open and free use of women were his own northern Methodist background;[57] and the experience and example of his wife Maria (Dyer) and her sister Burella. Daughters of a London Missionary Society missionary, they were brought up speaking the vernacular, and Maria was already teaching in Ningpo when Taylor met her.[58]

The CIM became a model for many other new societies, both world-wide and regional. As interdenominational missions, they had a low theology of ordination. Men were most often trained at the fairly new Bible Colleges or Mission Training Colleges, and if ordained it was within the society for which they worked. What was considered important was not the outward ceremony of ordination, but 'the mighty ordination of the pierced hands'.[59] In such organizations the position of women missionaries was in many ways different from that of women in denominational societies, where ordained men occupied leadership roles. But even in the older societies women were increasingly used as evangelists, and not always exclusively among women and children. The new Brethren

assemblies also commenced overseas missionary work in which
women were prominent as evangelists as well as teachers,
nurses and workers among women. 'The striking indifference
to clerical status and pastoral functions which marked the
revival and the organizations founded as a result was not simply the product of American influence, but also reflected the
influence of Plymouth Brethrenism, which was far more
pervasive at this time than is often realised.'[60]

However, when women missionaries returned to their
homelands, many of them experienced difficulty in addressing
church meetings while on deputation tours. In some cases they
could speak only to audiences of women; in few cases were
they allowed to speak from a pulpit.[61] Nevertheless, by the end
of the century there were a number of very well-known women
missionaries whose memoirs or biographies were widely read,
and a missionary calling offered enterprising young Christian
women an alternative and attractive avenue of service, despite
the continuing limitations.

It would appear that the arguments from Scripture were not
felt to be clear enough to prevent the ministry of women where
there was a clear spiritual calling. Social standing and the wish
for 'respectability' might inhibit them within their own culture
but were not seen as important while they worked within
another culture. When success confirmed a woman's calling,
her work was affirmed, but this success overseas could not
override prejudices in the homeland.[62]

Conclusion

During the course of the nineteenth century women became
better educated, better trained, and better able to work at any
number of different roles. In the churches they won respect
through their social involvement, their work as nurses, beginning with the Crimean War, and their work as missionaries all
over the world. At different times gifted women showed that
they had the calling of evangelists and prophets.

In the Anglican Churches and the leading Nonconformist
denominations, however, their official position did not change
significantly. Except in the Salvation Army, no woman could
hope to attain a leadership role. Gifts of preaching and teaching

had to be restricted to non-worship, and usually totally female, settings. A woman who in appearance and deportment did not conform to a well-defined feminine image found herself at a disadvantage. Most men in leadership roles in churches and church-related organizations were unable to concede that there were good scriptural precedents for the full ministry of women.

If the opposition to women had been confined to the possibility of their ordination to the priesthood or to the formal ministry of a denomination, we might assert only that opposition arose out of biblical interpretation and ecclesiastical tradition. But the continuing opposition to *any* widening of women's roles brings us back to our contention that the concept of the 'ideal Christian woman', engaged humbly in restricted feminine service, also intervened. At the end of the nineteenth century, the question of ordination had not arisen.[63] But when in 1897 Parochial Church Councils, which allowed for and encouraged lay participation in the affairs of an Anglican parish, were being set up, the bishops decided that elected councillors should be '*male* communicants of the Church of full age'.[64] In 1903, when a 'House of Laymen' was being set up, women were again excluded from participation, not only as delegates, but even as electors, unless they were also 'ratepayers'. The obvious unfairness – that a woman active in a church could neither elect nor be elected, but that any male ratepayer could participate – stimulated later 'church feminism'.[65] The actual question of women's ordination, raised in the *Church Times* as early as 1910, was frequently discussed, and just as frequently dismissed.

Yet, although many male evangelicals still questioned the propriety of female participation in any kind of leadership role, let alone actual ministry, the women themselves had begun to find their own way. They were now better prepared by education and training, and their capabilities had been proved in many spheres. Women had been seen to be effective preachers and evangelists, not only among other women, but also in mixed gatherings. They had served their country during the Crimean War and other wars; their work as deaconesses in the slums of Britain was known and appreciated. Missionary societies now recognized that their overseas ministry could not go on without the active participation of women. And evangelical women knew that they had the support of some, at least, of the men who had been their own teachers and mentors. The evangelical emphasis on 'the priesthood of all believers' was a particular strength. They could not now be stopped for reasons of propriety or prejudice; they were still willing to serve in the background, but where they felt that active leadership was appropriate, they were ready to demand and take up appropriate positions. We all today – both men and women – are their debtors.

Notes

1 For further discussion, see pp. 51–3 above.
2 For a helpful discussion of this view, and much more, see Monica Furlong, *A Dangerous Delight: Women and Power in the Church* (SPCK, 1991), especially chapter 2.
3 John Angell James (1785–1859), *Female Piety or the Young Woman's Friend and Guide through Life to Immortality*. It was so popular that it quickly went through ten editions up to 1864.
4 James, *Female Piety*, edn of 1852, p. 53.
5 Charlotte Mary Yonge, *Womankind* (1876), p. 1. Her famous novel for girls, *The Daisychain* (1856), preaches the same message, as the intelligent and scholarly heroine Ethel gives up her studies to become housekeeper and companion to her widowed father.
6 Charlotte Elizabeth [Tonna], *Personal Recollections* (1841), p. 67.
7 W. J. Townsend, H. B. Workman and George Eayrs, eds, *A New History of Methodism* (2 vols 1909), vol. 1, p. 34.
8 Townsend et al., *New History*, vol. 1, pp. 322–3.
9 Mary Bosanquet married John Fletcher ('Fletcher of Madeley') in 1781.
10 Zechariah Taft, *Thoughts on Female Preaching* (Dover, 1803). See also Mrs Mary Taft, *Memoirs of the Life of Mrs. Mary Taft, formerly Miss Barritt* (2 parts, Ripon, 1827).
11 George Eliot [Mary Ann Evans], *Adam Bede*, first published in 1859.
12 Deborah Valenze, *Prophetic Sons and Daughters, Female Preaching and Popular Religion in Industrial England* (Princeton UP, 1977), p. 51.
13 Townsend et al., *New History*, p. 455; cf. also Valenze, *Prophetic Sons and Daughters*, pp. 92–3.
14 See D. Colin Dews, 'Ann Carr and the Female Revivalists of Leeds', in Gail Malmgreen, ed., *Religion in the Lives of English Women 1760–1930* (Croom Helm, 1986): '. . . as early as the 1820s it was

114 *Gender Attitudes and the Contribution of Women*

clear that Wesleyan Methodism had finally rejected the use of women as preachers. Instead, the initiative passed to the Primitive Methodists and the Bible Christians, both basically lay-created churches with an informal view of the ministry . . .' (p. 72).

15 Wesley F. Swift, 'The women itinerant preachers of early Methodism.' *Proceedings of the Wesley Historical Society*, 28 (1952), pp. 89–94 and 29 (4), 1953, pp. 76–83.
16 Valenze, *Prophetic Sons and Daughters*, p. 278.
17 Townsend et al., *New History*, p. 413 (my italics).
18 Townsend et al., *New History*, p. 413.
19 Valenze, *Prophetic Sons and Daughters*, pp. 53–5, 89. See also Olive Anderson, 'Women preachers in mid-Victorian Britain: some reflexions on feminism, popular religion, and social change.' *The Historical Journal*, 12 (1969), p. 469.
20 On Ann Carr see D. Colin Dews, 'Female Revivalists', pp. 68–87.
21 Ann Carr and Martha Williams, *A Selection of Hymns for the use of the Female Revivalist Methodists. A New Edition with Additional Hymns* (1838). Martha Williams also wrote *Memoirs of the Life and Character of Ann Carr* (Leeds, 1841).
22 See Jocelyn Murray, 'Anglican and Protestant missionary societies in Great Britain: their use of women from the late 18th to the late 19th century.' *Exchange* (Leiden), 21 (1), April 1992, pp. 1–20, and 'Bibliography', pp. 21–8.
23 Quoted in Murray, 'Anglican and Protestant missionary societies', p. 12; letter to the London Committee of the SPFEE, dated 1835, in CMS Archives, University of Birmingham.
24 See Donald Lewis, *Lighten Their Darkness. The Evangelical Mission to Working-Class London, 1828–1860* (Westport CT: Greenwood, 1986), pp. 220–3.
25 See Catherine M. Prelinger, 'The female diaconate in the Anglican church: what kind of ministry for females', in Gail Malmgreen, ed., *Religion*, pp. 161–92.
26 Elspeth Platt, *The Story of the Ranyard Mission 1857–1937* (1937). Mrs Ranyard in her use of women was influenced by the work of missionary-trained Bible women in India and China.
27 Donald Lewis, '"Lights in dark places": women evangelists in early Victorian England', in W. J. Sheils and Diana Wood, eds, *Studies in Church History*, 27 (1990), pp. 415–27.
28 Robert Braithwaite, ed., *The Life and Letters of Rev. William Pennefather* (1878); Harriet J. Cooke, *Mildmay: or the Story of the First Deaconess Institution* (1892).
29 Prelinger, 'The female diaconate', pp. 167–8.
30 Braithwaite, ed., *Life and Letters*, p. 408.
31 James, *Female Piety*, p. 62.
32 F. de L. Booth-Tucker, *The Life of Catherine Booth, the Mother of the Salvation Army* (2 vols, 1897; 3rd edn 1924), pp. 83–5.
33 Booth-Tucker, *Catherine Booth*, vol. I, pp. 176–81.

34 Reprinted in England in 1856 from the 34th American edn.
35 Mrs [Catherine] Booth, 'Female Ministry, or Woman's Right to
    preach the Gospel', pp. 95–123 in her *Papers on Practical Religion*
    (1878). Mrs Booth herself did not preach publicly until 1860.
36 Acts 21.8: 'We went to the home of Philip the evangelist, who was
    one of the Seven. He had four unmarried daughters, who possessed
    the gift of prophecy' (NEB): was often used as a proof-text, by those
    who supported and by those who opposed the ministry of women.
37 W. R. Collett, *Woman's Work in the Church*, p. 27. For a comprehen-
    sive modern discussion of the issues involved in the biblical exegesis,
    with excellent references, see Willard M. Swartley, *Slavery, Sabbath,
    War and Women: Issues in Biblical Interpretation* (Scottdale, PA: Herald
    Press 1983), especially chapter 4, 'The Bible and Women', pp.
    150–91, and Appendix 3, pp. 256–69. Swartley discusses the argu-
    ments in terms of 'hierarchical' and 'liberationist' interpretations.
38 Booth, 'Female Ministry', pp. 105, 108–9.
39 Booth, 'Female Ministry', p. 121.
40 For the only comprehensive account of the revival, see J. Edwin Orr,
    The Second Evangelical Awakening in Britain (Marshall, Morgan and
    Scott, 1949).
41 Dr and Mrs Palmer sailed from New York to Liverpool in June 1859.
    They travelled and preached in England, Ireland, Scotland and
    Wales for four years. See *Four Years in the Old World: comprising the
    Travels, Incidents and Evangelistic Labors of Dr. and Mrs. Palmer in
    England, Ireland, Scotland and Wales* (New York, 1866).
42 Nancy A. Hardesty, *Women called to witness. Evangelical Feminism in
    the nineteenth century* (Nashville, TN: Abingdon 1984), p. 46.
43 Hardesty, *Women called to witness*, p. 55.
44 Hardesty, *Women called to witness*, pp. 62–4.
45 Hardesty, *Women called to witness*, p. 48.
46 George E. Morgan (son), *A Veteran in Revival: R. C. Morgan: his Life
    and Time* (1909).
47 Orr cites *The Revival* frequently, but in the whole of his book men-
    tions by name only two women as preachers and evangelists: Mrs
    Palmer and Mrs Booth.
48 *The Revival*, 25 Aug. 1864, p. 118.
49 See Fanny E. [Mrs H. Grattan] Guinness, *'She Spoke of Him': being
    recollections of the Loving Labours and Early Death of the late Mrs.
    Henry Dening* (1872).
50 Guinness, *'She Spoke of Him'*, chap. XV.
51 Report in the *Morning Herald*, reprinted in *The Revival*, 18 Aug.
    1864, p. 101. For further information on Jessie McFarlane, and also
    on Margaret Graham and Isabella Armstrong who were all promi-
    nent as evangelists in Scotland, see Neil Dickson, 'Modern prophet-
    esses: women preachers in the nineteenth century Scottish
    Brethren'. *Records of the Scottish Church History Society*, 25 (1993),
    pp. 89–117.

52 *The Revival*, 20 Nov. 1862, pp. 233–4.

53 *The Revival*, 31 Aug. 1865, pp. 129–30.

54 G. E. Morgan, *A Veteran in Revival*, p. 302.

55 It appears that many of the female evangelists themselves, happy about preaching to non-believers, were not prepared to argue for a woman's right to teach and pastor Christian congregations. Compare Dickson, 'Modern Prophetesses', pp. 106–7, discussing Isabella Armstrong's opinions.

56 Dickson mentions an Open Brethren assembly in Rhynie (Aberdeenshire) which continued (not without controversy) to allow the ministry of women throughout the 1880s and 1890s ('Modern Prophetesses', pp. 110–11, 115).

57 Murray, 'Anglican and Protestant Missionary Societies', pp. 18–19; Peter Williams, 'The recruitment of women missionaries', in Fiona Bowie, Deborah Kirkwood and Shirley Ardner, eds, *Women and Missions: Past and Present* (Oxford: Berg, 1993), pp. 45–53.

58 Murray, 'Anglican and Protestant Missionary Societies', pp. 18–19.

59 This phrase, which I have seen attributed to F. W. H. Meyer (*St. Paul*) actually comes from a poem by the Plymouth Brethren writer and translator Emma F. Bevan, 'The Gospel according to St. Paul' (*Hymns of Terstegen, Saso and Others*, 2 vols, 1894, p. 142).

60 Anderson, 'Women Preachers', p. 475.

61 See Williams, '*Women Missionaries*', p. 54, for a comment on Henry Wright, the Clerical Secretary of CMS, refusing, in 1878, to sit on a Mildmay Conference platform because women were to speak.

62 For a discussion of this question by a Brethren theologian, see Neil Summerton, 'The ministry and leadership of women', in *A Noble Task. Eldership and Ministry in the Local Church*, 2nd edn. (Carlisle: Paternoster Press, 1994), Appendix 2, pp. 119–32.

63 See Brian Heeney, *The Women's Movement in the Church of England, 1850–1988* (Oxford UP, 1988), especially pp. 116–38.

64 Heeney, *The Women's Movement*, pp. 95–7 (my emphasis).

65 Heeney, *The Women's Movement*, p. 99. The Church League for Women's Suffrage was founded in 1909, and by 1914 had over 5,000 members. See Brian Heeney, 'The beginnings of church feminism . . .' in Gail Malmgreen, ed., *Religion*, p. 272.

Chapter Six

Evangelicals and Education

EDWARD ROYLE

Education as a work of charity has always been an integral part of all Christian mission, so the historian of evangelical education faces several problems. Few institutions or approaches can be described as uniquely evangelical, and even when there were distinctive evangelical innovations, such as Sunday schools, these were often adopted by other Christians and their initial distinctiveness lost. Then there is the problem of distinguishing who the evangelicals were. Whilst in the Church of England it can be difficult to decide who *was* an evangelical, among Nonconformists the problem is to decide who was *not*. All sections of Methodism were products of the evangelical revival, and the major branches of Old Dissent – Baptists and Independents or Congregationalists – were also renewed by the revival. Even the Quakers, influenced by the Beaconites of Manchester or J. J. Gurney of Norwich, displayed some characteristics of evangelicalism. Ventures in education were often evangelical but their denominationalism was sometimes more significant. Educational conflict often took place *within* evangelicalism between Churchmen and Nonconformists. In Scotland, where many of the secessions from the Presbyterian Church of Scotland were evangelical in inspiration, in the opinion of one recent historian, 'the self-stylization "evangelical" came to be an avowal of Protestant orthodoxy' by the mid-nineteenth century.[1]

Two issues run through this chapter: to what extent did evangelicals preserve an exclusive witness, or seek instead to permeate wider institutions in collaboration with other Christians and an increasingly secular state; and to what extent did a

117

common evangelical faith transcend denominational rivalries? But first there is the myth that evangelicals were not interested in education at all.

Evangelical attitudes to education

It is easy to see why some contemporaries as well as subsequent historians have doubted the commitment of evangelicals to education. At a public meeting of leading evangelicals to establish Sunday schools in the city of York in 1786,

> It was unanimously agreed that such an institution is necessary to the rescuing of the children of poor parents from the low habits of vice and idleness, and initiating them in the principles of the Christian religion from which we may reasonably hope the rising generation will be made useful members to Society.[2]

Schools were a remedy for sin and social disorder, not to provide worldly learning. Even when dealing with the higher classes there was a suspicion of learning for its own sake, for the evangelical revival was born in part as a reaction against the arid intellectualism of rational theology. As John Wesley wrote of children in 1773, 'All our wisdom will not even make them *understand*, much less *feel* the things of God.'[3] Similar sentiments were expressed by the evangelical Churchman, Richard Cecil: 'However desirable and useful in its various respects learning may be, it is not essential to the Christian.'[4] These two quotations, though, exemplify the *inadequacy* of mere learning, not hostility to it. Wesley and Cecil were both learned men.

Indeed, one reason for the early evangelicals' mistrust of learning was the low quality of provision. Public schools and the ancient English universities were in the eighteenth century seen as dens of idleness and iniquity, not havens of righteousness and scholarship. Wesley was creating something of a cross between an improved public school and a reformed Oxford College when he set up his boarding school at Kingswood near Bristol in 1748. His aim was to create 'rational, scriptural Christians', not by rejecting secular learning but by using it to the greater glory of God.[5] True, this involved a harsh discipline that went against the enlightened educational ideas of the day and since, but the presumption that the educator started not with a *tabula rasa* of childhood innocence but the dangerous fruits of original sin was one that evangelicals shared with many other reformers.[6]

The idea that all learning was subordinate to the development of Christian faith could be both broadening and narrowing. It was broadening in the sense that much secular knowledge could be brought within the religious syllabus. A study of the periodical literature of evangelicalism shows how history, geography, natural history, geology, mythology and biography were all considered proper topics for discussion. However, the subordination of such topics to the demands of religious enlightenment was restrictive. Knowledge of controversial new ideas in history or geology, which might challenge accepted views of the Bible, was not encouraged. Like their secular counterparts, the utilitarians, evangelicals were inclined to mistake information for knowledge, and training for education.[7]

Education of the poor

Despite the limited objectives of evangelical educators of the poor, they offered more than those conservatives who thought it dangerous to provide them with any knowledge at all. Indeed, because evangelicals not only expected the poor to be able to read their Bibles, but also the tracts they issued to persuade them of the truths of the gospel and the errors of their ways, the teaching of reading to the poor was central to evangelical mission. From the late eighteenth century onwards, evangelicals provided an elementary education for the poor in at least two of the 'four Rs' – reading and religion.

In the earlier eighteenth century, this had been the work of the Society for the Promotion of Christian Knowledge (and its Scottish counterpart), but the society then lost its initial vigour. The Methodists also were slow to take the initiative and, although the distribution of tracts to the poor was discussed in 1782, a Tract Committee was not set up in the connexion for another forty years. The real inspiration for popular tracts came from Hannah More (1745–1833), a highly educated 'blue stocking' who experienced her evangelical conversion in the 1780s. Her *Village Politics*, written in 1792 to counter the

worst excesses of the French Revolution, led the Clapham
evangelicals in 1795 to set up 'A Repository of Cheap Publications, on Religious & Moral Subjects'. Written in the style of
chap-books, the tracts were bought and distributed by religious
people beyond the ranks of the evangelicals. Though their lasting effect on individuals is hard to judge, More's *The Shepherd
of Salisbury Plain* sold two million copies in four years and set
a fashion that many organizations followed in the nineteenth
century.[8]

The most important evangelical contribution to tract publication was the Religious Tract Society, founded in 1799. Along
with the Church Missionary Society and the Bible Society, it
was one of the great agents of evangelical mission and, like the
Bible Society, a part of that great upsurge of distinctively
evangelical (as opposed to denominational) activity that characterized the first hundred years of the revival. In towns and
cities across Britain, committees of evangelicals from all
denominations met locally to organize the distribution of tracts
– improving, moral tales that placed literature, and hence
education, at the front of missionary endeavour.

This activity assumed a widespread ability to read. Some
studies of literacy have claimed that the explosion in tract literature is itself evidence that a high proportion of the population
could read, although the level of signature-signing ability in
marriage registers (*not* the same thing as the ability to read)
suggests that in the rapidly expanding towns of industrializing
Britain standards of popular education fell in the later eighteenth century. The subsequent recovery has variously been
attributed either to Sunday schools or to the increasingly systematic provision of weekday schools by the National Society
for Promoting the Education of the Poor in the Principles of
the Established Church (1811) and the British and Foreign
Schools Society (1814).[9]

Sunday schools were the major distinctive contribution of
evangelicals to popular education. They emerged in the mid-
eighteenth century as much a response to the weekday
employment of children and the contrasting dangers of Sunday
idleness as to the pressing need to provide that saving ability to
read the Bible that many poor parents were failing to provide.
They spread rapidly following the publicity given by Robert

Raikes to his plan for Sunday schools in Gloucester in 1780.
By 1800 there were 200,000 children attending them; by
1851, over ten times that number – 13 per cent of the population. No institution of education touched so many children and
young people. By 1881, Sunday school enrolments totalled
over 5.7 million – 19 per cent of the population – and absolute
numbers peaked in 1911 at over 6 million. Protestant churches
of all persuasions shared in these figures, but the schools long
retained their evangelical ethos, not least because over half
the scholars attended places connected with Nonconformist
chapels.[10]

These schools were initially intended to occupy the whole of
Sunday and included compulsory attendance at public worship. Some taught writing as well as reading, but most did not
on the ground that writing was a secular pursuit inappropriate
for the Sabbath. In some large towns special buildings were
erected where interdenominational committees ran schools in
which former pupils continued as teachers. Elsewhere denominational chapel Sunday schools gained a semi-autonomous
existence for working-class people in a religious environment
otherwise dominated by the middle classes. In yet other –
usually smaller – places, Sunday schools were merely adjuncts
to chapels and churches, firmly controlled by parson, deacon
or elder. In Manchester in the 1830s the Statistical Society
found that over half the children who were receiving any
education at all were attending only Sunday schools. But as
the provision of weekday schooling increased, Sunday schools
were less concerned with literacy and their function among the
poor became more evidently religious and philanthropic.

Although Sunday schools and the weekday schools of the
religious societies were intended for the children of the lower
classes, standards of dress and cleanliness were expected that
put them outside the reaches of the lowest in society. This
became apparent to evangelicals working in the poorer areas of
Britain's towns in the 1830s and led to the establishment of
ragged schools. An advertisement in *The Times*, appealing for
funds for a ragged school run by the evangelical London City
Mission, drew Lord Ashley's attention to their work in February
1843. The following year he started the Ragged School Union
and the movement spread rapidly. The educational census of

1851 recorded 132 ragged schools with 23,643 children in England and Wales, and 21 schools with 1,977 children in Scotland; by 1867 there were 226 ragged Sunday schools, 204 weekday schools and 207 evening schools in London alone, with a total attendance of 26,000.[11]

Elementary schools and their teachers

The provision of weekday schools in England and Wales was increasingly the work of the British and Foreign Schools Society and – especially – the National Society, both aided from 1833 by state grants.[12] Neither the National Society nor the British Society was exclusively an evangelical body. Although the National Society represented the interests of the Church of England as a whole, it was influenced by High Churchmen from its foundation, though that did not exclude evangelical influences locally. In Lancashire, the evangelical Bishop J. B. Sumner of Chester worked through the National Society to restore the influence of the Church in the industrial districts against the competition of equally evangelical Nonconformists working through the less successful British Society.[13] The latter was founded by Quakers, Independents and some Anglicans, but it came to be associated mainly with Nonconformists – other than the Wesleyans, who had their own Education Committee that accepted government funds from 1847.

Educational provision was settling along denominational lines in the 1830s. The determination of the Whig government in 1839 not to give special favours to the Church of England led to a bitter conflict, with the Church of England asserting its proper place as the educator of the nation, and Nonconformists claiming freedom to compete with the Church on equal terms. However, following Ashley's failure to secure a compulsory Church education for children in the Factory Bill of 1843, he and other Churchmen recognized that denominationalism had won the day. Nevertheless, evangelical cross-currents persisted, especially in view of the increasing influence of high-church Tractarians in the National Society in the 1840s. Some Churchmen, including Francis Close (1797– 1882), one of the foremost evangelical clergymen of his generation, went as far as to support the Church of England Education Society as an alternative to the National Society in 1856. In contrast to the position he had adopted in 1843, he now advocated the cause of British schools, government inspection, state financial aid and compulsory (though not free) education.[14]

Along with Francis Close the two most outspoken advocates of evangelically-controlled education for the poor were Hugh McNeile of Liverpool and Hugh Stowell of Salford. Both men ran relentless campaigns against any proposals that would have diluted the Anglican and Protestant nature of popular schooling, whether the threat came from Liverpool Corporation's two non-sectarian schools, opened in 1836; or from the secular education proposals of the Lancashire Public Schools Association in 1850. Whether their actions were for the good of education locally is open to doubt but their vociferous campaigns for a Church of England education led eventually in each case to an acceptance of denominationalism and a determination to secure as a minimum the provision of evangelically-sound schools in a free market. By 1870, most Churchmen were prepared to regard as victory the compromise in Forster's Education Act that left the religious bodies free to run their own schools with public funding and set up non-sectarian schools run by locally elected school boards only where the denominations were unable to provide sufficient places. But the compromise was denominational and, although evangelical clergymen like E. A. Knox in Birmingham might chair school boards, there was no official place for purely evangelical activity.[15]

In Scotland, with its different tradition of parochial education, the opportunities for evangelical action lay in those parts of the country where the parochial system was failing – in the vast parishes of the Highlands and the expanding urban centres of central Scotland. In Glasgow, where Thomas Chalmers was attempting to make the parochial ideal function in the inhospitable climate of working-class St John's parish, David Stow and William Collins started church day schools in the 1820s. Stow and other members of the Glasgow Educational Society then went on to open a teacher-training college in 1836 which stood as a model for evangelicals throughout Britain. When Chalmers led most evangelicals out of the Established Church in the Disruption of 1843, they immediately began replicating the structure of the parent body, creating their own schools with training colleges in both Glasgow and Edinburgh. By 1865 there were some 570 Free Church schools in Scotland.[16]

The foremost English evangelical to stress the educational work of the Church was Francis Close in Cheltenham. He was active at all levels, founding some of the first infant schools in the country, opening an additional National School, presiding over the Cheltenham Diocesan Boys' School and starting a school for middle-class girls, as well as helping establish Cheltenham College (1841). Even more significantly for the evangelical contribution to education, in 1847 he was largely responsible for opening in Cheltenham an 'Institution for the training of pious Masters and Mistresses upon Scriptural and Evangelical principles'.

Elementary school teachers were drawn from a lower social class than clergymen, and their need for education and training was even more imperative. The main providers were the British Society, the National Society and, of increasing importance for the Church of England after 1839, colleges set up by diocesan education societies, but there was no guarantee that such places would be evangelically sound. Indeed, by the mid-1840s, with the National Society's executive dominated by Tractarians, its training college of St Mark, Chelsea, was suspect. Hence the widespread support in London and elsewhere for Close's venture in Cheltenham where, in 1849, Lord Ashley laid the foundation stone and McNeile preached the opening sermon for the new training college.[17]

The Congregationalists too began teacher-training at this time when their former theological college at Homerton fell vacant in 1850; and the following year the Wesleyans, who at first had sent their students to Glasgow, opened amid the slums of Westminster a training college modelled on Stow's method. Westminster was chosen so that would-be teachers would not lose contact with the sorts of children they were being trained to teach. In 1872 the training of women teachers was moved out to Battersea and then, in 1929, to Wimbledon. Westminster College itself went to Oxford after the Second World War.[18]

Although the provision of elementary schools by the religious bodies continued after 1870, the state steadily exerted greater control over standards in both local board schools and denominational schools. The cost of meeting these standards gradually led Nonconformists to relinquish most of their elementary schools to school-board and, after 1902, local-authority control. The continuance of public finance for religious – mainly Church of England and Catholic – schools under the 1902 Education Act aroused Nonconformist anger and left little room for a common evangelical approach to elementary schooling. In the remaining Church schools the evangelical contribution was restricted to the influence of the local clergyman and, within bounds, teachers. Those who wished to maintain a distinctive evangelical contribution to education turned to the increasingly important provision of secondary schooling for the middle classes.

Education for the middle classes

Almost all grammar and public schools at the end of the eighteenth century were Anglican, though only a few – like Hull when Joseph Milner was master between 1767 and 1797 – were under evangelical influence.[19] Most Nonconformist schools, other than those for the poor, were intended primarily for preachers' sons or to prepare preachers for their subsequent ministerial training. Kingswood school was reserved after Wesley's death for the sons of Methodist preachers, as was its northern equivalent, Woodhouse Grove near Leeds (1812). The Primitives' Elmfield College, York (1864), and the United Methodist Free Churches' Ashville College, Harrogate (1876), were broadly similar. The Congregationalists' oldest public school was Mill Hill in London (1808), to which were added schools for the sons of ministers and missionaries at Lewisham (1811), Silcoates near Wakefield (1831), Taunton (1847) and, for the daughters of ministers, Milton Mount (1871).

With the growth in middle-class wealth and social aspirations, the creation of a railway network and the restoration of parental confidence in private boarding schools, the number of 'public' schools rapidly increased from the 1840s. Influence clearly lay in founding schools for the expanding middle class. Close's Cheltenham College was the first response to this challenge, though the initiative then passed to a High Churchman,

Nathaniel Woodard, who set about raising money for a network of schools graded for the various classes, the first of which, at Shoreham (now Lancing College), was founded in 1847.

Cheltenham College was initially intended as a day and boarding school but soon became a mainstream public boarding school. Clifton College (1861) was similar, opened in another 'Simeonite' parish because Bristol grammar school did not take boarders. Other evangelical schools with the more limited ambition 'to wean away the professional and trading classes from Anglo-Catholicism or irreligion', were started through local initiatives. Some were founded by Clerical and Lay Associations, which were set up as informal evangelical regional organizations from 1858 onwards.[20] The Associations expressed a 'sincere and loyal attachment to the true principles of the English Reformed Church as distinguished on the one hand from doctrines and practices of a Romanizing tendency and from the Rationalistic free handling of Revelation on the other.'[21] In 1885 eighteen such Associations came together in a central Union to promote education on evangelical principles in rivalry with the high-church Woodard schools. Among their schools were Trent College, Long Eaton (1866), founded by the Midland Clerical and Lay Association in competition with Woodard's school at Denstone; Monkton Combe near Bath (1868), begun by the local vicar; Weymouth College, based on an earlier school begun at Melcombe Regis in 1879 by a group of local evangelical clergymen; and St Lawrence College, Ramsgate (1879), founded by the South-Eastern Clerical and Lay Association.

In 1882, the year of Francis Close's death, the Western Clerical and Lay Association decided to follow the example of Ramsgate and found an evangelical day school in or near a sympathetic evangelical parish. Cheltenham was eventually chosen and The Dean Close Memorial School was opened in May 1886 with a great evangelical celebration.

Despite the intentions of the founders, the proportion of day-boys at the school gradually fell and it became more like other public schools. The same was happening to the Nonconformists' schools as distinctions of wealth and class were added to earlier divisions of denomination and tradition. One Wesleyan public school, the Leys at Cambridge (1875), was opened as a traditional public school to offer an alternative to an Anglican education for children of middle-class Wesleyans seeking good secondary education preparatory to entry into the now-accessible universities of Cambridge or Oxford.[22] Though the Leys and The Dean Close Memorial School were both founded in the same evangelical tradition, they were also distinctively denominational creations. This trend continued into the twentieth century, when the most significant evangelical Anglican foundations were Canford and Stowe, both in 1923.

The education of the clergy

Evangelicalism implied a thorough grasp of theology and the early evangelicals sought to provide this for their ministers and preachers. This caused some tensions, especially in the ranks of Methodism where among the uneducated saints there was a suspicion of any learning that might undermine the spiritual equality of the gospel. Evangelicals within the Church, and in the older dissenting denominations, were more concerned to establish their credentials through learning. Education did not lead to faith, but out of faith came the desire for education.

An important role in promoting higher education was played from the later eighteenth century by the clerical societies. One of the earliest was the Elland Clerical Society, founded by Henry Venn in 1767. Ten years later the society started to provide funds for the university education of poor pious men wishing to take holy orders, and by 1800 fifty-six Elland pensioners had been groomed to strengthen the ranks of serious clergymen within the Church. The example set by the Elland Society was followed elsewhere, notably in Bristol (1795) and London (1816).[23]

Placing young evangelicals in the universities was not easy, especially after the expulsion of six Oxford undergraduates from St Edmund Hall in 1768 for 'methodistical' practices. Elland pensioners at first went to Magdalene, Cambridge, where William Farish was tutor; and then Queens' when Isaac, younger brother of Joseph Milner, became president in 1788. The attractiveness of Cambridge to evangelicals was confirmed when Charles Simeon (1759–1836) was appointed to a fellowship at

King's College in 1782. Not only did Simeon raise the standard
of theological education at Cambridge through his preaching
and after-sermon classes, he also helped transform the ministry of the Church in the parishes through the patronage of the
Simeon Trust, created to ensure livings for serious gospel clergymen. Francis Close was one such beneficiary at Cheltenham.[24]

The ancient universities of England were at this time the
almost exclusive territory of the Church of England. Though
Dissenters might attend Cambridge, there were few incentives
for them to do so. They had their own academies in which a
more practical education could be gained or they could go to
the ancient universities of Scotland. None of these institutions
was particularly congenial to evangelical attitudes; but in the
latter part of the eighteenth century new academies were
founded more in accord with the spirit of the revival. The
Countess of Huntingdon, who saw little of value in university-
educated men, set up her own college at Trevecca in
Breconshire. Her interest in supporting clergy training had
been stimulated by a New Jersey plan to found a college at
Princeton, and her college in Wales was opened by George
Whitefield on 24 August 1768. Among the earliest pupils were
two of the expelled undergraduates from St Edmund Hall.
Trevecca proved to be a powerhouse for the revival, training
evangelical ministers for the Countess's own chapels and the
growing number of Independent congregations stirred by the
preaching of Howell Harris and George Whitefield.[25]

Building on the work of Philip Doddridge at Northampton
(1729), the King's Head Society in London (1730) and James
Scott at Heckmondwike in Yorkshire (1756), new Dissenting
academies were founded from the later eighteenth century that
supported the Independents' claim to be the most educated of
orthodox Dissenters – places like John Conder's Mile End
Academy (1754), moved in 1768 to Homerton where the Independents' most distinguished tutor, John Pye Smith, taught
from 1806 until 1850; and Gosport (1789), where David
Bogue opened an academy which became a leading missionary
college. In 1850, when the three London colleges of Homerton,
Highbury and Coward were amalgamated to form New College,
there were provincial colleges in Rotherham, Bradford,
Manchester, Plymouth and Birmingham in England, Brecon

in Wales and Glasgow in Scotland. The tutors at these academies were influential scholars and teachers who ensured that
almost without exception the pulpits of Congregational Inde-
pendency were filled by college-educated men.[26]

As denominational boundaries hardened after 1800, Baptists
too began to open new academies to ensure an educated pastorate. Bristol had been open since 1770, but when William
Steadman moved north to begin Horton Academy, Bradford,
in 1805 he lamented, 'Most of the ministers are illiterates,
their talents small, their manners dull and uninteresting, their
systems of divinity contracted, their maxims of church government rigid, and their exertions scarcely any at all.'[27] Gradually
the case for an educated ministry was accepted, as other new
colleges were opened in Abergavenny (1807) and Stepney
(1810), with Horton becoming Rawdon College in 1859. The
expanding intellectual aspirations of the Baptists can be
charted in the location of Stepney College: in 1856 it was
moved to Regent's Park to be closer to London University and
by the 1880s there were proposals to move it again, this time
to Oxford or Cambridge.[28]

The Methodists were the slowest to develop their own
institutions of higher education, despite Wesley's proposal to
add an 'academical course' to his school at Kingswood. It is
not that he was opposed to learned preachers – he provided
lists of recommended reading for them as well as establishing
book stocks in London, Bristol and Newcastle – but only in
1834 did the Wesleyan Conference finally agree a plan for a
Theological Institution, opened the following year in the
former premises of the Hoxton Academy in London. Students
also attended lectures at King's College in the Strand. In 1842
a northern branch of the Institution (the Methodists disliked
the word 'college') was begun at Didsbury in Manchester
and the Hoxton enterprise was moved out to Richmond-on-
Thames. The other Methodist connexions were not far behind.
Shebbear College was opened by the Bible Christians in 1841,
to provide a school, teacher training and preacher training; the
New Connexion Methodists had Ranmoor College, Sheffield
from 1864; the United Methodist Free Churches opened Victoria Park College, Manchester (1876), and the Primitives
Sunderland (1868) and Manchester (1878). The attraction of

the latter city was the non-sectarian Owen's College (later the University of Manchester).[29]

While the Dissenters and Methodists were making progress with their own arrangements for the education of their preachers, evangelicals in the Church of England continued to rely upon the traditional education offered at Oxford and Cambridge, supplemented by Trinity College, Dublin, and, from 1829, King's College, London. Durham was not a significant provider of graduate clergy until after 1869. Two of the earliest Anglican colleges, St Bees (1816) and St Aidan's, Birkenhead, were founded by evangelical Bishops of Chester but, like St David's College, Lampeter (1822), they were not so much concerned with increasing the learning of the clergy, as with providing non-graduate clergy in areas of shortage, and their status was low. The first theological colleges for graduates, Chichester (1839) and Wells (1840), were both high-church and even when Cuddesdon, near Oxford, was founded in 1854 there was still no similar college under evangelical control. Litton Hall was opened with help from Lord Shaftesbury in 1855 for both Anglican and Nonconformist evangelicals, but the venture failed in 1860. More successful was the London College of Divinity, started with funds provided by Alfred Peache, a wealthy Gloucestershire clergyman, in Kilburn in 1863 and moved to Highbury in 1865. Nevertheless, evangelicals suspected theological training outside the universities as leaning towards the high-church position and no evangelical bishop established a college for his own diocese after Sumner's foundation of St Aidan's in 1846.

When Oxford and Cambridge were divested of most of their remaining Anglican monopolies in 1871, and undergraduate degrees in theology were instituted, it was still High Churchmen who took the initiative, founding Keble at Oxford in 1870 and Selwyn at Cambridge seven years later. These were colleges in all but name, opened to provide an Anglican community for undergraduates in what were now non-sectarian universities, though one of their principal aims was to provide a relatively cheap education for future clergy. In response, evangelicals adopted a more exclusive strategy, opening graduate halls in which to ensure a theologically correct education at the universities. Wycliffe Hall was opened in Oxford in 1877, followed by Ridley Hall, Cambridge, in 1881, but an attempt by the Elland Society and others in the 1890s to found a graduate college in Hull failed because all who wanted that kind of education could already go to Wycliffe or Ridley.[30]

By the 1870s the context of educational provision was changing, not only in the universities but also more widely. Although the suspicion persisted that evangelical approaches to learning were conservative and narrow, evangelicals, both Churchmen and Dissenters, had succeeded in establishing an educated pastorate capable of matching the increasing expectations of their middle-class congregations.

Higher education and evangelical mission in the twentieth century

The dilemma of evangelicals in the twentieth century has been how to preserve a distinctive presence in an increasingly secular world in which the provision, control and supervision of education are directly or indirectly the work of the state.

Different traditions within evangelicalism have responded differently. Evangelical Nonconformists, excluded from mainstream institutions until the late nineteenth century, then claimed as equals with other traditions their place in the world of learning and consequently put at risk their evangelical distinctiveness. Thus the Congregationalists' Spring Hill College, Birmingham, was transformed into Mansfield College, Oxford (1886), the Presbyterians opened Westminster College in Cambridge (1899), Cheshunt took its Hertfordshire name to Cambridge (1905), the Methodists opened Wesley House there (1926) and the Baptists' Regent's Park College finally arrived in Oxford in 1927.[31]

In contrast to this movement among Nonconformists towards assimilation, in the Church of England evangelical suspicion that special institutions were the preserve of Roman and Anglo-Catholics gave way to support for such establishments for educating both clergy and lay evangelists in the purity of evangelical truth. The danger was not assimilation but schism. The most ambitious and least exclusive achievement in the inter-war years was St Peter's Hall, founded in Oxford in 1928 'to promote religion and education generally and

especially to assist students of limited means, to encourage
candidates for Holy Orders and missionary work abroad, and
to maintain the principles of the Church of England as set forth
in the Book of Common Prayer'. Apart from the coded implications of the last phrase (a reference to the Prayer Book controversy of the 1920s) this was the same motivation that had
inspired High Churchmen to set up Keble and Selwyn in the
1870s and like them it subsequently shed its denominational
role and became a fully integrated college of the university.[32]

Evangelical colleges were also associated with the University
of Durham, where St John's Hall had been opened in 1909.
Two such external institutions were Oak Hill College in South-
gate, and the Bible Churchman's Missionary Society College
in Bristol. The latter was set up by conservative evangelicals in
1925 following a split in the Church Missionary Society. The
Bible Churchmen's Missionary Society (which also opened a
college for women in Bristol in 1930), itself then suffered a
split, prompting the former first principal to open Clifton
Theological College in 1932. Despite this tendency to fracture,
the overall effect was to double the provision of places for evangelical theological training between the wars.[33]

The determination of evangelicals to maintain their distinctive witness also led to several institutions for lay evangelists.
Cliff College in Derbyshire grew out of the work of Thomas
Champness, a Wesleyan Minister in Rochdale, who began training lay evangelists in 1886. Under its principal, Thomas Cook,
it became a centre of the holiness movement that spread from
America in the 1870s and found its classic expression in the
Keswick Convention of 1875.[34] Another institution to grow out
of the Keswick movement at the end of the nineteenth century
was the Bible Training Institute at Glasgow. Similar institutions
in the twentieth century have included the Bible College of
Wales (1924) and London Bible College (1943), the latter
being associated with the Christian Union movement in
higher education.[35]

The Cambridge Inter-Collegiate Christian Union (CICCU)
was founded in 1877. Other universities, including Edinburgh
and Oxford, followed and formed the British College Christian
Union in the 1890s. The latter became the Student Christian
Movement (SCM) in 1905, though its change of title betrayed

a widening outlook that caused CICCU to disaffiliate in 1910. After the failure of reconciliation talks in 1919, Cambridge and similar student groups in other universities then formed links that led to the Inter-Varsity Fellowship (IVF) in 1928. Despite the weakness of evangelicalism in the church at large between the wars, the IVF experienced growth as Christian Unions spread to several of the newer provincial universities. After the Second World War the expansion of evangelicalism in the universities continued, stimulated by the Billy Graham mission of 1954. Scholarship was not neglected, with study centres being opened at Tyndale House, Cambridge (1945) and Latimer House, Oxford (1960). In the 1960s and 1970s, Christian Unions were a leading force in the resurgence of evangelicalism both within and beyond the Church of England, while the SCM collapsed as an effective student organization.[36]

Conclusion

Questions of strategy have been implicit in the evangelical mission since the eighteenth century – exclusive identity or permeating influence, secular scholarship or faith in the Bible simply understood. The experience of educational history suggests no single approach.

   In the eighteenth century, the task seemed simple when weaknesses in existing religious and educational provision presented evangelicals with opportunities for distinctive action. During the nineteenth century, different strategies developed. With denominational lines crossing theological positions and the state taking an increasing part in the provision and funding of schools, the scope for evangelical action was circumscribed. This led some evangelicals to question whether education should remain part of their mission at all. In the twentieth century, with changing attitudes towards class, doubts have also been raised about the morality of involvement in private education. As a result, direct evangelical activity in schooling has become marginal.

   In higher education, as universities have undertaken an increasing role in theological training in the period since 1870, many former evangelical institutions also have lost their distinctiveness. The response of conservative evangelicals – especially

in the Church of England – has been to turn to their own institutions for some protection against the liberalism of university
theology.[37] This strategy has proved successful since the 1920s
in building up evangelical strength. Similarly, the rise of
Christian Unions, separate but within secular institutions, has
been the response to the need for a distinctive position among
non-theological students. Paradoxically, therefore, as the special
evangelical contribution to the educational needs of society has
declined, education has itself been used to define a special
identity for evangelicalism in society. Whether this quest for a
separate identity has had a broadening or a narrowing effect on
the work of mission remains a matter for debate.

Notes

1 C. Brown, *The Social History of Religion in Scotland since 1730*
   (Methuen, 1987), p. 17.
2 J. Howard, *Historical Sketch of the Origin and Work of the York
   Incorporated (Church of England) Sunday School Committee*, second
   edition (York, 1896), p. 7.
3 Quoted in H. D. Rack, *Reasonable Enthusiast: John Wesley and the Rise
   of Methodism* (Epworth Press, 1989), p. 354; see also A. H. Body,
   John Wesley and Education (Epworth Press, 1936).
4 C. Cecil, ed., *Original Thoughts on Various Passages of Scripture being
   the substance of sermons preached by the late Rev. Richard Cecil, A.M.*
   (1848), p. 649, quoted in D. Rosman, *Evangelicals and Culture*
   (Croom Helm, 1984), pp. 208–9. For Cecil, see L. E. Elliott-Binns,
   The Early Evangelicals: a Religious and Social Study (Lutterworth
   Press, 1953), pp. 244–5. Rosman's book contains the most thorough
   examination of this complex question.
5 Rack, *Reasonable Enthusiast*, p. 356. For the Methodist contribution
   to education see F. C. Pritchard, 'Education' in R. Davies, A. R.
   George and G. Rupp, eds, *A History of the Methodist Church in Great
   Britain* (4 vols, Epworth Press, 1965–83), vol. 3, pp. 279–308.
6 The classic fictional description of the harshness of an evangelical
   boarding-school education, based on her experiences of Cowan
   Bridge school for clergy daughters, is Lowood in Charlotte Brontë's
   Jane Eyre. For Thomas Arnold's views on education and sin, see T.
   W. Bamford, ed., *Thomas Arnold on Education* (Cambridge UP,
   1970), pp. 8–12.
7 Rosman, *Evangelicals and Culture*, pp. 220–34.
8 See M. G. Jones, *Hannah More* (Cambridge UP, 1952) and S.
   Pedersen, 'Hannah More meets Simple Simon: Tracts, Chap-books

and Popular Culture in Late-Eighteenth Century England', *Journal of British Studies* 25 (1986), pp. 84–113. For a critical evaluation of the religious tract, see V. E. Neuburg, *Popular Literature: a History and a Guide* (Harmondsworth: Penguin, 1977), pp. 249–64.

9 V. E. Neuburg, *Popular Education in the Eighteenth Century* (Woburn Press, 1971), esp. pp. 93–113; L. Stone, 'Literacy and Society in England, 1640–1900', *Past and Present* 42 (Feb. 1969), pp. 69–139; M. Sanderson, 'Literacy and Social Mobility in the Industrial Revolution in England', *Past and Present* 56 (Aug. 1972), pp. 75–104; and the subsequent debate between M. Sanderson and T. W. Laqueur in *Past and Present* 64 (Aug. 1974), pp. 96–112.

10 For a contemporary assessment of Sunday schools in 1851, see *British Parliamentary Papers: 1851 Census: Report and Tables on Education in England and Wales* (1853–1854), pp. lxxi–lxxix and cxxi-ii; and *Report and Tables on Religious Worship and Education in Scotland* (1854), p. 37. For the history of Sunday schools, see P. B. Cliff, *The Rise and Development of the Sunday School Movement in England, 1780–1980* (Redhill: National Christian Education Council, 1986); and T. W. Laqueur, *Religion and Respectability: Sunday Schools and Working Class Culture, 1780–1850* (New Haven and London: Yale UP, 1976). Laqueur's interpretation is challenged by M. Dick, 'The Myth of the Working Class Sunday School', *History of Education* 9 (1980), pp. 27–41.

11 E. Hodder, *The Life and Work of the Seventh Earl of Shaftesbury, K.G.* (3 vols, 1886), vol. 1, pp. 481–7; *Report and Tables on Education in England and Wales* (1853–1854), p. cxxiii, and *Report and Tables on Religious Worship and Education in Scotland* (1854), p. 36.

12 The best introduction to the history of elementary education is J. Murphy, *Church, State and Schools in Britain 1800–1970* (Routledge and Kegan Paul, 1971). See also C. K. F. Brown, *The Church's Part in Education 1833–1941 with Special reference to the Work of the National Society* (National Society and SPCK, 1942) and H. J. Burgess, *Enterprise in Education: the story of the work of the Established Church in the education of the people prior to 1870* (National Society and SPCK, 1958).

13 M. Sanderson, 'The National and British School Societies in Lancashire 1803–1830: the roots of Anglican supremacy in English education' in T. G. Cook, ed., *Local Studies in the History of Education* (Methuen, 1972), pp. 1–36.

14 For Close's educational interests, see M. Hennell, *Sons of the Prophets: Evangelical Leaders of the Victorian Church* (SPCK, 1979), pp. 112–17.

15 For McNeile, Stowell and Knox, see K. Hylson-Smith, *Evangelicals in the Church of England, 1734–1984* (Edinburgh: T & T Clark, 1988), pp. 145–50, 272–3. For McNeile in Liverpool, see J. Murphy, *The Religious Problem in English Education: the Crucial Experiment* (Liverpool UP, 1959) and for Stowell in Manchester, see S. E.

Maltby, *Manchester and the Movement for National Elementary Education* (Manchester UP, 1918).

16 H. Corr, 'An Exploration into Scottish Education', pp. 292, 294, in W. H. Fraser and R. J. Morris, eds, *People and Society in Scotland: Volume II, 1830–1914* (Edinburgh: John Donald, 1990), pp. 290–309.

17 Hennell, *Sons of the Prophets*, pp. 116–17; Burgess, *Enterprise*, pp. 119–29.

18 Pritchard, 'Education', p. 290. One incidental contribution of Westminster College to educational history is the leading part played by its students in the formation of the National Union of Teachers.

19 J. Lawson, *A Town Grammar School Through Six Centuries: a history of Hull Grammar School against its local context* (Oxford UP, 1963), pp. 163–84.

20 There is a convenient summary of the work of the Clerical and Lay Associations in R. J. Evans, 'Town, Gown and Cloth: an essay on the foundation of the school', in M. A. Girling and L. Hooper, eds, *Dean Close School: the first hundred years* (Cheltenham: Dean Close School, 1986), pp. 1–39. The quotation is from p. 14. See also G. R. Balleine, *A History of the Evangelical Party in the Church of England* (1908), p. 273.

21 Quoted in Evans, 'Town, Gown and Cloth', p. 8.

22 Pritchard, 'Education', pp. 296–8.

23 There is a brief account of these societies in F. W. B. Bullock, *Voluntary Religious Societies, 1520–1799* (St Leonards on Sea: Budd and Gillatt, 1963), pp. 241–2.

24 For evangelicalism at eighteenth-century Oxford and Cambridge, see Elliott-Binns, *Early Evangelicals*, pp. 351–65; for Simeon, see the short sketch in K. Hylson-Smith, *Evangelicals*, pp. 70–6.

25 G. W. Kirby, *The Elect Lady* (Trustees of the Countess of Huntingdon's Connexion, 1972), pp. 40–6. The College moved to Cheshunt in 1792 and Cambridge in 1905. It was amalgamated with the Presbyterians' Westminster College, Cambridge, in 1968. See also E. Welch, ed., *Cheshunt College, the Early Years*, Hertfordshire Record Society Publication 6 (1990), pp. vi–xiv.

26 See R. T. Jones, *Congregationalism in England, 1662–1962* (Independent Press, 1962), pp. 140–3, 176–9.

27 Quoted in A. C. Underwood, *A History of the English Baptists* (Baptist Union, 1947), p. 175.

28 For the Baptist colleges, see E. A. Payne, *The Baptist Union: a short history* (The Carey Kingsgate Press, 1958), pp. 39, 94, 211.

29 Pritchard, 'Education', pp. 286–7, 291–3.

30 Details of the Church of England colleges are given in A. Haig, *The Victorian Clergy* (Croom Helm, 1984), esp. pp. 27–115; and Hylson-Smith, *Evangelicals*, pp. 182–5.

31 See F. M. Turner, 'Religion', pp. 295–7 in B. Harrison, ed., *The History of the University of Oxford. VIII: The Twentieth Century* (Oxford: Clarendon Press, 1994), pp. 293–316; and C. N. L.

Brooke, *A History of the University of Cambridge. IV: 1870–1990* (Cambridge UP, 1993), pp. 141–6. For the symbolism of Mansfield's new building, see C. Binfield, '"We claim our part in the great inheritance": the message of four Congregational buildings', pp. 203–14 in K. Robbins, ed., *Studies in Church History*, Subsidia 7 (1990), pp. 201–23.

32 Hylson-Smith, *Evangelicals*, pp. 268–9; Turner, 'Religion', p. 304.
33 Hylson-Smith, *Evangelicals*, pp. 252, 267–9.
34 W. J. Townsend, H. B. Workman and G. Eayrs, eds, *A New History of Methodism* (2 vols, 1909), vol. 1, pp. 463–4; H. D. Rack, 'Wesleyan Methodism 1849–1902', pp. 162–3, in Davies, George and Rupp, eds, *Methodist Church in Great Britain*, vol. 3, pp. 119–66.
35 D. W. Bebbington, *Evangelicalism in Modern Britain* (Unwin Hyman, 1989), p. 260.
36 Bebbington, *Evangelicalism*, pp. 188, 259–61; A. Hastings, *A History of English Christianity, 1920–1985* (Collins, 1986), pp. 86–92, 200–1, 453–8, 552–4.
37 For both these trends at Oxford, see Turner, 'Religion', pp. 295–7, 304–5.

Chapter Seven

Nonconformist Evangelicals and National Politics in the Late Nineteenth Century

KENNETH D. BROWN

In considering the part played by evangelicals in British politics during the decades prior to the First World War the historian immediately runs into two fundamental questions. The one – what is meant by the term 'politics'? – can be simply if somewhat arbitrarily resolved. It is here taken to mean the national political process involving parliament, party, lobbying and electioneering. The second – with which particular individuals are we concerned? – is more difficult to resolve.

Within the Church of England, evangelical influence reached its apogee around the middle of the century. At that time about a third of the clergy were reckoned to be evangelicals and between 1815 and 1865 several of their number were appointed to bishoprics. The evangelical political presence was also very apparent. More than a hundred evangelical MPs sat in the House of Commons in the fifty years between 1782 and 1832. Following their participation in the successful campaign for the abolition of slavery, they made regular interventions in public life, leaving barely a single contemporary need or institution untouched. Partly under their influence parliament was turned into the vehicle for a succession of national crusades with the result that the political process itself was imbued with profound moral and religious overtones. 'I voted today', recorded Henry Thornton, 'so that if my Master had come again at that moment

I might have been able to give an account of my stewardship.'[1] In these years the evangelicals' greatest achievement, it has been suggested, 'was to have established politics as an honourable profession for honest men rather than as a playground for party hacks.'[2] By the end of Queen Victoria's reign, however, evangelicals were very much on the defensive within the Church of England. Between 1865 and 1900 only six were appointed to bishoprics and by the turn of the century evangelical leadership depended very heavily on men of an older generation. Evangelical energies were increasingly distracted by internal debates about Christian socialism, the nature of church government, and ritualism. Some became involved in the holiness movement associated with the Keswick conventions. By the time Edward VII ascended the throne in 1901, the Anglican evangelicals had, in the words of their most recent historian, become 'quite seriously dispirited, uncertain of their role within the church and in society, and without that cohesion, purposefulness and energy which had characterised them in the halcyon days of the past.'[3]

With the obvious exception of Unitarianism, Nonconformity had always been more uniformly evangelical than the Church of England. Methodism had been born during the eighteenth-century evangelical revival, a movement which had also had a profound impact on the older Baptist and Congregational forms of Dissent. Nonconformists' political activity in the first three-quarters of the nineteenth century had been directed mainly into efforts to remove the political and civil disabilities under which they laboured. With the progressive lifting of these burdens, politically-minded Dissenters were able to concentrate on wider concerns. By the 1870s 'the Nonconformist conscience', as it was later termed, was an increasingly potent force in public life.[4] Free Church leaders moved in the highest political circles. Nonconformist campaigns, for example against the Balkan atrocities or the 1902 Education Act, secured enormous publicity. It was the Nonconformists' network which sustained the Liberal Party in the provinces. Above all, it was their votes which helped to return an estimated 200 Free Churchmen to the House of Commons elected in 1906. The Prime Minister, Henry Campbell-Bannerman, acknowledged the importance of this support when he suggested that the

Liberals had been 'put into power by the Nonconformists'.[5] Clearly, by the end of the nineteenth century, Nonconformity provided the main channel through which evangelical influence flowed into the nation's political life. It was, it has been recently remarked, 'Free Church liberalism' that provided 'evangelicalism's cutting-edge'.[6]

Yet it was precisely in this same period that Nonconformist evangelicals began to withdraw from social and political involvement. The early twentieth century witnessed what has been called 'the great reversal'.[7] While it would be unwise to exaggerate the speed and degree with which this change occurred there can be no doubt that by the time of the First World War theological, social, intellectual, and political change had all conspired to make it more difficult for Nonconformist evangelicals to exercise the sort of corporate political influence enjoyed by their Anglican counterparts in the early years of the nineteenth century. In seeking to explain this, the historian can identify two key developments: change in theological thinking and change in the political system. To each there were several facets.

In the first half of the century most Nonconformists regarded themselves as evangelical. The term itself undoubtedly embraced a wide range of theological convictions running all the way from predestination to free will. The Wesleyan Arminian, Jabez Bunting, agonized for some time over whether Sarah Maclardie's early Calvinistic upbringing disqualified her as a potential wife. His subsequent happy – though sadly shortlived – marriage to Miss Maclardie, indicated, however, that such differences did not outweigh other, more important beliefs that drew them together.[8] Within mainstream Nonconformity and to a lesser extent among Anglicans, evangelicalism implied a common subscription to a core of theological beliefs – the need for individual salvation, a particular regard for the Bible, a stress on the centrality of Christ's atoning work on the cross, and a belief that the gospel needed to be actively expressed.[9] The emphasis was not so much on systematic belief but rather on individual experience which led to a particular way of life. Translated into political terms this manifested itself in a series of interdenominational campaigns directed against obstacles to and substitutes for the gospel, and aimed also at the elimination of sin. By sin was understood immorality and a life-style contrary to Scripture. Thus the anti-slavery campaign was driven not so much by humanitarian motives as by a conviction that the institution was inherently sinful. At a lower level an evangelical Baptist pastor, William Brock, persuaded his congregation to rebuke or expel a number of individuals who had been involved in corrupt practices during a parliamentary election.[10] Although it would be idle to suggest that agreement on specific policies necessarily followed, in general evangelicals were all working from this same set of underlying religious convictions. From mid-century onwards, however, this common base began to crumble, undermined by three new, but interlinked, waves of thought.

Older interpretations tend to lay a lot of stress on the first of these waves, that arising from the work of Charles Darwin on natural selection and evolution. *The Origin of Species*, it was remarked in 1940, for example, 'came into the theological world like a plough into an ant-hill. Everywhere those rudely awakened from their old comfort and repose swarmed forth angry and confused.'[11] Such work appeared to challenge, implicitly if not directly, foundational evangelical notions about the nature of man, personal responsibility for sin, judgement, hell, and even the historical personage of Jesus. Above all, Darwin's notion of natural selection appeared inconsistent with what seemed the strongest argument for Christian belief – the view that the adaptation of a species to its mode of life was evidence for the activity of a beneficent creator. It was a long time before the average chapelgoer became unduly agitated by these questions or, indeed, before the issue resolved itself into a straightforward conflict between Darwin and the Bible. Darwinism may not have been so corrosive of faith as older writers have suggested but it did contribute to a more sceptical intellectual climate and produce internal divisions within evangelicalism.

A second, and more damaging solvent was compounded from Romanticism, German theology, and the English school of poetry. All served to undermine the evangelicals' trust in the Enlightenment emphasis on evidences, scientific method, and a structured universe governed by cause and effect. The controversies frequently generated by new ideas sometimes served to divert energies into internal disputes rather than outwards into the public life of the nation. From as early as 1851 Congregationalists were disturbed by controversies over the inspiration and authority of the Bible. In the autumn of 1877 they were rocked again when James Picton presented a paper entitled 'The relations of theology to religion'. His argument – that the essence of religious communion should be based on feeling rather than credal uniformity – provoked a heated response from the traditionalists on the grounds that it was precisely this sort of approach which had wrecked the spiritual life of the German churches.[12] The Wesleyan Revd J. Agar Beet was twice censured by the annual conference for expressing unorthodox ideas of hell, while fundamentalists in the denomination also questioned the evangelical credibility of George Jackson when he was appointed to the chair of Homiletics and Pastoral Theology at Didsbury College in 1912.[13]

Similar disunities were also generated by the third wave of new thought, which was produced by the evangelicals' own attempts to come to terms with the changing social and economic world in which they lived and to formulate agendas for political involvement. This 'New Evangelicalism', as its real initiator, R. W. Dale, minister of Carr's Lane Congregational Chapel in Birmingham, called it, was 'formulated to rescue Nonconformity from irrelevance in a rapidly changing environment, and to help Nonconformists to retain by assertive action an identifiable communal life as they accommodated their religion to secular prosperity.'[14]

There were several dimensions to this process. One aspect involved the progressive dismantling from 1828 of the legal and civil disabilities imposed on Nonconformists. However, this also removed a most potent focus for political activity. Another aspect was the commercialization of leisure which combined with the growing involvement of the state in welfare and education to deprive the churches of some of their major social functions. Rising living standards gave the populace greater freedom to search out alternative social and leisure activities. While some churches responded in kind by trying to compete in the provision of such facilities, others were highly critical of what they regarded as an unwholesome mixing of the sacred and the secular. A neat cameo of this is provided by the experience of the leading Methodist Hugh Price Hughes whose grandmother admonished him for playing cricket. She could not 'think that such a pastime is fitting for a future Wesleyan preacher'.[15]

Theologically, the growing emphasis on secular responsibilities and involvements, as found in Dale's early writings, ultimately resulted in the atonement losing the central place which it had enjoyed in orthodox evangelical doctrine. It was subsumed now in the incarnation. By the mid-1870s, however, there were signs that Dale was backtracking, alarmed by the divisions to which his well-intentioned reformulation of evangelical doctrine was giving rise. These differences became more public when the Leicester meetings of the Congregational Union in 1877 were upstaged by a parallel conference organized by Congregational dissidents. The following year the Union reaffirmed its commitment to uphold and extend Evangelical Religion. But the genie had been let out of the bottle. As a denomination the Congregationalists continued to drift towards a much more diffuse and liberal version of Christianity. So, though to a far lesser extent, did some Baptists; at least, the fear that this might happen was voiced in 1887 by their best-known preacher, C. H. Spurgeon. In that year he accused the Baptist Union of compromising evangelical truth, thus sparking off the Down Grade controversy. Spurgeon was alarmed by the implications of the new theology and where it might ultimately lead. In venting his concern he was effectively criticizing many of his brethren whose evangelical theology was stoutly traditional.

Spurgeon's censures received little support from his fellow ministers but the Down Grade controversy did suggest that even the relatively cautious Baptists were by no means immune to the uncertainties created by the new modes of theological thought which were making such headway within Congregationalism. A broader spectrum of evangelicalism and evangelical activism was opening up which many found difficult to accommodate within their older, more narrowly focused versions. For example, the increasing emphasis that was placed on the environment as a contributory factor in individuals' sinfulness cut right across the traditional evangelical emphasis on personal responsibility for sin. Their consistent response to the social

problems arising from urbanization had been to emphasize the
necessity of a personal encounter with Christ. From the 1870s
the emphasis began to shift from Christ the atoning saviour to
Christ the incarnated exemplar and teacher. This was the
message offered by the president of the Brotherhood movement. 'As we get a firm grasp of the ethical teaching of the
Carpenter of Nazareth, we are convinced that it contains those
principles of life and conduct which alone will give a perfect
solution to every social problem . . . social salvation.'[16] When he
got on to the atonement he was far too vague for orthodox
evangelical taste. 'We will not, therefore, stultify ourselves by
limiting our ideas concerning this great theme . . . we will seek
to be permeated with its spirit.'[17] Not surprisingly, perhaps, he
was forced to admit that his movement was faced with the
danger of schism between those who wanted nothing at their
meetings but the old gospel and those who preferred the
emphasis to be on social and political issues such as housing
and unemployment. In the eyes of the traditionalists within the
Nonconformist churches this ran the risk of diluting evangelical
spirituality. Many voices were raised in favour of re-empha-
sizing the old orthodoxy and this tension became ever more
apparent as the nineteenth century turned into the twentieth.
Thus the president of the Bible Christian conference urged his
hearers in 1902 to 'let nothing divert our attention – no question of philosophy, no postulation of criticism, no political
agitation – from our supreme mission of preaching Christ and
saving sinners.'[18] In similar vein the Methodist Samuel
Chadwick insisted that 'Conversions . . . solve the social problem. Environment is but the shadow of character, and the
surest way to change the shadow is to begin with the man.'[19]

Once it was conceded that the environment played at least
some part in encouraging a tendency to sinfulness, so social
reform became an inevitable component of the effort to eliminate sin. This was readily acceptable to those who came to
embrace immanentist theology, the notion that God was in
everything and everyone. 'Every kindness that you show to the
drunkards,' wrote Hugh Price Hughes, 'to the harlots . . . to the
starving poor . . . is a kindness shown to Jesus Christ.'[20] In the
late nineteenth century, collectivist solutions were more widely
espoused, urged on by the demands of newly enfranchised

workers, some of whom had benefited from the collective
action pursued by their trade unions. But this created difficulties for those who found it hard to reconcile the individualism
implicit in their theology with the notion of collective responsibility for social problems. For example, when in 1883 Andrew
Mearns denounced social conditions in the capital in *The Bitter
Cry of Outcast London*, the reaction of his fellow Congregationalist Samuel Morley was to suggest that most of the misery
experienced by the London poor was self-inflicted.[21] Many, of
course, did manage to translate their traditional emphasis on
the conscience of the individual into the collective conscience.
A few, including John Clifford, called themselves socialists. J.
E. Rattenbury, a Wesleyan minister, even advanced the view
that evangelicalism and socialism were compatible.[22] Yet collectivism and socialism were frequently decried – at least in the
popular press – as godless. St. Loe Strachey, for instance,
claimed that socialism would mean the 'overthrow of the
Christian moral code in regard to marriage and the relation of
the sexes, and must end in free love and promiscuity.'[23]
Another contemporary noted that Edwardian electors were
frequently bombarded with popular political leaflets declaring
that 'a vote for a Labour candidate is a vote against God'.[24]
Nothing could have been more calculated to frighten off those
evangelicals who had ventured a little way down the road of
collectivist political remedies to contemporary social problems.
The *Methodist Weekly* ceased publication in 1903, its readers
alienated by the socialism of its new editor, the Revd Samuel
Keeble. The establishment of the Free Church Socialist League
provoked a storm of orthodox evangelical protest. 'The ministry that departs from the great mission of saving sinners',
declaimed the Revd George Freeman, 'is a discredit in the
world and a degradation to itself.'[25]

Together the intellectual waves generated by Darwinism,
Romanticism, and the 'New Evangelicalism' weakened the ability of evangelicals to sustain a powerful corporate influence in
political life. Energies were absorbed by internal wranglings.
The opening up of a broader spectrum of evangelical thought
meant that they were no longer able to speak with a united, and
therefore powerful, voice. As Spurgeon put it with some feeling: 'it is mere cant to say "We are all Evangelicals": we are all

Evangelicals, and yet decline to say what Evangelical means.'[26] Above all, perhaps, they were pushed onto the defensive because so many of the widely accepted evangelical verities were no longer generally held to be self-evident truths. Increasingly, evangelicals were addressing a world, both inside and outside the church, in which they had first to establish their initial premises, rather than one which accepted them *de facto*. In this regard the position of the evangelicals in the late nineteenth century was beginning to resemble that of all churchmen in the twentieth. They were no longer able to approach the pulpit as a throne from which to expound the meaning and implications of their beliefs. Rather it was more of a witness box from which the beliefs had to be proven and defended. Accordingly, their interventions in public life lost something of the force they had earlier derived from being rooted in widely accepted theological premises.

But it was not only changes in theological thinking which thus made it increasingly difficult for evangelicals to exert a serious political influence. In the early nineteenth century their political influence was greatly enhanced by the symbiotic relationship existing between their theology and the contemporary political system. In terms of political goals, evangelicals wished to eliminate sin and obstacles to the propagation of the gospel. In turn, this view of their proper role in society dictated political tactics. The favoured *modus operandi* was public campaigns. These were conducted through mass meetings, concentrated on single issues, and were essentially negative in the sense that they were directed at eliminating specific evils by pressurizing parliament. Nonconformists generally and evangelicals in particular were seen as negative influences – anti-slavery, anti-Catholic, and anti-Establishment, for example. It was, said one late nineteenth-century activist, 'not his business to propose schemes of redress or to suggest legislative measures . . . [but to] denounce abuses and wrongs and shams and inequalities.'[27] These were forms of activity well suited to a political culture in which the electorate was small, and parties were weak, both ideologically and institutionally. It is no surprise, therefore, that similar tactics were adopted by other significant pressure groups such as the Chartists, the Anti-Corn Law Leaguers, the National Education League, the United Kingdom

Alliance, the Peace Society and the Liberation Society. Thus, a particular theological stance combined with a particular political structure to afford the evangelicals considerable influence in contemporary politics.

In the last two decades of the nineteenth century, however, the British political system began to assume a more recognizably modern form. The general election of 1880 is usually recognized as the turning point, for it was the first to be fought as a national campaign between two clearly defined political parties. Thereafter, the trend was towards a parliament increasingly dominated by party. This process culminated in the creation of a mass electorate by the further extension of the franchise in 1918 and the shift away from communal to class-based politics. For three reasons this was bound to have an adverse effect on the ability of evangelicals to influence politics in any corporate way. First, Nonconformist numbers had failed to keep up with population growth. The progressive extension of the franchise to the mass of the working classes, the least religiously active segment of the population, was bound to reduce the overall significance of Nonconformists within the electorate. By extension, the influence of the evangelicals was also proportionately decreased, although this point should not be pressed too far, since only about two thirds of adult males were on the electoral register in 1900, despite the franchise extensions of 1867 and 1884. Second, the shift to class-based politics weakened the effectiveness of communal groups like the Nonconformists and – again by extension – the evangelicals. Class exposed differences of emphasis and opinion within a group whose unifying focus had been provided by involvement in chapel life. Third, the growing dominance of party in the political process reduced the effectiveness of extra-parliamentary campaigning of the sort which had been so effective in the earlier part of the nineteenth century.

There had always been a tension within evangelical Nonconformity about the validity of political activity. Early nineteenth-century leaders such as John Pye Smith had argued that it was a Christian duty to be politically involved. 'As teachers of religion', he proclaimed, 'we are bound to be teachers of politics.'[28] Thomas Binney, another well-known Congregational leader, agreed: 'Politics are a branch of morals and the Bible is the most political of books.'[29] On the other hand, Dr Chalmers of Glasgow expressed his opposition to political involvement by ministers on the grounds that he had seen too many 'who, as platform orators, have figured much at these meetings, [and] have been sadly drawn off from keeping their own vineyards.'[30] It is worth noting in this respect that throughout the nineteenth century the level of political involvement by Nonconformist ministers was probably much lower than is sometimes appreciated. A man like Alfred Cooke, a Baptist who remained totally uninvolved in the public life of Luton during a ministry which lasted for half a century, was perhaps more typical than has hitherto been appreciated.[31] Impressions have been distorted by the high profile political activity of the few.

But when evangelicals spoke of eschewing politics they usually tended to mean the pulpit and party politics. Wesley, for instance, had urged a no-politics rule on his followers, and Methodist ministers generally found it difficult to get deeply involved because of the operation of the itinerant system. But this did not prevent Wesley's successor, Jabez Bunting, from speaking out on political affairs, most notably in opposition to the grant to the Roman Catholic seminary at Maynooth in Ireland. It was not politics *per se* but rather their appearance in the pulpit that an early principal of the Wesleyan Theological Institute found distasteful. The pulpit, he averred, 'is sacred to better purposes than the discussion of political subjects; and my business in the pulpit is with men's souls and not with matters of state.'[32] In his presidential address to the Baptists in 1867 John Aldis argued that the 'less we have to do with politics the better' – by which, he explained, he meant not that they should abrogate responsibilities as citizens and patriots but rather that they should not employ religious organizations for political ends.[33] The Methodist, Gervase Smith, agreed. Addressing newly ordained ministers in 1875 he urged that 'If you accept my counsel you will sedulously avoid all political confederations and party politics. They will eat into your soul as doth a canker. But there are great protestant and Evangelical subjects constantly rising up, with which you should be well acquainted, and concerning which you should seek to form a careful and upright judgement.'[34] A year or two later the

Wesleyans' annual conference address urged local societies to keep in mind that politics could be divisive and that the honour of Christ, not party success, should be the cardinal validating motive behind any political action. Similarly, it was party politics that the Presbyterian, Monro Gibson, had in mind in 1895 when he urged the National Free Church Council to steer clear of political activity. In 1892 Henry Stedwicke, a Congregationalist, expressed the hope that whatever views Nonconformists had of political and social issues 'our ministers will refrain from taking any active part in electoral contests of a purely party character', since immense harm had been done by their involvement in the 1885 and 1886 elections.[35]

Yet such involvement was the logical outcome of the 'New Evangelicalism', and Stedwicke's letter, therefore, prompted a swift response from two more Congregationalists who wrote to say that Scripture itself did not support his position.[36] This was certainly more to the editor's taste. Returning to the topic some time later, he roundly castigated the abstainers. 'There are many', he wrote, 'to whom the very name of politics is an offence . . . superficial pietists in whose eyes to take an active interest in politics is regarded as an iniquity but slightly removed from the seven deadly sins.'[37] Among Baptists there was a similar division. Whereas some ministers in the denomination deprecated political controversy, John Clifford was so active in the Liberal Party that in 1903 he topped the poll in the elections for the executive of the National Liberal Federation.

Such differences were brought into sharper focus by the emergence of the modern party system. It became increasingly difficult to maintain the distinction between issues and parties. The dilemma was well illustrated in the career of the Wesleyan, Hugh Price Hughes. As pastor of an important London chapel, editor of the *Methodist Times*, the most dynamic of contemporary preachers, and first president of the National Free Church Council, Hughes constantly reiterated the need for Nonconformists to remain unfettered by party ties. In practice, however, this was more rhetoric than reality, and the Nonconformists became ever more closely identified with the Liberal Party. As Brian Stanley has argued: 'Nonconformists appealed to long-established principles of evangelical political action in order to align Nonconformity with a set of social policies and accordingly *with the political party which proposed those policies.'*[38]

For some Nonconformist evangelicals such an identification was quite acceptable. But at the same time it did add yet another potentially divisive dimension to those already created by new theological thinking. This could serve only to weaken further political effectiveness. For one thing, party politics implied loyalty to a leader. Gladstone's high moral tone and biblical emphasis made him the object of veneration among Nonconformists, notwithstanding his high churchmanship. But in the main his successors, Rosebery, Campbell-Bannerman, and Asquith, had adult connections that were tenuous, if that, with Nonconformity, and weaker still with evangelicalism. David Lloyd George was a practising chapelgoer who frequently sought to capitalize on his Baptist background, but his personal integrity fell far short of the high standards demanded by the evangelical credo. One Presbyterian academic commented that 'one does not like to see the finance of England in the hands of a man who cannot be trusted to give an exact statement of anything.'[39]

A second implication of party politics was commitment to programmes, not all the features of which might be acceptable. This was why in 1886 the thirty-eight Free Church ministers who supported a petition in favour of the Irish Home Rule Bill refused to sign a wider political manifesto. Third, the growth of formalized parties inevitably meant that the organization rather than the faith would have first claim on an individual's loyalty. This was certainly true, for instance, of Samuel Morley, proprietor of the *Daily News*, and J. J. Colman, MP for Norwich, both of whom were willing to back the Liberal Party, even on matters which went against their religious interests. Such an order of priority was distasteful to those like Dale who felt that faith should not be compromised for the sake of preserving the party's interests. His was increasingly a minority view, however. The Nonconformist MPs, it has been observed, 'conceived of themselves primarily as party politicians and only incidentally as the proponents of distinctive religious views.'[40] It was noted, for example, that of the two hundred or so Liberal Nonconformist members returned in 1906 only about seventy or eighty bothered to attend meetings of the parliamentary

Nonconformist lobby.[41] It followed from this, too, that issues
and principles were often ignored in the struggle to hold on to
power. This was hinted at in W. H. Mills' *Grey Pastures*, the hero
of which, John Ogden Nash, viewed his Congregational chapel
and the Liberal Party as 'final goals in themselves.'[42] The Revd
Arthur Guttery assured his father who had expressed concern
lest ends and means became similarly confused, that 'you must
not fear, however, that I shall ever forget that my chief work is
to preach the Gospel. My most powerful motive for entering so
largely into Temperance and political work is that it increases
the audiences and influence of my church.'[43] Some years later,
the Revd C. S. Horne's friends were persuaded only reluctantly that their minister could maintain the paramountcy of his
pastoral work even while serving as a member of parliament.[44]

Furthermore, the rise of party exposed differences of
emphasis and allegiance between denominations, again weakening the cohesion of evangelicalism. Wesleyans had always
been less politically active than other Nonconformist evangelicals, partly because of their closer links with Anglicanism,
partly because of Wesley's no-politics legacy. When Compton
Rickett invited prominent Nonconformist ministers to meet
Campbell-Bannerman and Herbert Gladstone in 1902 he
invited mainly Congregationalists because they 'take a more
prominent part in political work than Methodists'.[45]

Even within denominations it is true that while the majority
supported the Liberals, there were important minorities who
did not. A Nonconformist Unionist Association existed during
this period, for instance. Others could happily give their support to the Labour Party. Of twenty-three Baptist MPs elected
before the First World War three were Labour representatives.
About eight of the Labour MPs elected in 1906 were active
Nonconformists, including Arthur Henderson, a powerful lay
figure amongst the Wesleyans, who was elected party chairman
in 1908.[46] While it is clear that the policies of the Edwardian
Labour Party were essentially very similar to those of the
Liberals, there were – in theory at least – important differences
of principle between the two. If the New Liberalism envisaged
a much greater role for the state in the tackling of social problems it most certainly did not go as far as the infant Labour
Party which was, in the words of Philip Snowden, 'the only

party which has a comprehensive principle as its basis and a distinct social ideal to be reached by the application of this principle. . . . The efforts of the Labour Party in parliament will be directed to this end alone, to applying collectivist principles to the treatment of every question.'[47] In this way, therefore, party political differences had the potential to divide evangelicals. The involvement of the Revd John Wilson in founding the Woolwich Labour Party provoked much adverse comment from members of his congregation, 'who thought the cobbler should stick to his last'.[48]

They were by no means alone. Even in the immediate afterglow of their greatest political intervention, the general election of 1906, Nonconformists themselves were increasingly inclined to question the validity of political activity. The retreat was at once heralded and symbolized by the appearance in 1910 of the anonymous but highly influential *Nonconformity and Politics*. Its message was simple and evidently evoked a ready response within significant sections of the Nonconformist community.

> Modern Nonconformity, in making corporate political action bulk so largely upon its programmes, is forsaking its first ideals. It does a work which was never committed to its hands, and leaves undone, or at best put (*sic*) poorly done, the work for which it was ordained. . . . In the political activity of modern Nonconformity power is deflected upon wrong lines, a mass of thought and earnestness which should be devoted to one set of ideals hurls itself in hot haste upon another – the forsaken and forgotten ideals meanwhile pleading vainly for service from those who have sworn to give it – and the very raison d'être of Nonconformity passes out of sight and memory with those who bear the Nonconformist name.[49]

In a way, perhaps, this symbolized the evangelicals' recognition that their ability to exert a powerful corporate influence on national political life had been seriously diluted by the developments described above. Broad social and economic change was in any case tending to marginalize churchmen of all varieties. For evangelicals this process was made more acute by the fissiparous effects of the evolution of theological thought and by the emergence of the modern party system. These of course were lengthy processes and British society continued for some years to reflect its evangelical inheritance. As individuals evangelicals continued to make their presence felt at both the local and national levels of politics. But by the time of the First World War it was no longer possible to suggest, as had been done by a contemporary of the newly crowned Queen Victoria, that the evangelicals 'make all the noise now'.[50]

Notes

1 Quoted in I. Bradley, *The Call to Seriousness. The Evangelical Impact on the Victorians* (Jonathan Cape, 1976), p. 166.
2 Bradley, *Call to Seriousness*, p. 177.
3 K. Hylson-Smith, *Evangelicals in the Church of England, 1734–1984* (Edinburgh: T & T Clark, 1989), p. 227.
4 On this see D. W. Bebbington, *The Nonconformist Conscience: Chapel and Politics, 1870–1914* (Allen and Unwin, 1982).
5 Quoted in *The Times*, 17 June 1931, and cited in S. Koss, *Nonconformity in Modern British Politics* (Batsford, 1975), p. 74.
6 D. Hempton and M. Hill, *Evangelical Protestantism in Ulster Society, 1740–1890* (Routledge, 1992), p. 189.
7 D. O. Moberg, *The Great Reversal* (Scripture Union, 1973).
8 T. P. Bunting, *The life of Jabez Bunting* (1859), pp. 150–5.
9 This definition is proposed by D. W. Bebbington, *Evangelicalism in Modern Britain* (Unwin Hyman, 1989), pp. 2–17.
10 C. M. Birrell, *Life of William Brock* (1878), p. 141.
11 L. J. Henkin, *Darwinism and the English Novel, 1860–1910* (1940 edn), p. 62. Quoted in R. Young, 'The impact of Darwin on conventional thought', in A. Symondson, ed., *The Victorian Crisis of Faith* (SPCK, 1970), p. 17.
12 F. J. Powicke, *David Worthington Simon* (1912), pp. 99–101.
13 D. Bebbington, 'The persecution of George Jackson: a British fundamentalist controversy', in W. J. Sheils, ed., *Studies in Church History*, 21 (1984), pp. 421–33.
14 M. D. Johnson, *The Dissolution of Dissent, 1850–1918* (Garland, 1987), p. 7.
15 D. P. Hughes, *The Life of Hugh Price Hughes* (1904), pp. 30–1.
16 W. Ward, *Brotherhood and Democracy* (1910), p. 33.
17 Ward, *Brotherhood*, p. 174.
18 W. J. Michel, *Brief Biographical Sketches of Bible Christian Ministers and Laymen* (Jersey, 1905–6), p. 253.
19 N. G. Dunning, *Samuel Chadwick* (1934), p. 54.

20 Hugh Price Hughes, *Social Christianity* (1889), p.88.
21 R. Helmstadter, 'The nonconformist conscience', in P. Marsh, ed., *The Conscience of the Victorian State* (Hassocks: Harvester, 1979), p. 166. See also p. 157 below.
22 J. E. Rattenbury, *Six Sermons on Social Subjects* (1908).
23 *Spectator*, 19 Oct. 1907.
24 R. Bray, *Labour and the Churches* (1912), p. 18.
25 *Anti-Socialist* (Sept. 1909), p. 90.
26 Quoted in I. Sellers, *Nineteenth-Century Nonconformity* (Arnold, 1977), p. 28.
27 J. G. Bowran, *The Life of Arthur Thomas Guttery DD* (1922), p. 63.
28 J. Medway, *Memoirs of the Life and Writings of John Pye Smith DD LLD FRS FGS* (1853), p. 95.
29 W. O'Neill, *Notes and Incidents of Home Missionary Life and Work* (1870), p. 13.
30 G. Redford and J. A. James, eds, *The Autobiography of the Rev William Jay* (1855), p. 113.
31 See my analysis in *A Social History of the Nonconformist Ministry in England and Wales, 1800–1930* (Oxford UP, 1988), pp. 198–221.
32 J. Entwisle, *Memoir of the Rev Joseph Entwisle. By his son* (Bristol, 1848), p. 91.
33 *Baptist Handbook* (1867), p. 163.
34 A. O. Smith, *The Rev Gervase Smith DD* (1882), p. 241.
35 *Independent and Nonconformist*, 8 Jan. 1892.
36 *Independent and Nonconformist*, 15 Jan. 1892.
37 *Independent and Nonconformist*, 29 Aug. 1895.
38 B. Stanley, 'Evangelical social and political ethics: an historical perspective', *Evangelical Quarterly*, 62 (1990), p. 29. My italics.
39 R. Buick Knox, 'Professor John Gibb and Westminster College, Cambridge', *Journal of the United Reformed Church History Society*, 3 (1986), p. 334.
40 Koss, *Nonconformity*, p. 117.
41 *Baptist Times*, 25 Feb. 1910.
42 W. H. Mills, *Grey Pastures* (1924), p. 1.
43 Bowran, *Guttery*, p. 46. He was as good as his word, refusing several invitations to stand as a Liberal parliamentary candidate.
44 Koss, *Nonconformity*, p. 107.
45 Quoted in Koss, *Nonconformity*, p. 36.
46 See my 'Nonconformity and the British labor movement: a case study', *Journal of Social History*, 8 (1975), pp. 113–20.
47 P. Snowden, 'The Labour Party and the general election', *Independent Review*, 7 (1905), p. 139.
48 F. S. Clayton, *John Wilson of Woolwich* (n.d.), p. 46.
49 A Nonconformist Minister, *Nonconformity and Politics* (1910), pp. 3–4.
50 Quoted in Bradley, *Call to Seriousness*, p. 13.

Chapter Eight

The Social Gospel: A Case Study

IAN M. RANDALL

It is often maintained that the 'social gospel' was a phenomenon which originated in America and there is also a widespread perception that it was something which drew evangelical Christian leaders away from their historic principles and priorities. Both assumptions will be questioned in this chapter. It is true that the social gospel gained great prominence in America, but it had its own distinctive origins, development and characteristics in Britain, where Christian socialism had emerged independently in the mid-nineteenth century in a movement associated with F. D. Maurice. Christian socialism became more deeply rooted from the late 1870s.[1] Typically it entailed a rejection of evangelical categories of sin and individual salvation. The origins of an evangelical social gospel are, however, also to be found in the 1870s and 1880s. British evangelical leaders such as the Baptist John Clifford and the Wesleyan Hugh Price Hughes who began to think in terms of a social gospel were prepared to draw from newer thinking, but their fundamental conviction was that traditional evangelistic passion was entirely compatible with a broader framework which embraced ministry to all aspects of society.[2] During the 1890s, crucial shaping of this thinking took place and the social gospel remained an important, if divisive, feature of evangelicalism in Britain up to the First World War. From then on, social concerns were increasingly marginalized in the evangelical constituency. As early as the 1880s, however, a divergence began to open up between those evangelicals who involved themselves in, and those who withdrew from the world. The evangelical leader who became the foremost advocate of a gospel which bridged the main 'pietist' and 'activist' streams was F. B. Meyer (1847–1929), a Baptist minister and Nonconformist statesman whose national influence was at its peak from about 1890 to 1914. Meyer became the epitome, in this period, of an evangelical social gospel moulded by both conservative and progressive evangelical thought. During a time when, as we have seen in the previous chapter, effective evangelical political influence was in decline, Meyer illustrates the continuing vitality of evangelicalism's broader engagement with society.

Origins

J. C. Carlile, a journalist and Baptist minister, described the social gospel as 'simply the social application of the Gospel'.[3] The perception that the gospel had profound social implications was a tradition inherited from the eighteenth century, an important early influence being the remarkable charitable work of the German pietist, August Francke, at Halle.[4] Earlier nineteenth-century evangelicals launched numerous political crusades for the removal of social sores felt to be at odds with the gospel and also had a commitment to voluntary philanthropy.[5] The emphasis, however, was emphatically individualistic. Lord Shaftesbury, for example, was wary of the idea of state provision of housing at nominal rents in case it proved to be destructive of moral energy.[6] While the poor should benefit from the generosity of the rich, they must not become dependent on the institutionalized charity of a public welfare system. It was in the 1870s and 1880s that doubts began to surface about the apparent inconsistency of such a stance. The state was becoming increasingly acceptable to evangelicals as a legislator against such wrongs in society as prostitution, the drink trade and mass gambling.[7] What was now being explored was whether social wrongs – essentially viewed as sins – could be more widely defined and whether society as a whole could be mobilized by the gospel to care for the needy.

R. W. Dale, the leading Birmingham Congregationalist

minister, played an important part in laying foundations for new ways of thinking about the gospel and society. He was indebted to George Dawson, a Baptist minister who moved away from evangelical orthodoxy and began his own congregation, the Church of the Saviour, which many of Birmingham's intelligentsia attended. While Dale did not concur with the Unitarian tendency of Dawson's thinking, he did for a time attend Dawson's church and imbibed ideals for public life which were to enable him to become the foremost spokesman for the 'civic' or 'municipal' gospel.[8] Dale's influence on the life of Birmingham was immense and he contributed to a marked degree to the position the city achieved as a model of good housing and sanitation due to effective local government. Laws to prevent exploitation or to improve health were, Dale argued in 1883, as much part of the redemptive work of Christ as the preaching of forgiveness. In the same year, A. W. Fairbairn, who was Chairman of the Congregational Union and later Principal of Mansfield College, Oxford, suggested that social and industrial questions were integral to the mission of the churches. The year 1883 marked the climax of this first wave of the incoming tide of the social gospel. Andrew Mearns, Secretary of the London Congregational Union, published in September of that year a short, explosive book, *The Bitter Cry of Outcast London*. There was widespread horror as the facts of poverty, misery and sexual degradation in London became apparent. The *Christian World* called for people to be rescued from 'surroundings which render their salvation all but hopeless'.[9] Even the *Christian*, representing a more devotional and socially conservative evangelicalism, spoke of *The Bitter Cry* bringing to light a situation which filled Christians with 'shame and deep concern'.[10] Many evangelicals, in common with others in the nation, began to call for state action over housing conditions, partly because of the links being made with incest and prostitution. *The Bitter Cry* was probably the single most powerful weapon in the armoury of the advance guard of the social gospel.[11] Doubts were being raised among evangelicals about whether it was possible to solve massive social problems purely at an individualistic level, without changing – at least in certain aspects – society itself.

In the late 1880s the pressure to re-think evangelical social strategy became more intense. B. F. Westcott, the respected liberal Anglican thinker (later Bishop of Durham), identified, in 1887, the gospel of the kingdom as the 'social Gospel'.[12] In 1889 the Christian Social Union (CSU) was formed under Westcott's presidency and had increasing influence on Anglican social thought. Other leading non-evangelical Christian social-ists were the Anglo-Catholic Stewart Headlam, who led the Guild of St Matthew, and Henry Scott Holland, an energetic Canon of St Paul's Cathedral. The same period saw evangeli-cals facing up to social questions. A wave of social concern was prompted in part by the industrial disputes of 1888–9, espe-cially the London Dockers' Strike. John Clifford was quick to respond. In October 1888 he gave a speech to the Baptist Union Assembly which stressed the theme of the social gospel, and in the following year he asserted that Christian brotherhood would, in his view, gain by the strike.[13] But Nonconformists as a body were seen as having failed to produce a coherent policy on the industrial struggle. Ben Tillett, one of the dockers' lead-ers, while praising the mediation of Cardinal Manning, Roman Catholic Archbishop of Westminster, alleged that with one or two exceptions, such as Clifford, Nonconformists had been 'conspicuous by their lukewarmness'.[14] Carlile was a member of the Strike Committee and had a branch of the Union named after him, but S. H. Booth, the Secretary of the Baptist Union, and C. H. Spurgeon, minister of the Metropolitan Tabernacle (whom Tillett dismissed as 'rather an old autocrat'), both expressed worries about Carlile's involvement. F. B. Meyer was, however, willing, at Carlile's invitation, to speak to the dockers, and his address was so effective that his audience unexpect-edly called for 'another turn'. The very fact that Manning brought about a resolution of the dispute was a challenge to evangelicals to seek a broader framework for their social thought and to some, such as Hugh Price Hughes, it had by 1890 become abundantly clear that Christ came to save human society as well as individuals.[15] In the same year, William Booth, the founder of the Salvation Army, published his *In Darkest England and the Way Out*. By that time the platform for the social gospel was in place.

Development

Both in Britain and America the social gospel assumed a more significant role in the 1890s. The emphasis it brought was consistent with a developing view of society as not simply a collection of individuals but a community with a corporate life. It also reflected fashionable concern for social reform. The growth of the social gospel can, however, be understood only if it is seen as primarily a religious phenomenon. The philosophical base was an understanding of spiritual need rather than a theory about society. At main church services, Hughes insisted (in answer to a critic), we 'preach the Gospel', while at special Sunday afternoon meetings the social aspects of Christianity were tackled. It was quite evident, said Hughes, that political and social reforms without spiritual reforms would be a 'melancholy disappointment'. Similarly F. B. Meyer's stated goal in 1897 was the evangelistic one of seeing the mass of the people 'hail the religion of Jesus Christ', which he believed could happen as it was linked with 'liberty and righteousness and truth'.[16] While Meyer's starting point was mission, his experience of working among London's poor in the 1890s led him in the direction of radical politics. In 1898 Meyer supported Fred Smith, an Independent Labour candidate for North Lambeth (and a member of the Salvation Army), and in the following year Meyer was described as 'practically a Christian Socialist'.[17] For some evangelicals Christian socialism meant Anglo-Catholicism, and the thinking of Stewart Headlam, for example, was indebted to the concept of baptism as a 'sacrament of equality' and to the adoration of the Virgin Mary as a reminder of the sacredness of humanity as revealed in Jesus.[18] This was far from the thinking of evangelicals, but there were Free Church leaders who were prepared, in their attempt to formulate a Christian message for society, to investigate and perhaps remould the social thinking of those from other backgrounds. R. F. Horton, a Congregational minister known for his broader evangelical views, underlined the influence upon his social thinking of the book *Progress and Poverty* by Henry George, an economist who argued for a greater role for the state.[19] Clifford cited Richard T. Ely, an American social gospel exponent; Hughes drew from T. H. Green's idealist philosophy and from Westcott's distaste for 'tyrannical individualism'; while another

Methodist leader, John Scott Lidgett, was indebted to F. D. Maurice.[20] Meyer was so committed to the new social impetus that the *Christian World* described his 'evolution' – during the 1890s and beyond – from a spiritual director to a social strategist, as 'one of the most striking psychological phenomena of our time'. But there was no question, for Meyer, of the traditional gospel being abandoned as a result of the quest for new formulations.

It was clear to Nonconformist leaders of the 1890s that unremitting campaigns should be waged against societal sins, especially drinking and impurity. Meyer had emerged as a leading advocate of what was called 'gospel temperance' during his ministry at Melbourne Hall, Leicester, in the 1880s. He combined evangelism with ambitious social programmes, including the rehabilitation of ex-prisoners and the reclamation of drunkards. These two emphases were linked in Meyer's mind since he saw drink as being the usual cause of crime.[21] By 1883 Meyer was arguing that God had been using the temperance movement to sow seeds which were producing a spiritual harvest. Leicester's drink trade began to decline as a result of Meyer's activities. From 1892, as minister of Christ Church, in Lambeth, one of London's poorest areas, Meyer planned a massive assault on the notorious local brothels. Through the efforts of Meyer's team of 'Christian Stalwarts' in gathering evidence and submitting it to the police, 700–800 brothels were closed during the period 1895 to 1907.[22] This was part of a national campaign as a result of which prosecutions were brought against, on average, 1,200 brothels each year from 1885 to 1914.[23] Fulmination against drink and immorality was at the core of 'the Nonconformist conscience', a term first used in 1890 when Clifford and Hughes pressed for Charles Stewart Parnell, the Irish political leader, to be relieved of his position on account of his adultery. In the early twentieth century Meyer was viewed by some as the personification of the Nonconformist conscience. Out of a passion for individual righteousness a more comprehensive, though fairly negative view developed about the relationship between morality and social welfare. The 1890s saw a distinctively evangelical proclamation of a moral law and a social gospel which called for public life to embody the rule of Christ.

Conversionism remained an important part of this revisionist scheme. At the Baptist Union Assembly in 1891, Clifford argued that a man whose life was sweated out of him sixteen hours a day could not be expected to seek his own spiritual welfare. Clifford's message was received, generally, with enthusiasm. In 1896 the Wesleyan, Samuel Keeble, who like Horton represented a broader evangelical position, wrote in *Industrial Day-Dreams* that the social gospel was as sacred and indispensable as the individual gospel. The two, he asserted, were complementary.[24] Evangelicals were aware that their traditional patterns of mission had not met with much success among working class communities and that it was necessary to conduct a reappraisal. One result of the attempt to widen the scope of the gospel was the formation of networks of societies – religious, educational and social – centred on the local church. In the 1880s Meyer's version of this 'institutional church' model at Melbourne Hall influenced the development of the Methodist Central Halls.[25] Building on his Leicester experience, Meyer attempted, at Christ Church, to find still more ways of applying the gospel to the unreached sectors of society. Having consciously set his face against separate mission halls, he adopted a 'departmental' strategy, structuring the various meetings within the life of the church in such a way as to make them culturally relevant to his target audiences. Meyer's show-piece was his Sunday afternoon Brotherhood which he began in 1893 and saw grow to 800 men. This working class congregation was a concrete expression of Meyer's belief that the gospel created a new social reality, a brotherhood. The men were his brothers (Meyer described 'brethren' as 'cant' used by clergy) and Meyer, never one to adopt complete egalitarianism, was the 'skipper'.[26] Samuel Collier's Methodist Central Hall in Manchester exhibited a similar integration of the spiritual and the social, using Meyer's work as an example, and Collier's church membership rose from 93 in 1887 to 1,484 in 1895.[27] Evangelists like Meyer and Collier were unashamedly conversionist. But attracting and keeping, as Meyer did, some of the roughest men and boys in Lambeth (the name hooligan came from a family called Hooligan, discovered by Meyer's staff) was only realistic in the context of a holistic approach to the gospel.

Divergence

At the same time as some evangelicals were highlighting social issues, others were seeking to withdraw from the world into a form of 'deeper life' spirituality. Beginning with large meetings held in Oxford in 1874, when 1,500 attended, and Brighton in 1875, when 8,000 came together, a new inter-denominational holiness movement became a major force in British evangelicalism.[28] The network which subsequently developed was known as the Keswick movement because its focus was an annual convention held in that Lake District town. Most Keswick leaders were Anglicans who were at best ambivalent about Nonconformist socio-political action, and when Meyer first spoke at Keswick, in 1887, there was concern about his activities as a temperance campaigner.[29] Despite the tradition of philanthropy which evangelical Anglicanism inherited, there was increasing reluctance to confront serious social needs. For some, this resulted from their own restricted experience. Social evil for them was at the level of 'viciousness on the croquet lawn'.[30] The message of liberty, equality and brotherhood could also be seen as a threat to such bulwarks of society as hierarchy and rank. It was true that Bishop Handley Moule, Keswick's most respected theologian, joined the CSU in 1900 and Stewart Holden, who was the dominant figure at Keswick in the 1920s, followed Meyer in his willingness to tackle social questions.[31] Nevertheless, more typical of the social stance of Keswick was Prebendary Webb-Peploe, a member of the Anti-Socialist Union of Churches. Hugh Price Hughes, while committed to Wesleyan holiness teaching's relevance to social issues, was wary of Keswick on the grounds of its lack of social application. Meyer on the other hand became, from 1887, one of Keswick's central figures. At the 1888 Baptist Union Assembly, when Clifford was proclaiming the social gospel, Meyer spoke on cultivating the devout life, a typical Keswick theme.[32] From the 1890s Meyer was the chief international spokesman for Keswick teaching, and his position as the leading Nonconformist speaker on a predominantly Anglican Keswick platform was also a strategic one.[33] His achievement was to become a major holiness teacher who at the same time pursued a path of social and at times political action.

How did Meyer resolve the apparent tension between a
gospel which was social, in the sense that it was for society, and
a message for believers which strongly emphasized their personal relationship with God? Meyer, in common with other
evangelical advocates of the social gospel, began with the individual. When he introduced a call for social justice into a
Keswick address in 1900 he used the example of a wealthy
man who had attended the convention for eighteen years but
who, in his business life, had a 'grinding disposition'.[34] This
man regretted later that he had not applied what he had heard
at Keswick to his business affairs. But by 1909 Meyer was
tracing a progression in his own social thinking which had
resulted in his placing an increasing emphasis on collective,
rather than individual action. Employing the example of the
good Samaritan to illustrate how to deal with the problem of
drink, Meyer said that whereas he used to pick up mauled travellers (victims of drink) between Jerusalem and Jericho, he now
called on Pilate (the state) to 'blow up with dynamite the caves
in which the bandits hide'.[35] The Keswick constituency felt
more comfortable about joining Meyer in prayer over temperance matters than it was about his militant tendencies, although
Meyer was praised in Keswick circles for his co-operation with
A. F. Winnington-Ingram, the Bishop of London, on social
issues.[36] The *Christian* commented with some satisfaction in
1906 that secularism was a rapidly failing force, and contrasted
its impotence with the power of the Cross, which was, it stated,
'the life of the Social Gospel'.[37] Meyer went further, insisting
that the Spirit's anointing was 'not simply to preach the Gospel
to the poor, but to heal the broken-hearted by removing causes
of heartbreak; to proclaim liberty to the captive of the sweater's
den.'[38] Keswick's focus on Jesus and the Spirit had given Meyer
a fresh framework for a call to social action.

The social gospel increasingly highlighted differing priorities
in evangelical agendas. There were those who saw conversion
as the first requirement, from which social improvements
would flow, and those, like Meyer, who believed (as he put it)
that while the primary mission was to proclaim the reconciling
grace of God, there was a parallel requirement to bring in the
kingdom of God on earth. Meyer spoke of 'betterment' or 'the
salvation . . . of the whole man' as the goal of the human race.[39]

R. Mudie Smith, a Baptist social investigator, similarly maintained in 1904 that a gospel which did not concern itself with
man's body, mind and environment, as well as his soul, was a
contradiction in terms.[40] Two years later Meyer, as President of
the Baptist Union, was arguing for the redemption of individuals but also of the state.[41] Given his ability to identify with
both the pietistic and the activist wings of evangelicalism,
Meyer was ideally placed to formulate an evangelical theological understanding of the social gospel and at the same time to
explore the possibilities for a new social vision.

Theological themes

The themes which characterized the social gospel in America
have been summarized as a conviction that the principles of
Jesus could guide social life; a stress on the immanence of God;
a belief in the goodness and worth of human beings; a view of
the gospel as a message of the kingdom; a belief in progress,
and a commitment to the ethic of love.[42] In Britain the most
prominent theological themes were the kingdom of God, the
centrality of the life and teaching of Jesus, and the wider mission of the church. The kingdom of God, for Meyer, was a
'kingdom of social justice'. Particularly in the period from
1900 to 1914 Meyer saw the proclamation of the kingdom as
having profound social implications. In 1906 he declared that
politics was an effort to 'illuminate the public mind with the
ideals of Christ's kingdom'. Clifford also emphasized the redis-
covery of the message of the kingdom of God and the way in
which this brought a new understanding of the state as 'essentially a spiritual organism'. Meyer believed that the state had a
part to play in the righting of 'the wrongs which make the few
rich and the many poor' and advocated pressure being brought
to bear on the state to 'level up women's wages'.[43] When
employers refused to pay workers a living wage this should be
addressed, Meyer argued in September 1911, by 'particular
preaching', not generalities. Yet Meyer could, in the following
month, suggest that the detailed application of the principles of
the kingdom were outside the competence of the ministry. 'Do
not let us meddle with the great public questions', he told
Scottish Baptists. Pastors should give themselves to visiting,

study, and prayer, and should touch public life through those they educated. Despite its inconsistencies, Meyer's theology of the kingdom saw God actively fulfilling his purposes outside narrowly spiritual realms. A banker might not open his bank with prayer, and a workman might not have psalms as background music, but if they were 'open to the Spirit of Truth and Righteousness' they might be doing as much to 'secure that God's Kingdom should come' as the 'priest or revivalist'.[44]

Jesus was crucial, in social gospel thinking, as a demonstration that God was immanent in human affairs. The idea of God's immanence was taken to an extreme by R. J. Campbell, minister of the City Temple, who published views in 1907 which verged on pantheism. Meyer and Campbell shared a common affirmation of the importance of the trend towards collectivism,[45] and Meyer's gospel also had immanentist overtones. Christ was moving, he suggested in 1906, to an end which he had in view, with the church aiding him in the work of reconstruction and securing the values of the kingdom. Mankind was described by Meyer as being on a 'spiral staircase of ascent' drawing closer to the one who was transcendent yet 'Immanent in all'. On the other hand Meyer insisted, in a vigorous reply to Campbell, that to teach only God's immanence led to an abyss, in which God was no longer Father and creator.[46] Emphasis on the Fatherhood of God should not be dismissed as an example of vague universalism. It was set in the context of an awareness of God as Jesus understood him. For Clifford, God was 'holy Father', redeeming mankind through Christ and bringing people into a new brotherhood. While Meyer saw the emerging new society as a human quest for brotherhood, he insisted, in 1907, that it was essential to recognize both God's Fatherhood and Christ as the 'Eternal Brother'. He rejoiced, in 1908, that the 'humanitarian side' of the gospel was coming to the fore. With Jesus as his paradigm, Meyer's hope was the missionary one of seeing the gospel 'incarnated again' in the community.[47] But he did not allow incarnational theology to marginalize the doctrine of the atonement. Meyer's gospel had at its heart the 'peace-giving conception of God in Christ bearing the curse and shame', although he did question the concept of the cross as something which 'pacified and mollified the Father's anger'.[48] The cross was, Meyer said in 1910,

a 'tidal wave out of the heart of God', and in 1913 he went so
far as to envisage Jesus redeeming all the sentient orders of
being.[49] Both the ministry and the sacrifice of Jesus had social
as well as individual dimensions.

For the social gospel to be authentic, Meyer was convinced
that it had to be expressed in appropriate ecclesiological settings.
The question which Meyer set himself to answer, especially at
Christ Church, was whether working people could be integrated, with the more 'wealthy and illustrious', into church life.[50]
At first the older church members resented his approach and
although many were subsequently reconciled to him, Meyer
announced (no doubt with a measure of exaggeration) in 1905
that Christ Church's rich congregation had either gone to
heaven or to the suburbs.[51] Institutional churches, with their
networks of societies should, he argued in 1902, be open every
night for the service of the various groups of people in the
neighbourhood.[52] Without abandoning his view that the pulpit
should major on the central doctrines of the faith, rather than
on social issues, Meyer came to believe by 1907 that some of
his previous ideas had been 'too restricted and too respectable'
and that the election of members of parliament, as well as the
problems of the inner life, were matters of legitimate interest in
church life.[53] One way through which Meyer attempted to
embody the social gospel was by the Brotherhood movement.
Having started and led his Brotherhood congregation at Christ
Church, Meyer went on to argue that the wider movement was
a channel for 'great social ideals' to be 'infiltrated' with the
gospel of Christ.[54] He was convinced that all great revivals
resulted in social and political reconstruction.[55] It was vital,
therefore, for churches to work out the social implications of
the gospel if their spiritual message was to carry credibility.

Social vision

In the period when the Nonconformists were contributing to
the idea that the state should create a better society and to the
progress of the New Liberalism, they were still, with few exceptions, evangelicals. Meyer's social vision was of the church
engaged in both spiritual and social activities.[56] His social

themes were human dignity, equality and freedom of conscience. During the 1880s, in Leicester, Meyer discovered how hard it was for men coming out of prison to find employment. In order to employ some of them and so help them find dignity through work, he set up in business as 'F. B. Meyer, Firewood Merchant'. He stressed that this project and other entrepreneurial efforts had the ultimate aim of producing 'devotion to Christ' and claimed that through his rehabilitation and support structures many men had been converted and the prison population reduced.[57] In 1898 Meyer was involved in setting up a colony at Lingfield in Surrey, which had the aim of helping the urban unemployed. In Lambeth, in 1905, Meyer opened the 'Old Nelson Coffee-House' as an alternative to the local public houses. It was his observation that in localities where public houses flourished the children had no shoes and women were poorly clothed.[58] Restoration of dignity, for Meyer, meant dealing with the environment, whereas there were evangelicals who attributed poverty and other problems to the moral weakness of the poor person. Addressing the Free Churches in 1908, Meyer challenged them to go beyond soup kitchens and blankets to a concern with justice, and in the following year called for state action over housing conditions where people were living 'like pigs in a sty'. Meyer insisted that he had no sympathy with Christians who spoke only of heaven 'while the wrongs of earth are unredressed'.[59]

A second goal was equality. Nineteenth-century measures had done much to remove the sense among Nonconformists that they were second-class citizens. The government's Education Bill of 1902, however, provoked them to intense activity, since it gave Anglicans certain privileges, including the funding of Church schools from public money. In June 1902 Meyer dismissed the government's policy as 'absurd and retrograde' and controversy broke out in *The Times* in 1904 over Meyer's allegations that Nonconformist children in village schools were suffering discrimination.[60] Equality for women was also part of Meyer's message. In 1906 he criticized Christians who drew 'handsome dividends' from companies which paid women a 'wretched wage' and he proposed a world-wide trade union for women and a boycott of traders who did not pay adequate wages. 'Let us teach society', he concluded, 'to realise that we are our sisters' keepers.' Whether or not Meyer's rhetoric had any effect is not the main point. The fact is that his gospel was wide enough to include the issue. Against the background of the campaign for votes for women, Meyer stated in *The Times* 1913: 'Woman suffrage has got to come'.[61] The 'war between the sexes' was proving disturbing to Meyer. His ultimate solution for all inequalities was not conflict but was the evangelical message of reconciliation.

Freedom of conscience was an integral part of Meyer's gospel. At times this spirit could become partisan. In 1904 he described the evangelical party in the Church of England as 'narrow', contrasting this with the 'free air breathed by Nonconformists'.[62] Meyer's emphasis, however, was on freedom from repressive political regimes and policies. On an extended visit to South Africa in 1908 he had seen the oppression suffered by the native races and had discovered that 'Christianised and educated' native people were full of 'yearnings for purity, truth, and usefulness'. Meyer was outraged that they should be dismissed as 'niggers' and treated as 'deserving only to be horsewhipped or killed'.[63] In the following year, back in Britain, Meyer inveighed against the domination of the House of Lords, which he described as 'warped by class prejudice'.[64] His concern was for the will of the people to be heard. Meyer's last great effort on behalf of liberty of conscience was in the First World War. Together with other Free Church leaders, Meyer became uneasy about the way conscientious objectors were being treated. On 5 May 1916, he addressed the Quaker Meeting for Sufferings as part of an attempt to mobilize and unite the churches on the issue and thereby to influence the government. He subsequently visited COs who had been sent to France and sentenced to death for resisting military orders.[65] By this stage Meyer, although not a pacifist, was defending those who had 'steered by the pole star of conscience against adverse currents', and was advocating 'absolute exemption' for objectors (from civilian as well as military duties). He suggested that the CO would be an 'Apostle and Prophet' of a future spirit of peace.[66] For Meyer, there was invariably an evangelistic dimension. During this period he worked in conjunction with the No-Conscription Fellowship and it is likely that his book *The Majesty of Conscience* incorporated material supplied by Bertrand Russell who was an NCF collaborator.[67] After the war Meyer felt that COs should be using their experiences to press for changes in the prison system, making it 'regenerative', rather than 'punitive'.[68] Regeneration, in the sense of renewed human existence as well as spiritual awakening, was Meyer's ultimate vision for the whole of society.

The gospel and socialism

Most evangelicals who embraced the social gospel were not socialists. There were exceptions such as John Clifford and the group of Methodist ministers led by Samuel Keeble who formed the socialist Sigma Club. Even a deeply committed socialist like Keeble was, however, wary of aspects of socialism, such as its low view of the family. Many Free Church ministers did accept the need for a collectivism which addressed human-itarian needs and which offered, as Meyer put it, the 'coral island' of a 'golden age' of liberty, equality and brotherhood.[69] It was this island which he saw emerging from the surface of the stormy waters. But at the same time the idea of an all-pervasive state system was generally rejected. Some evangelicals, such as those who gathered at Baptist Church House in 1909 to form a Nonconformist Anti-Socialist Union, could be un-compromising in their opposition.[70] The attempts of many to chart a middle way have been dismissed as weak humanitari-anism, destructive of the intellectual and moral strength of evangelicalism. On the other hand, incarnationalism can be seen as properly contributing to an evangelical theology of involvement. It has also been argued that the evangelical ener-gy which was present in the revivalism of the early part of the twentieth century was partially channelled into social change.[71] The social gospel attempted to chart a course that avoided both strict state control and ultra-individualism, while affirm-ing the role of both the state and the individual.

In 1906 Meyer asserted that a society was being created in which the aspirations of the mass of the people would be ful-filled. He went so far as to aver that even revolutionary social change was due to 'Divine impulses'. This included revolutions in their 'wildest forms'. It was far better, however, for the

Christian Church to lead a movement for the 'helpless and defenceless'. Such a Christian body, Meyer believed, was destined to be the church of the future. Meyer's hopes for social change were not far removed from mainstream Nonconformist thinking, but Meyer was more attracted to the message of socialism than were most of his fellow Baptists and he tried to persuade his denominational colleagues that they shared with Labour a concern for peace, old age pensions and better housing. Meyer insisted, however, that the Labour Party needed to be 'alive with the Spirit of Christ'.[72] In 1909 Meyer accepted that he had fallen from his position as 'a sort of sky-pilot', confined to spiritual matters.[73] Yet the essence of the evangelical message, as Meyer saw it in 1914, was that external circumstances should be dealt with but that it was the 'new heart' which was essential.[74]

Conclusion

Although the social gospel had well-known American devotees, it was also an important feature of British Christian thinking. Meyer, who was one of the most prominent leaders of the mainstream evangelical constituency of his day, portrayed God's purposes in broad terms. While attempting to address his gospel to society at large, he was fervently conversionist, basing his whole evangelistic approach on the Bible and especially on the person and work of Christ. Today Meyer is best known by most evangelicals as a Keswick devotional speaker and writer. In the 1920s his socio-political activities declined and his energies were directed towards the premillennial Advent Testimony and Preparation Movement which he began in 1917. Meyer's changing priorities reflected the increasing tendency for evangelicals in the first half of the twentieth century to withdraw from the world. Immediately after Meyer's death in 1929 the conservative wing of evangelicalism, while lauding his association with D. L. Moody, Keswick and Advent Testimony, chose to ignore his massive socio-political endeavours. A deep pessimism about the affairs of this world, and especially about political remedies, was taking over conservative evangelicalism in the inter-war years. Meyer's contribution, in the period before the First World War, was to show that

evangelical spirituality of the Keswick variety could be combined with a message for society. Certainly Meyer's social
gospel had weaknesses. Like others of his time he had a tendency to reflect current political values and was stronger on
generalities than on specifics. On the other hand, he did not
present glib solutions, as if the gospel had a simple answer to all
life's problems.[75] Rather, Meyer attempted to convey a message,
and actively to carry out a ministry, which was true to the
Bible, relevant to individuals and designed to influence the way
society functioned. It was this kind of boldness, tinged with a
degree of over-confidence, which helped to shape an evangelical social gospel.

Notes

1 See E. Norman, *The Victorian Christian Socialists* (Cambridge UP,
   1987); and E. Norman, *Church and Society in England, 1770–1970*
   (Oxford UP, 1976), chap. 5.
2 D. W. Bebbington, *Evangelicalism in Modern Britain: A History from
   the 1730s to the 1980s* (Unwin Hyman, 1989), p. 212.
3 J. C. Carlile, *My Life's Little Day* (1935), p. 49.
4 W. R. Ward, *The Protestant Evangelical Awakening* (Cambridge UP,
   1992), pp. 61–2.
5 For further details see the chapters in this volume by Brian Dickey
   and David Hempton, above, pp. 17–58.
6 D. M. Thompson, 'The Emergence of the Nonconformist Social
   Gospel in England', in K. Robbins, ed., *Studies in Church History*,
   Subsidia 7 (1990), p. 258.
7 D. W. Bebbington, *The Nonconformist Conscience: Chapel and Politics,
   1870–1914* (Allen and Unwin, 1982), chap. 3.
8 G. Parsons, 'From Dissenters to Free Churchmen: The Transitions
   of Victorian Nonconformity' in G. Parsons, ed., *Religion in Victorian
   Britain: Vol. 1: Traditions* (Manchester UP, 1988), p. 93. On Dale see
   also pp. 142–3 above.
9 *Christian World* (hereafter *CW*), 28 Dec. 1883, p. 917.
10 *Christian* (hereafter *C*), 25 Oct. 1883, p. 6.
11 P. d'A. Jones, *The Christian Socialist Revival, 1877–1914* (Princeton
   UP, 1968), pp. 7–8; Bebbington, *Nonconformist Conscience*, pp. 42–4.
12 The address was given by Westcott at Westminster Abbey. B. F.
   Westcott, *Social Aspects of Christianity* (1887), p. 96.
13 *British Weekly* (hereafter *BW*), 12 Oct. 1888, p. 386; 13 Sept. 1889,
   p. 323.

14 *BW*, 27 Sept. 1889, p. 352.
15 D. W. Bebbington, 'The City, the Countryside and the Social Gospel', in D. Baker, ed., *Studies in Church History*, 16 (1979), p. 417; H. P. Hughes, *Social Christianity* (1890), p. 55. See also for Hughes, W. M. King, 'Hugh Price Hughes and the British "Social Gospel"', *Journal of Religious History*, June 1984, pp. 66–82.
16 *Free Church Year Book* (1897), p. 159.
17 *London Leader*, 26 Feb. 1898, p. 4; Interview with H. G. Turner, Meyer's Private Secretary, on 19 July 1899: Booth Collection, B271, p. 79 (held in the library of The London School of Ecnomics).
18 Norman, *Victorian Christian Socialists*, pp. 108–9.
19 R. F. Horton, *An Autobiography* (1917), p. 81.
20 Thompson, 'John Clifford's Social Gospel', p. 207; King, 'Hugh Price Hughes', pp. 69–71; R. J. Helmstadter, 'The Nonconformist Conscience', in G. Parsons, ed., *Religion in Victorian Britain, Vol IV: Interpretations* (Manchester UP, 1988), p. 89.
21 F. B. Meyer, *The Bells of Is: Or Voices of Human Need and Sorrow* [1894], p. 41. See also pp. 75–6, 121.
22 *Free Church Year Book* (1908), p. 179.
23 P. McHugh, *Prostitution and Victorian Social Reform* (Croom Helm, 1980), pp. 28–9.
24 S. E. Keeble, *Industrial Day-Dreams* (1896), pp. 62–3.
25 W. Y. Fullerton in *The Life of Faith* (hereafter *LF*), 7 Feb. 1912, p. 141; W. Y. Fullerton, *F. B. Meyer: A Biography* [1929], p. 115.
26 M. J. Street, *F. B. Meyer: His Life and Work* (1902), p. 92; Fullerton, *Meyer*, pp. 108, 110–11; Turner interview, Booth Collection, B271, p. 79; C. Binfield, *George Williams and the YMCA* (Heinemann, 1973), p. 303; *BW*, 19 Oct. 1905, p. 37.
27 G. Jackson, *Collier of Manchester* (1923), pp. 68, 125.
28 See Bebbington, *Evangelicalism*, Chapter 5.
29 F. S. Webster in *LF*, 25 July 1917, p. 813.
30 J. C. Pollock, *The Keswick Story* (Hodder and Stoughton, 1964), p. 16; K. Hylson-Smith, *Evangelicals in the Church of England, 1734–1984* (Edinburgh: T & T Clark, 1989), pp. 209, 260.
31 I. M. Randall, 'Spiritual Renewal and Social Reform: Attempts to Develop Social Awareness in the Early Keswick Movement', *Vox Evangelica*, 23 (1993), pp. 67–86.
32 Published as F. B. Meyer, *The Cultivation of the Devout Life* (1888).
33 See W. B. Sloan, *These Sixty Years: The Story of the Keswick Convention* (1935), p. 33; S. Barabas, *So Great Salvation: The History and Message of the Keswick Convention* (Westwood, NJ: Fleming H. Revell, 1952), p. 186 and also W. H. Griffiths in C. F. Harford, ed., *The Keswick Convention* (1907), p. 233.
34 *LF*, 4 April 1917, p. 336; J. B. Figgis, *Keswick from Within* (1914), p. 112.
35 *Free Church Year Book* (1909), pp. 29–30.
36 *LF*, 4 April 1917, p. 336; Figgis, *Keswick*, p. 112.

37 *C*, 17 May 1906, p. 10.
38 *BW*, 4 Oct. 1906, p. 630.
39 *BW*, 26 April 1906, p. 70; *CW*, 26 Sept. 1907, p. 6.
40 D. W. Bebbington, 'The City, the Countryside and the Social Gospel', p. 418.
41 *Baptist Times* (hereafter *BT*), 27 April 1906, p. 308.
42 R. T. Handy, ed., *The Social Gospel in America, 1870–1920* (New York: Oxford UP, 1966), pp. 10–11.
43 *BW*, 26 April 1906, p. 70; *Free Church Year Book* (1909), p. 29.
44 *BT*, 27 April 1906, p. 308.
45 R. J. Campbell, *The New Theology* (1907), pp. 74, 253–4; Meyer in *BW*, 4 Oct. 1906, p. 629.
46 F. B. Meyer, *In Defence of the Faith* (1907), p. 69.
47 *Free Church Year Book* (1908), p. 33; *Free Church Year Book* (1902), p. 94.
48 Meyer, *In Defence of the Faith*, p. 73; F. B. Meyer, *The Soul's Wrestle with Doubt* (1905), p. 50.
49 F. B. Meyer, *At the Gates of the Dawn* (1911), p. 74; F. B. Meyer, *Life and the Way Through* (1913), p. 140.
50 *C*, 16 May 1907, p. 11.
51 *BW*, 19 Oct. 1905, p. 37; Turner Interview, B271, pp. 83, 93.
52 *Free Church Year Book* (1902), p. 93.
53 *BW*, 1 June 1905, p. 195; *CW*, 7 Feb. 1907, p. 24.
54 *CW*, 12 April 1906, p. 11; Binfield, *George Williams*, p. 303.
55 *Free Church Year Book* (1904), p. 33.
56 *The Times*, 22 June 1907, p. 12.
57 Meyer, *Bells of Is*, pp. 73, 89–90, 102.
58 *BW*, 7 Sept. 1905, p. 509; *The Times*, 18 Oct. 1907, p. 13.
59 *BW*, 17 March 1904, p. 611.
60 *CW*, 12 June 1902, p. 3; *The Times*, 18 April 1904, p. 12; 28 April 1904, p. 10. For Nonconformist resistance to the Education Act see J. E. B. Munson, 'A Study of Nonconformity in Edwardian England as revealed in the Passive Resistance Movement against the 1902 Education Act', unpublished D.Phil. thesis, University of Oxford, 1973.
61 *The Times*, 27 June 1913, p. 68.
62 *BW*, 17 March 1904, p. 611.
63 F. B. Meyer, *A Winter in South Africa* (1908), pp. 197–9.
64 *CW*, 9 Dec. 1909, p. 3.
65 Minutes of the Meeting for Sufferings, 5 May 1916 (56, 1912–16); *The Times*, 22 June 1916, p. 7, and J. Vellacott, *Bertrand Russell and the Pacifists in the First World War* (Brighton: Harvester, 1980), p. 74.
66 *The Times*, 9 June 1916, p. 9; 22 June 1916, p. 7; 7 July 1916, p. 10; F. B. Meyer, *The Majesty of Conscience* [1917], pp. 16, 19.
67 Vellacott, *Pacifists*, p. 213.
68 *The Tribunal*, 8 Jan. 1920, No. 182, pp. 5–6.
69 *BW*, 26 April 1906, p. 20.

174   *The Social Gospel*

70 P. d'A. Jones, *Christian Socialist Revival*, p. 392.
71 For these views see Helmstadter, 'The Nonconformist Conscience',
    pp. 84–93; Thompson, 'Nonconformist Social Gospel', pp. 276–7; S.
    E. Koss, '1906: Revival and Revivalism', in A. J. A. Morris, ed.,
    Edwardian Radicalism 1900–1914 (Routledge and Kegan Paul, 1974).
72 *BW*, 4 Oct. 1906, p. 611.
73 *Free Church Year Book* (1909), p. 30.
74 *The Times*, 29 April 1914, p. 6.
75 See J. Munson, *The Nonconformists: In search of a lost culture* (SPCK,
    1991), p. 119; Helmstadter, 'The Nonconformist Conscience', p. 65;
    D. J. Tidball, 'Evangelical Nonconformist Home Mission, 1796–
    1901', unpublished Ph.D. thesis, University of Keele, 1981, p. 309.

Chapter Nine

The Decline and Resurgence of Evangelical Social Concern 1918–1980

DAVID BEBBINGTON

In the years immediately following the First World War, evangelicals in Britain were often active in humanitarian causes. The tradition of social commitment associated with the names of Wilberforce and Shaftesbury was still upheld in many quarters, and certainly there was little rejection in principle of Christian concern for the betterment of the underprivileged. The chief reservation, heard mainly in more conservative sections of the movement, was merely that evangelism was the pressing priority. 'Social and philanthropic effort', wrote the founder of the Faith Mission in 1918, 'have their places in the improvement of character and surroundings in this earthly sphere, but such is secondary to that which is spiritual.'[1] In many cases church leaders from the evangelical tradition showed no qualms at all about identifying with the cause of the people's welfare. Thus J. E. Watts-Ditchfield, Bishop of Chelmsford from 1914 to 1923, was celebrated during the war for the extent of his belief in social improvement.[2] Stuart Holden, an Anglican clergyman soon to be chairman of the Keswick Convention, was outspoken in asserting the 'righteous demands of the miners' during the 1921 coal strike. 'The Church', he claimed in a sermon, 'has assisted the privileged classes to keep Labour in chains.'[3] Although by no means all evangelicals would have gone so far, Holden's statement illustrates that advanced forms of radicalism were tolerated in the movement. Evangelicalism and social reform remained entirely compatible.

Throughout the twentieth century, furthermore, the tradition of their blending was never wholly extinguished. Liberal evangelicals who tried to combine older evangelical emphases with modern knowledge and liturgical awareness never ceased to engage with the social questions of the day. Thus one of their spokesmen wrote in 1921 that they preached a social as well as an individual gospel, attacking the evils of bad housing, inadequate wages and commercial bargaining as frequently as personal sins.[4] A leading figure among them, Guy Rogers, played a full part in the Industrial Christian Fellowship during the 1920s.[5] Liberal evangelicals commonly maintained a robust social commitment down to their disappearance as a party in the 1960s. More conservative bodies also persevered in doing good on an organized basis. The Salvation Army, which enforced its evangelical doctrinal standards during the whole of the century, 'recognised', according to its official historian, 'with divine impartiality the needs of body and spirit'.[6] The extensive institutional philanthropy of the Church of Scotland was organized and staffed largely by evangelicals who often held distinctively conservative theological views.[7] Likewise, even the Cambridge Inter-Collegiate Christian Union, near the heart of the conservative evangelical network, supported the charitable activities of the Cambridge University Mission in Bermondsey. There were thinkers such as Henry Wace, Dean of Canterbury, and Josiah Stamp, a Wesleyan civil servant turned businessman, who expounded carefully conceived social opinions in substantial consistency with traditional political economy.[8] The author of the Inter-Varsity Fellowship's compendium of systematic theology, *In Understanding be Men* (1936), Archdeacon T. C. Hammond, two years later also published a booklet on social ethics called *Perfect Freedom*. The conservative evangelical tradition that from the 1960s began to drop the word 'conservative' as superfluous never entirely lost its social conscience. Any recognition of the weakening of social commitment in that tradition must be qualified by the admission that, in some quarters and in some measure, there persisted a willingness to engage with social issues in theory as well as practice.

Yet the inter-war period witnessed a definite decline of the
sense of social responsibility among conservative evangelicals.
In part the trend was merely a prolongation of inherited reservations that were powerful in the evangelical party of the
Church of England. When, in 1908, its annual Islington
Conference had been given over to social questions, some had
regretted the diversion from ecclesiastical and spiritual issues.
There was a risk, wrote a clerical correspondent of *The Record*,
the leading evangelical Anglican newspaper, of their being
duped by the enemy of God and man into alliances inimical to
true Christianity.[9] But by 1924, when the mainstream
Protestant churches combined to sponsor the Conference on
Christian Politics, Economics and Citizenship (COPEC), attitudes had hardened. E. L. Langston, vicar of Emmanuel
Church, Wimbledon, launched a withering attack on the conference in *The Record*. COPEC, he argued, offered no solution
to the problem of redeeming a lost and fallen world, for which
the only answer was the message of free salvation. 'We fear', he
concluded, 'that C.O.P.E.C. and the Social Gospel will take the
place in many pulpits of the Gospel of the Grace of God.'[10] For
the first time in the 1920s it became conventional wisdom in
conservative theological circles that the social gospel was a
substitute for the gospel of personal regeneration rather than
its complement. Evangelical enthusiasm for social reform went
into eclipse at the very epoch when, fostered by Charles Gore
and William Temple, High Church commitment to the cause
shone out in full brilliance. For many years it was customary to
deprecate Christian involvement in the issues of society at
large. 'Law, politics, education, economics, science, social service are all of value', admitted an evangelical in 1946, 'but
without Christ they fail utterly to make a better nation or
happy people.'[11] Others, such as an Elim Pentecostal evangelist
in 1943, were even more sweeping. 'You cannot preach', he
wrote, 'if you leave out sin. You cannot preach if you begin with
. . . social service, or reform. I am not interested in the reformation of the world.'[12] The bugbear of the social gospel drove
many evangelicals into deliberate avoidance of any efforts to
deal with the ills of society.

Why did such a retreat take place? A major reason was the
spread of premillennial views in the evangelical constituency.

During the First World War, encouraged by the apocalyptic circumstances, there took place an upsurge of belief that the second coming of Jesus Christ was imminent. In 1917 there was created an Advent Testimony Movement under the leadership of the now venerable Baptist minister F. B. Meyer, once an eager advocate of social reform but by this time much more reserved on the question. Helped by the advocacy of the Brethren (the so-called Plymouth Brethren) and the popularity of the Scofield Bible, first published in 1909, the dispensationalist version of premillennial teaching made rapid headway. Dispensationalists taught that no events were to intervene before the sudden and unexpected return of Christ to earth, first to collect true believers and then to set right all the wrongs of earth in a display of kingly power.[13] According to this way of thinking, the idea that Christians should be striving to build the kingdom of God on earth, a commonplace in COPEC circles, was a dangerous error. Thus a book by A. E. Garvie, a Congregationalist theologian of social gospel convictions, was condemned by a premillennialist reviewer because it was rooted in 'the conception that the kingdom of God is to come on the lines of God's present dealings with men and nations. The thought of the return of Christ as the centre of the coming kingdom is ignored.'[14] The same charge of dishonour to the coming king was the basis of E. L. Langston's critique of COPEC, and of many other explanations by the theologically conservative of why social service was not the task of the believer. It was a doctrinal error, they held, to suppose that the church should establish the kingdom. 'COPEC', as Langston put it, 'is the natural result of Modernism.'[15] Social commitment was shunned because it seemed to be bound up with a false eschatology.

The enormous influence of Keswick teaching had a similar effect. By the beginning of the twentieth century the sanctification doctrine of the convention had become normal among evangelical Anglicans and had spread into other denominations.[16] The general tendency of the movement, despite the social engagement of exceptional figures such as F. B. Meyer, was to encourage watchfulness about matters of personal behaviour rather than any sense of responsibility for life beyond the ecclesiastical sphere. The central imperative was greater consecration, which would lead to 'a holiness revival'. Then, according to a writer in 1923, no longer would church halls be used for questionable amusements.[17] No broader impact on society was expected or even envisaged. The weekly newspaper associated with Keswick, *The Life of Faith*, might call at election time for MPs of noble ideals or see voting as part of the Christian's obligation to king and nation, but it was lukewarm about COPEC and had doubts about the whole notion of a social mission for the church.[18] Stuart Holden, the Keswick leader most favourable to social reform, taught that once Christians knew their God they could labour 'toward the doing of His will on earth as it is done in heaven', but even he reaffirmed that Keswick 'does not attempt to solve the world-problems in its message'.[19] The movement associated with the convention was broadly wary of current expressions of Christian social responsibility.

It was by no means solely theological influences that inhibited the social witness of evangelicals between the wars. They were also diverted into other public causes by the exigencies of the hour. Evangelicals in the Church of England, and to a lesser extent those outside it, were confronted by the rising ascendancy of the Anglo-Catholic party. The revision of the Book of Common Prayer, a process long under way, culminated in the appearance of a liturgy that seemed to make crucial concessions to the Romanizers. Evangelicals mobilized through rallies, organizations and literature against the threat to the national church. Although the revised Prayer Book was rejected by an upsurge of Protestant feeling in parliament in 1927 and 1928, evangelical Anglicans continued to feel an imperative to maintain a standing protest against growing catholic strength.[20] Likewise many of the more conservative among the evangelicals tried to resist the advance of the liberal theological views that they branded modernism. Denial of biblical miracles, doubts about the virgin birth, belief in Darwinian evolution and, supremely, higher criticism of the Bible roused them to public action. The Fraternal Union for Bible Testimony, for example, was organized following an Albert Hall rally in 1923 to counter error by 'an intelligent and positive presentation of an evangelical position'.[21] Others, some of whom were proud to be called fundamentalists, wanted to assert the evangelical position but were less intelligent and less positive in their methods.[22] The two spectres of Romanism and modernism haunted many evangelicals of this generation. It is hardly surprising that they found less time than their ancestors in the faith to take initiatives for the healing of social ills.

If the struggle against Anglo-Catholicism was mainly a preoccupation of evangelicals in the Church of England, another reason for the recoil after 1918 from churchly attempts to solve the problems of society was the erosion of the political influence of evangelical Nonconformists, and especially their leaders. The decline of Nonconformist church membership that had set in since 1906 was now attributed to over-absorption in politics.[23] Even before the First World War there had been a swing of opinion against the secular activity of pressing for social reform as an inferior alternative to more directly spiritual work. To describe the deliverance of the poor as the first duty of the church, declared the *Methodist Recorder* in 1912, was a lie uttered by 'the subtle and eternal spirit of deceit'. 'Our fathers', it went on, 'were much more concerned about the glory of God and the dishonour done to him than about any social problems.'[24] It became received wisdom among the inter-war leaders of the denominations with an evangelical heritage that the church, as a distinctively spiritual community, should beware of squandering her strength on the passing issues of the hour. For the Congregationalists S. M. Berry, the secretary of the Union from 1923 to 1938, emphasized churchly concerns in the denomination. M. E. Aubrey, secretary of the Baptist Union from 1925 to 1951, took strong exception to the effort of Lloyd George through the 'Council of Action' in 1935 to mobilize the Free Churches in the causes of peace and full employment.[25] Although the tendency to retreat from politics was less marked in Methodism, even Henry Carter, the secretary of the Methodist Temperance and Social Welfare Department and a man wholly committed to Christian social responsibility, tried to steer his denomination away from advocating prohibition.[26] For each of them the spectre of over-politicization in a previous generation loomed large. The church, they believed, had a vocation that transcended temporal concerns.

A more sharply focused worry about politics was the fear of

socialism, an apprehension which had already been apparent before the First World War.[27] Anglicans in whom principles of social deference had been deeply ingrained were alarmed by those who seemed to advocate 'the pulling down of the existing structure and the setting up of something else.'[28] Anxiety was particularly acute among the leisured gentlemen and retired officers of the armed forces who often formed a majority of the lay element on evangelical committees during the inter-war years. A 'red scare' ran deep in the wake of the Russian Revolution in 1917. The revolution was an 'atheistical outburst of blood and torture beyond description', according to A. H. Burton, the Brethren editor of *The Advent Witness*, and thereafter, he claimed, industrial chaos in Britain was 'being engineered by the Communists of Moscow'.[29] It was hard to identify the Labour Party with international Communism while its organizing genius, Arthur Henderson, was a devout anti-Communist Wesleyan and so many of its early MPs were Methodists, yet some saw little to distinguish between the parties of the left. When it came to the General Strike of 1926, *The Life of Faith* carried an article of 'Startling Disclosures' about the great plot against the British Empire being masterminded by an international Jewish gang of atheists based in Russia.[30] Paranoia was perhaps to be expected in so unsettled an era, but its consequence was plain: there should be no tampering with social reconstruction, for that would be to play into the hands of the hidden revolutionaries. The social gospel was in part a victim of anxieties that swung much of the evangelical community politically to the right.

There was a further political reason for the eclipse of evangelical social commitment. Increasingly it was becoming difficult for the churches to exert any leverage on the formulation of policy. As Prime Minister between 1916 and 1922, Lloyd George had been careful to consolidate his political base by tokens of favour to Free Churchmen, especially J. H. Shakespeare of the Baptist Union, but the growth of the government machine under his premiership was an early stage in the apparently unstoppable trend of the state to expand its role. With the advance of a corporate bias in the political system there went a greater role in the formulation of policy for economic pressure groups such as employers and trade unions but a corresponding decline in the impact of non-economic organizations such as the churches.[31] The increasing provision of welfare facilities by state-sanctioned agencies at local level had an even more significant effect. From the laying of the foundations of the welfare state in the decade before the First World War, traditional religious forms of social work became redundant. Free meals provided in church halls were superseded by subsidized school dinners; district visiting was supplanted by trained social workers. Christian organizations retired in the face of more efficient competition.[32] At the same time prosperous businessmen who had previously funded local charitable efforts, often through the churches, withdrew their patronage, partly because the state was taking more from their pockets in taxation.[33] It is true that the acute unemployment of the inter-war years prompted churches to make fresh forays into welfare provision: the Church of Scotland, for instance, opened several halls for the unemployed in Glasgow in the early 1930s.[34] Nevertheless the trend in all the churches was to abandon expressions of social concern that had been normal in the previous century. Evangelicals were participating in a wider ecclesiastical response to the growth of the state.

If most of the factors tending to discourage evangelical social involvement operated over the long term, many of them were accentuated by the crisis of the First World War. The apocalyptic atmosphere promoted adventism; the associated upsurge of working-class militancy, especially in the immediate wake of the war, increased fears of revolution; the heavier taxation of upper- and middle-class incomes diverted money from philanthropy. Plans for post-war reconstruction compelled evangelicals to crystallize their understanding of social reform, the more liberal favouring it, the more conservative showing mounting suspicion. The change was particularly evident in the fundamentalist circles that formed the hard core of conservative evangelicalism. In 1914, on the eve of war, the Bible League, a crusading fundamentalist body, held a summer school at which one of the talks was on 'Citizenship';[35] after the war it disregarded the subject. The Wesley Bible Union, a rallying ground for Methodist fundamentalists, sympathized in principle with the church exerting an influence in the world, but when in 1917 reconstruction entered the public agenda it voiced its reservations. There had recently, its magazine noted, been a concentration by the church on social and political reform to the neglect of spiritual agencies. The influence of the church, it went on, was mightiest when it showed that it 'expects no effective reconstruction of human society except through the regeneration of the individual'. To suppose otherwise was to be led away by 'the Modernist apostasy'.[36] The Wesley Bible Union was setting its face against social work as an end in itself. It was during the final stages of the war and its aftermath that the social gospel became indissolubly linked with theological liberalism.

A final factor affecting the attitudes of evangelicals towards social involvement was their sheer weakness. They were dimly aware that their collective influence over the tone of British life had been slowly declining since the middle years of the previous century. Since that juncture the nation might have been growing more respectable, but it had not been growing more evangelical. High churchmanship and agnosticism had asserted themselves while evangelical growth rates had slowed, halted and begun to plummet. Although parliament contained a higher proportion of evangelicals, at least from the Nonconformist denominations, than during the nineteenth century[37] and although some of them, including Sir Thomas Inskip for the Conservatives and Ernest Brown for the Liberal Nationals, reached high office in the years between the wars, in society at large the evangelical presence had faded. There were successful businessmen such as Charles Wass, a Primitive Methodist coal merchant from Birkenhead, and Joseph Rank, a Wesleyan flour miller originally from Hull,[38] but the proportion of evangelicals in the population, though impossible to calculate accurately, had undoubtedly fallen and was continuing to fall. Methodist membership, to take one major contributor to evangelical strength, rose slightly in the 1920s but slipped back further in the 1930s.[39] Bare membership figures, which were rarely corrected downwards, masked a declining body of committed worshippers. Not only were numbers low: evangelicals were also remarkably uncoordinated. There was often little contact between Anglicans and Nonconformists, however similar their Christian outlook, and the Evangelical Alliance had shrunk to a condition of insignificance.[40] Consequently evangelicals were in no position to exert any major social influence. They formed a marginal and apparently decaying sector of British life.

For all these reasons, voluntary and involuntary, evangelical Christians of the more conservative variety became distanced from the social activism of their forefathers. At mid-century the predominant view was that the proper Christian response to social needs was at best indirect: to preach the gospel, to look for conversions and to hope for improvements in conditions as a result. Basil Atkinson, a member of staff at the Cambridge University Library and a senior stalwart of the Christian Union there, voiced the current orthodoxy in 1949. 'The commission of the Christian', he told a Graduates' Fellowship reunion, 'is to gather out of the world by evangelization a people to Christ's Name. No other commission has ever been given to the Church, and no other purpose for the existence of the Church is mentioned in the New Testament.' Hence the spread of the gospel was the only criterion for assessing humanitarian work. 'If social amelioration is a means to evangelization it is good. If it is treated as an end in itself it is bad.' Normally, he assumed, social reform was no more than a diversion from evangelistic endeavour. How then did Atkinson account for the earlier evangelical tradition of social involvement? 'The evangelicals at the time of the Revival', he explained, 'were often to be found visiting prisons. Their object was not prison reform in the abstract but the personal salvation of the prisoners.' Conveniently forgetting the achievement of Elizabeth Fry, he concluded with the restatement of an argument often heard in the 1920s. 'The only successful way of bringing about social reform', he contended, 'is by means of personal evangelism. The conversion of a drunkard means a clean-up of his home.'[41] Atkinson represented a phase when conservative evangelicals were single-mindedly preoccupied with the spread of the gospel. A critique of the movement published in 1957 admitted that the Inter-Varsity Fellowship bore a 'splendid witness' to the gospel for the individual. 'But what', it asked, 'has it to say about God's world, and the problems of our social life?'[42] The expected answer was nothing.

Nevertheless there were already stirrings within the Inter-Varsity Fellowship itself. After Atkinson's address to the 1949

reunion an alternative view of Christian socio-political responsibility was put by D. R. Denman, then a young lecturer in
estate management at Cambridge and subsequently Professor
of Land Economy there. The prophet Daniel, he pointed out,
served in high office; Joseph 'administered to the economic
and social needs of Egypt's millions'. Arguing that any supposed division between the spiritual and the secular was imag-
inary, Denman advocated the cultivation of a Christian mind
that should encompass the whole of God's world. Social service was legitimate so long as the Christian walked with his
God.[43] A new generation was looking at the issue in a fresh
light. At the same time a group of industrialists led by Alfred
Owen of Rubery Owen, the West Midlands engineering firm,
began to explore the implications of the Christian faith for
business. 'In a true sense', wrote Owen in 1949, 'Christ was a
business man',[44] and so Christian service in business was certainly possible. Although at first the primary objective was
evangelistic, the enterprise eventually blossomed in the late
1950s into Christian Teamwork for the application of principles of the faith to industrial problems.[45] In 1964 Frederick
Catherwood, an elder of Westminster Chapel and later an
MEP, summarized recent thinking in *The Christian in Industrial
Society*. Soon enthusiasm for social involvement quickened. In
1967 the Keele congress of evangelical Anglicans, under the
bold leadership of John Stott, rector of All Souls, Langham
Place, made the uncompromising statement that 'Evangelism
and compassionate service belong together in the mission of
God';[46] in the following year the Evangelical Alliance created a
relief fund for Third World aid (TEAR Fund); and in 1969 the
Shaftesbury Project was founded to stimulate thought and
action about social problems from an evangelical perspective.
Before long local congregations that had once shied away from
any activity not wholly evangelistic were sponsoring play-
groups, old people's clubs and fund-raising for international
aid without any inhibition. With John Stott codifying the social
ideals of the movement in his *Issues facing Christians Today*
(1984), active humanitarian concern was restored to favour in
the evangelical community.

How can the post-Second World War recovery of an active
social conscience be explained? It was partly the result of a

reversal of the trends of the 1920s in popular theology. In the 1950s and 1960s the gloomy belief that this world-order was about to be swept away in divine judgement and was therefore not worth improving, gradually faded. Advent Testimony rallies secured smaller audiences, the alternative postmillennial and amillennial positions gained ground and even many Brethren abandoned dispensationalism. The associated Keswick teaching also went into decline. It was not that the convention closed down, though many of the lesser Keswick meetings did come to an end, but rather that the distinctive message of holiness by faith slowly disappeared. The validity of the convention's theory of sanctification could no longer be assumed among conservative evangelicals after a vigorous onslaught against it by the young theologian J. I. Packer in 1955.[47] The Keswick sanction for otherworldliness gradually melted away. So the two currents of theological opinion that had helped to sweep social concern aside earlier in the century became much less powerful.

Other theological convictions came into favour. Like his mentor Martyn Lloyd-Jones, minister of Westminster Chapel, J. I. Packer looked back for inspiration to the Reformed theology of the seventeenth century. The Puritan Conferences of the 1950s and 1960s and the Banner of Truth Trust that sprang from them spread a taste for Calvinism among a younger generation of evangelicals.[48] Some of them could hardly fail to be swayed by the Puritan vision of a godly commonwealth upholding high standards of righteousness. A few went further, to the Dutch tradition of Reformed social theory massively embodied in the writings of Hermann Dooyeweerd, for their guidance on the application of Christian principles to modern society. It was this body of thought that spurred Alan Storkey to create the Shaftesbury Project. Alongside the Reformed revival from the 1960s was the even more influential movement of charismatic renewal. Disseminated through the existing denominations through the Fountain Trust, renewal also generated a vigorous set of house churches.[49] Charismatics suffered from few of the inhibitions that had affected the conservative evangelicals of an earlier day. In looking to Scripture with fresh eyes they discovered teaching about aspects of mission that had previously been neglected. The charismatic emphasis on divine healing for the mentally disturbed, for instance, soon led to care for those with psychological handicaps.[50] Theologically, too, there was innovation. The largest grouping of house churches, called Harvestime and later Covenant Ministries, for instance, adopted postmillennial teaching in its journal *Restoration*. Consequently the magazine portrayed a vision of a progressively renewed society.[51] It is hardly surprising that, when Alan Storkey stood as a parliamentary candidate at the October 1974 election, a high proportion of his supporters were charismatic Christians.[52] Like the reinvigorated Reformed tradition, charismatic renewal often encouraged greater social activism.

Contact with Christians outside their own ranks tended to draw evangelicals in the same direction. In the earlier post-war years it was common for those in the evangelical tradition to look askance at the ecumenical movement, fearing it merely concealed a drift towards Rome. Gradually, however, there was a softening of attitudes. The Keele congress discussed church unity sympathetically and even concluded, in the wake of the Second Vatican Council, that there were new possibilities of dialogue with the Roman Catholic Church.[53] Full participation in the affairs of the Church of England, another Keele emphasis, entailed co-operation with churchmen of higher and broader persuasion, and evangelicals in many denominations often discovered common ground with other Christians through local Councils of Churches. Consequently the social commitment of many Catholics and more liberal Protestants was brought afresh to the attention of evangelicals. They realized, as the Keele statement put it, 'to our shame that we have not thought sufficiently deeply or radically about the problems of our society.'[54] TEAR Fund was in part a response to the success of Christian Aid in more committed ecumenical circles. Likewise the Uppsala assembly of the World Council of Churches, held in 1968, provoked evangelicals into serious reflection on the place of socio-political action by defining the mission of the church partly in those terms.[55] In a more diffuse way literature produced by other schools of thought also had an effect on the evangelical community. As early as 1949 an essay in the Inter-Varsity Fellowship's magazine for graduates commended social reform on the basis of historical analysis drawn from R. H. Tawney and unqualified admiration for the work of William Temple.[56] Similarly the topic of 'Christian Worldliness' was borrowed as a theme for Keele from the writings of the church historian Alec Vidler.[57] Evangelicals could not remain immune to currents of social thought flowing in adjacent channels.

Nor could they avoid being influenced by developments elsewhere in the evangelical world. At a much earlier date than in Britain, the theologian Carl Henry put social issues on the agenda of the American movement with his book *The Uneasy Conscience of Modern Fundamentalism* (1947).[58] Although Henry's volume had no appreciable effect on the other side of the Atlantic, the journal he edited from 1956, *Christianity Today*, enjoyed a small but select circulation in Britain, confirming among its readers the importance of public responsibility.[59] Literature from the United States made a broader impact in the later 1960s, particularly when, in 1968, Sherwood Eliot Wirt's *The Social Conscience of the Evangelical* was published in London as well as in America. More radical views were fostered by the writings of the American Mennonites J. H. Yoder and Ronald Sider and by the example of the Sojourners Community in Washington, DC. Worldwide contacts also helped. The Evangelical Alliance was in touch with its American equivalent, the National Association of Evangelicals, in part through the World Evangelical Fellowship that was established in 1951.[60] From ten years later, Anglican evangelicals had their own global body, the Evangelical Fellowship in the Anglican Communion.[61] International co-ordination of the evangelical movement culminated in the Congress on World Evangelization held at Lausanne in 1974. There Billy Graham, the magnetic figure most responsible for the gathering, summoned the participants to discuss social responsibility, and the resulting Lausanne Covenant duly affirmed that 'evangelism and socio-political involvement are both part of our Christian duty'.[62] A series of lesser international consultations held from 1966 onwards tried to thrash out in more detail the proper relationship between the two, the best known report issuing from the Grand Rapids conference of 1982.[63] At first North Americans troubled by race riots and Vietnam were the pacemakers; subsequently Latin American personalities such as Samuel Escobar and René Padilla rose to prominence, urging drastic conclusions more like those of liberation theologians. In the context of such discussions leaders of British evangelical opinion were swept along by the new tide of enthusiasm for social engagement.

The divisions evident in the international movement between the more and the less radical came to be paralleled within Britain. In the years immediately after the Second World War apolitical tendencies were strong. At the 1950 general election a correspondent of the popular evangelical weekly the *Christian* argued in the manner of Basil Atkinson that Christians should not vote, and the Baptist denominational newspaper, though appearing on election day, entirely ignored the event.[64] Evangelicals of conservative theological views, insisting on 'the importance, rights and responsibilities of the individual',[65] were often at a loss in a novel collectivist age. With the catastrophic decline of the Liberal Party, most of them – except, probably, those in the ranks of Methodism – gave their tacit allegiance to the Conservative Party. In 1981 52 per cent of the senior figures forming the Evangelical Group in the General Synod of the Church of England were willing to identify themselves in private as Conservatives.[66] From the 1970s onwards, however, some were eager to play a more overt role in partisan politics. Prominent individuals such as Brian Griffiths, Director of the Centre for Banking and International Finance at the City University, urged economic prescriptions associated with Margaret Thatcher's brand of Conservatism as the means of national regeneration. In 1980 Griffiths advocated 'dismantling the corporate state'.[67] On the other hand different leaders saw increased public spending as the only way to grapple with the urban deprivation of the age. This was true, for example, of David Sheppard, who drew on his earlier experience as warden of the Mayflower Centre in the East End of London, as well as his concerns as a bishop, to write his widely circulated book *Built as a City* (1974). So strongly was collectivist opinion represented in the official statement on 'Power in our Democracy' at the Nottingham Evangelical Anglican Congress in 1977 that a right-wing group led by Brian Griffiths and a Conservative MP felt bound to compose an alternative document.[68] Political diversity was in large measure a result of the resurgence of social commitment, but it must also be ranged among its causes. Alignment with the parties of left and right meant that the articulation of their social policies now came more naturally to many evangelicals.

Another political reason for the mobilization of the movement on social issues was the entry of the state into moral provinces that the churches had supposed to be their own. Evangelical Nonconformists who had traditionally denounced gambling were pained when a Conservative government introduced Premium Bonds in 1957 and a liberalizing Betting and Gaming Act three years later. More alarming was the deluge of legislation on more personal moral questions during the 1966 parliament. In 1967 abortion was legalized and homosexual acts between consenting adults decriminalized; in 1968 theatre censorship was abolished; and in 1969 divorce by consent was introduced. Already the onset of permissiveness in the media had provoked resistance from Mary Whitehouse and her National Viewers' and Listeners' Association, set up, with extensive evangelical support, in 1965.[69] Now the apparent repudiation by parliament of its role as the guardian of national morality roused rank-and-file Christians of many traditions in protest. In 1971 Mary Whitehouse and a diverse group of fellow-campaigners organized a Festival of Light in which local beacons were lit and a rally against permissive morality was held in Trafalgar Square.[70] As the movement evolved into CARE Trust and CARE Campaigns it increasingly emerged as a definitely evangelical organization with the twin purposes of research and public protest. In 1973 Raymond Johnston, soon to become director of CARE Trust, told his fellow evangelical Anglicans that 'we . . . need to recover the social message of the Bible'.[71] What incited Johnston, a traditionalist at heart, and many of his contemporaries to take that stance, however, was not the set of social issues attractive to left-wingers. Rather it was the revolution in moral standards sanctioned by the legislature in the swinging sixties. The growth in attention to the problems of the day was by no means a left/liberal monopoly. Those with a conservative social philosophy were equally spurred into action by the emergence of the permissive society.

Behind the moral change of the era lay the process of secularization. The ethical teaching of the churches was repudiated only after their claim on the sympathies of the people had already vanished. No longer were church links cherished even by those who attended merely for rites of passage. The proportion of marriages celebrated in church in England and Wales fell from two-thirds in 1966 to under a half in 1980.[72] The number of those who were willing to identify with the Protestant churches decreased too. From a post-war peak of some 5,407,000 in 1956, church membership in the major denominations declined to 4,311,000 in 1970 and continued to fall thereafter.[73] Religion retreated to the margins of society. There was a twofold consequence for evangelicals. On the one hand, the place of religion in social institutions was challenged. Evangelical teachers in schools, for example, often found themselves alone in wanting to preserve religious education and a Christian assembly. Through the Association of Christian Teachers and other bodies, they considered the issues thrown up by their professional responsibilities in the context of a changing society. Likewise, with the observance of Sunday being steadily eroded, the Jubilee Centre at Cambridge took up its public defence, initially with conspicuous success. The inexorable advance of the secular made Christians more willing to stand up and be counted. As another result of secularization, on the other hand, the proportion of evangelicals in religious institutions increased. The decay of traditional churchgoing, no longer buttressed by custom and deference, meant that evangelicals became progressively more powerful as a sector of the religious world. By 1989 they formed as high a proportion as 28 per cent of adult churchgoers in England.[74] Their buoyant temper made them ready to explore fresh fields including the social implications of the faith. The increasingly secular tone of national life undergirded many of the other forces pushing evangelicals in the same direction.

The tendency of the younger evangelicals to upward social mobility, assisted above all by higher education, also had a similar effect. The expansion of the Inter-Varsity Fellowship is a good index of the change. In 1938 there were 37 affiliated Christian Unions; in 1948, 82; in 1958, 190; in 1968, 352; and in 1978, 554.[75] The enormous growth of post-war higher education enabled the children of evangelical families to rise in the social scale and, supplemented by converts drawn into

Christian Unions, to take a strategic place in the evangelical community. Educated laypeople with secular concerns began to share leadership with those trained for the ministry in theology. Some were graduates in sociology; many others through their professional duties encountered the problems of modern society. These constituted the rank and file of the Shaftesbury Project and the readers of *Third Way*, a magazine founded in 1977 to relate the faith to social and cultural issues in a discerning manner. It was not that the Inter-Varsity Fellowship pursued any deliberate policy of resensitizing the evangelical social conscience. Although the Fellowship's magazine was the first in the conservative theological orbit to take up questions of socio-political involvement from the late 1940s, it showed initial reluctance to sponsor the Shaftesbury Project in the late 1960s and when, in 1970, its general secretary, Oliver Barclay, encouraged the formation of a Christian mind on public issues in his book *Whose World?* he felt bound to write under a pseudonym. Through its very existence rather than through any conscious plan, the Inter-Varsity Fellowship produced reflective graduates who broadened the horizons of the evangelical community. Greater engagement with social questions was the result.

During the twentieth century there was therefore a double bend in the trajectory of conservative evangelical attitudes to social concern. Between the wars there was a turn towards the position of Basil Atkinson, that Christians were to concentrate solely on evangelism. Later there was another change of mind, summed up by John Stott, the most potent individual influence on the process, as a shift from merely expecting that there would be social consequences of obeying the gospel commission to holding that social responsibility was itself a part of the commission.[76] It would be wrong to exaggerate either alteration of course. Some evangelicals, especially on the more liberal fringe of the movement, never abandoned their commitment to the problems of the wider society. Evangelical Nonconformists tended to be reminded from time to time by their denominational bureaucracies about pressing social problems, and the Church of Scotland issued a remarkable series of reports on church and society during the Second World War.[77]

It was among the conservative evangelicals of the Church of England and in the sects, especially the Brethren and the Pentecostalists, that the repugnance to social activism was strongest. In those quarters, however, and to a less marked extent elsewhere, interest in social affairs reached a nadir in the years around the Second World War. It was therefore in the same quarters that the awakening to a sense of social responsibility was most sharply felt.

The twofold process of decline and resurgence has to be explained in terms of factors of several types. Theology was necessarily important in a movement committed to the maintenance of truth. The progress and decay of premillennial and Keswick doctrine, giving ideological justification for otherworldliness, correlate closely with the downswing and upswing of social concern; Reformed and charismatic teaching helped to sustain the upswing. Ideas about the proper mission of the church also affected the process. A preference for anti-catholic and anti-modernist campaigning, together with a Nonconformist reaction in favour of spiritual values, diverted evangelical groupings between the wars, whereas ecumenical and international influences afterwards drew them back towards active philanthropy. The political environment, however, was also a significant force. It tended to discourage social action in the earlier period because of a widespread fear of socialism and the state's novel entry into the welfare field. In the later period the rise of more left-wing bodies of evangelical opinion, together with protest against public sanction for permissive morality, did much to mobilize the movement. But most fundamental was the changing place of evangelicalism within society at large. The cataclysm of the First World War indirectly provoked much of the evangelical recoil from humanitarian affairs; the sheer weakness of the movement consolidated the withdrawal. Conversely later in the century its growing relative strength, coupled with the emergence of a graduate lay leadership, thrust it back into social questions. Although the evangelical movement had a theological dynamic of its own that did much to transform its attitudes, it was also shaped by the socio-political context. If the effect was at first to eclipse the tradition of Wilberforce and Shaftesbury, it was subsequently to restore it. Although their names had never ceased to be honoured, by the last quarter of the twentieth century their deeds were once more being imitated unashamedly by their evangelical successors.

Notes

1 I. R. Govan, *Spirit of Revival: The Story of J. G. Govan and the Faith Mission* (Edinburgh: Faith Mission, 1938), p. 173.
2 Alan Wilkinson, *The Church of England and the First World War* (SPCK, 1978), p. 248.
3 *British Weekly*, 21 April 1921, p. 49.
4 *Record*, 3 March 1921, p. 149 (F. Mellows).
5 Gerald Studdert-Kennedy, *Dog-Collar Democracy: The Industrial Christian Fellowship, 1919–1929* (Macmillan, 1982), p. 40.
6 Frederick Coutts, *The History of the Salvation Army: 7: The Weapons of Goodwill, 1946–1977* (Hodder and Stoughton, 1986), p. 18.
7 L. L. L. Cameron, *The Challenge of Need: A History of Social Service by The Church of Scotland, 1869–1969* (Edinburgh: Saint Andrew Press, 1971).
8 Norman Anderson, *An Adopted Son: The Story of my Life* (Leicester: Inter-Varsity Press, 1985), p. 213; M. Anderson, 'Economic Science in Evangelical Social Thought: A Missing Dimension of the English Christian Social Movement', *Lucas: An Evangelical History Review*, 15 (1993).
9 *Record*, 7 Feb. 1908, p. 125 (F. D. Stammers).
10 *Record*, 18 Sept. 1924, p. 591.
11 *Advent Witness*, Jan.–Feb. 1946, pp. 97f. (Allister W. Smith).
12 *Elim Evangel*, 1943, p. 481, quoted by B. R. Wilson, *Sects and Society: A Sociological Study of Three Religious Groups in Britain* (Heinemann, 1961), p. 29n.
13 D. W. Bebbington, 'The Advent Hope in British Evangelicalism since 1800', *Scottish Journal of Religious Studies*, 9 (1988), pp. 107–9.
14 *Life of Faith* [hereafter *LF*], 10 June 1925, p. 660.
15 *Record*, 18 Sept. 1924, p. 591.
16 D. W. Bebbington, *Evangelicalism in Modern Britain: A History from the 1730s to the 1980s* (Unwin Hyman, 1989), chap. 5.
17 *LF*, 11 April 1923, pp. 405f. (Dr James Little).
18 *LF*, 28 Nov. 1923, p. 1408; 15 Oct. 1924, p. 1228; 16 April 1924, p. 445; 4 June 1924, p. 656.
19 *LF*, 22 July 1925, p. 814.
20 Bebbington, *Evangelicalism in Modern Britain*, pp. 204f., 221f.
21 *LF*, 30 Jan. 1924, p. 122.
22 D. W. Bebbington, 'Martyrs for the Truth: Fundamentalists in

Britain', in Diana Wood, ed., *Studies in Church History*, 30 (1993), pp. 417–51.

23 See above, pp. 147–52. See also D. W. Bebbington, *The Nonconformist Conscience: Chapel and Politics, 1870–1914* (Allen & Unwin, 1982), chaps 7 and 8.

24 *Methodist Recorder*, 4 June 1912, p. 3.

25 W. M. S. West, 'The Reverend Secretary Aubrey: Part I', *Baptist Quarterly*, 34 (1992), pp. 204–12.

26 G. T. Brake, *Policy and Politics in British Methodism*, 1932–1982 (Edsall, 1984), pp. 434ff.

27 See above, p. 145.

28 *Record*, 26 March 1925, p. 214 (Prebendary A. W. Gough).

29 F. W. Pitt, *Windows on the World: A Record of the Life of Alfred H. Burton, B.A., M.D.* (Pickering & Inglis, n.d.), p. 78.

30 *LF*, 26 May 1926, pp. 547f.

31 Keith Middlemas, *Politics in Industrial Society: The Experience of the British System since 1911* (André Deutsch, 1979), pp. 373f.

32 Jeffrey Cox, *The English Churches in a Secular Society: Lambeth, 1870–1930* (New York: Oxford UP, 1982), pp. 197–201.

33 Stephen Yeo, *Religion and Voluntary Organisations in Crisis* (Croom Helm, 1976).

34 *Life and Work*, April 1934, p. 163.

35 *Journal of the Wesley Bible Union*, March 1915, p. 61.

36 *Journal of the Wesley Bible Union*, July 1917, pp. 159f.

37 For the Baptists, see D. W. Bebbington, 'Baptist Members of Parliament in the Twentieth Century', *Baptist Quarterly*, 31 (1986).

38 D. J. Jeremy, *Capitalists and Christians: Business Leaders and the Churches in Britain, 1900–1960* (Oxford: Clarendon Press, 1990), p. 348.

39 Robert Currie et al., *Churches and Churchgoers: Patterns of Church Growth in the British Isles since 1700* (Oxford: Clarendon Press, 1977), p. 143.

40 J. B. A. Kessler, *A Study of the Evangelical Alliance in Great Britain* (Goes, Netherlands: Oosterbaan & Le Cointre, 1968), pp. 87f.

41 *Christian Graduate*, March 1949, pp. 6f.

42 Gabriel Hebert, *Fundamentalism and the Church of God* (SCM Press, 1957), p. 27.

43 *Christian Graduate*, March 1949, pp. 7–11.

44 *Christian Graduate*, June 1949, p. 60.

45 Jeremy, *Capitalists and Christians*, pp. 220–7.

46 Philip Crowe, ed., *Keele '67: The National Evangelical Anglican Congress Statement* (Falcon, 1967), p. 23.

47 J. I. Packer, '"Keswick" and the Reformed Doctrine of Sanctification', *Evangelical Quarterly*, 27 (1955).

48 'Introduction', in D. M. Lloyd-Jones, *The Puritans: Their Orgins and Successors* (Edinburgh: Banner of Truth Trust, 1987).

49 Edward England, *The Spirit of Renewal* (Eastbourne: Kingsway,

196   *Decline and Resurgence of Social Concern*

1982); Peter Hocken, *Streams of Renewal: The Origin and Early History of the Charismatic Movement in Great Britain* (Exeter: Paternoster, 1986); Andrew Walker, *Restoring the Kingdom: The Radical Christianity of the House Church Movement* (Hodder & Stoughton, 1985).

50 Bebbington, *Evangelicalism in Modern Britain*, p. 242.

51 *Restoration*, Jan.–Feb. 1986, pp. 12–16. I am grateful for this reference to Timothy Larsen.

52 I am grateful for this point to Alan Storkey.

53 Crowe, ed., *Keele '67*, p. 39.

54 Crowe, ed., *Keele '67*, p. 26.

55 D. J. Tidball, *Contemporary Evangelical Social Thinking – A Review* (Nottingham: Shaftesbury Project, 1977), pp. 5f.

56 W. J. H. Earl, 'Christianity and Social Theory', *Christian Graduate*, Sept. 1949, pp. 70–4.

57 Anderson, *Adopted Son*, p. 213.

58 George Marsden, *Reforming Fundamentalism: Fuller Seminary and the New Evangelicalism* (Grand Rapids, Mich.: Eerdmans, 1987), pp. 79–82.

59 Carl F. H. Henry, *Confessions of a Theologian: An Autobiography* (Waco, Texas: Word Books, 1986), chaps 9–15.

60 D. M. Howard, *The Dream that would not Die: The Birth and Growth of the World Evangelical Fellowship, 1846–1986* (Exeter: Paternoster Press, 1986).

61 John Stott, 'World-wide Evangelical Anglicanism', in J. C. King, ed., *Evangelicals Today* (Guildford: Lutterworth Press, 1973).

62 *Church of England Newspaper*, 26 July 1974, p. 1. Athol Gill, 'Christian Social Responsibility', in C. René Padilla, ed., *The New Face of Evangelicalism: An International Symposium on the Lausanne Covenant* (Hodder and Stoughton, 1976), p. 87.

63 Christopher Cope, 'The Relationship between Evangelism and Social Responsibility in Evangelical Thought from the Wheaton Conference of 1966 to the Wheaton Conference of 1983', unpublished M.Phil. (Theol.) thesis, University of Manchester, 1990; *Evangelicalism and Social Responsibility: An Evangelical Commitment* (Exeter: Paternoster Press, 1982).

64 *Christian*, 3 February 1950, p. 7 (E. K.); D W. Bebbington, 'Baptists and Politics since 1914', in K. W. Clements, ed., *Baptists in the Twentieth Century* (Baptist Historical Society, 1983), p. 78.

65 *Christian Graduate*, June 1948, p. 1.

66 K. N. Medhurst and G. H. Moyser, *Church and Politics in a Secular Age* (Oxford: Clarendon Press, 1988), p. 236.

67 Brian Griffiths, *Morality and the Market Place* (Hodder and Stoughton, 1982), p. 124.

68 John Capon, *Evangelicals Tomorrow: A Popular Report of Nottingham 77, the National Evangelical Anglican Congress* (Glasgow: Collins, 1977), p. 110.

69   Max Caulfield, *Mary Whitehouse* (Mowbrays, 1975).
70   John Capon, . . . *and There was Light: The Story of the Nationwide Festival of Light* (Lutterworth Press, 1972).
71   *Church of England Newspaper*, 12 Jan. 1973, p. 1.
72   *Social Trends*, 1982 edn (HMSO, 1981), p. 193.
73   Currie *et al.*, ed., *Churches and Churchgoers*, p. 32.
74   Peter Brierley, ed., *Prospects for the Nineties* (MARC Europe, 1991), p. 23.
75   Douglas Johnson, *Contending for the Faith: A History of the Evangelical Movement in the Universities and Colleges* (Leicester: Inter-Varsity Press, 1979), p. 338.
76   John Stott, *Christian Mission in the Modern World* (Falcon, 1975), p. 23.
77   D. C. Smith, *Passive Obedience and Prophetic Protest: Social Criticism in the Scottish Church, 1830–1945* (New York: Peter Lang, 1987), pp. 373–81.

Afterword
Hope For the Future?

CLIVE CALVER

As the year 2000 rapidly approaches one is entitled to ask whether evangelicals have really learned anything from their past. Contemporary evangelicals often display a reluctance to examine their heritage. To use the word 'history' in an average evangelical congregation invites widespread groans of dismay. This is unfortunate because Christianity is an historical faith. It is founded on events that actually happened. The sure knowledge of the God who has fulfilled his promises in the past is the basis for our confidence to face the future.

Christians possess roots in the past and to ignore their existence is to risk reducing faith to the level of personal opinions or beliefs. Religion without history is grounded on feelings rather than facts. Modern liberal scholarship, with its rejection of 'the Jesus of history' in favour of the 'Christ of faith', has suggested further uncertainties about the value of this field of investigation. According to this school of thought, what matters is religious experience rather than the search for historical truth.

Similarly, the prominence of tradition within the Catholic sector of the church has created a suspicion among evangelicals of too great an emphasis on past experience. Today and tomorrow have become all-important, yesterday has been largely forgotten.

This compilation of essays has been produced in an attempt

to redress such an imbalance. It has not been written in a vacuum, for academic study of our past has relevance to our present and future. Those prepared to open their eyes and acknowledge its importance are those who benefit most. The poet Steve Turner summed up this perspective quite brilliantly when he wrote:

History repeats itself
Has to
No-one listens.[1]

To neglect the lessons we could be learning from the experience of previous generations is little short of open folly and a mark of reluctance to acknowledge the debt of gratitude we owe to our spiritual predecessors.

This does not mean that we are bound up in a mechanistic cycle of historical repetition – far from it. We are not condemned to repeat the mistakes of the past, nor are we automatically guaranteed to improve on the legacy of previous generations, but we do have much to learn from them.[2]

In the years since 1980, evangelicals in the United Kingdom have participated in some significant changes. David Bebbington's definition of evangelical distinctives as conversionist, activist, biblicist and crucicentrist has contributed to a major shift in understanding and attitudes.[3]

Fresh styles of worship, an acceleration in church planting and a new commitment to social responsibility have all played their part in producing numerical increase among evangelicals in all denominations.[4] Perhaps the most crucial factor of all has been the growth of community involvement among evangelicals. As evangelicals of this generation have begun to depart from an inherited policy of self-imposed isolation, they have emerged from their comfortable ghettos to grapple with the needs of contemporary society.

Unlike the stereotyped image of America's 'religious right', evangelicals in the United Kingdom have remained stubbornly independent in their choice of party allegiance. This political variety has been emulated by the differing means of social expression that evangelicals have employed.

While it is far too early to examine the long-term consequences of this development, no book of this nature, which

examines past failures and achievements, should avoid a brief
analysis of some significant activities taking place among evangelicals today. For many have begun to acknowledge again
that:

> the view that personal evangelism should be our exclusive
> concern falls short of being the full message of the Bible.
> The message includes a strong theme, which runs right
> through Scripture, that God's people have responsibilities
> in the world as well as in His Kingdom. Put another way,
> we have a mission to our culture and society as well as to
> individuals.[5]

Many of the new initiatives that have emerged over the last two
decades owe their genesis to the energies of individual pioneers
determined to chart a fresh course for the future. Most
acknowledge that their ideas are not original, but they are following the example of others, particularly from the nineteenth
century, who once demonstrated that evangelistic concern and
social compassion could walk together.

The development of The Evangelical Alliance Relief Fund
(Tear Fund) in the 1970s was to make a critical contribution
towards the reawakening of the evangelical social conscience.
Focusing primarily on relief and development work overseas,
its professionally qualified staff assist partner churches and
societies in attacking the basic causes of poverty, suffering and
disadvantage, rather than just treating the problems they
cause.[6] With a budget of around £20 million it stands as a flag-
ship for what can be achieved from very humble beginnings.

No longer does Tear Fund stand alone in this area of
ministry. Similar initiatives, originating in the United States,
include World Vision and Samaritan's Purse, and, from the
United Kingdom, has emerged the younger movement 'Christmas Cracker'. The latter was formed in 1987 by a Baptist
minister, Steve Chalke, and an Asian businessman, Ram
Gidoomal. They employed a simple slogan for its seasonal
cafeterias and restaurants, 'Eat Less, Pay More'. By 1994 it
had released over £3 million for overseas projects.[7]

The lack of space prevents adequate coverage of a burgeoning number of new projects, based in the UK, designed to
alleviate poverty and suffering by contributing to medical,

physical and spiritual needs in situations as diverse as Romania, Bosnia, Poland and Hong Kong. Suffice it to say that entrepreneurial evangelical initiatives are being launched on a regular basis in order to meet shorter-term needs. Similarly, many mission societies have begun to introduce both the language and practices of social concern as an integral part of their activities.

Nor is the phenomenon of evangelical philanthropy limited to overseas situations. Shortly after the energetic Anglican clergyman, George Hoffman, set up Tear Fund in 1968, a proposal emerged for a parallel structure to operate in the United Kingdom. In 1995 the United Kingdom Project, a fund to be administered by Tear Fund in association with the Evangelical Alliance, offers a fresh focus on 'the materially poor and socially vulnerable' in the United Kingdom. This initiative is not designed to develop its own projects but to support the work of existing organizations in this field.[8] This parallels existing trusts and the Anglican Church Urban Fund, which is designed to support the ministry of parishes in Urban Priority Areas.

Such a fund is not likely to be short of worthwhile applications. While the Salvation Army has consistently demonstrated the need for church-based social action in the local community others have been slow to follow their example. Yet recent developments have indicated a distinct wind of change blowing in that direction. Large numbers of local churches have become convinced of the need for a more holistic attitude to Christian ministry and become actively involved in areas of social action.

On a recent visit to a Baptist church in the north of England, I was impressed to learn of their drop-in centre, church cafeteria, works with the unemployed and single parents, and community enterprise schemes. Frankly, I had been unaware of their considerable involvement in this field. Perhaps the reason is that increasing numbers of churches are recognizing a direct responsibility to serve the needs of the community as a whole – not just of their own congregation.

Sir Fred Catherwood, former Vice-President of the European Parliament and President of the Evangelical Alliance, has been instrumental in encouraging the foundation of Christian Action Networks. The CANs provide the means for churches in specific towns or cities to link their individual caring initiatives together in order that they may support one another and provide an effective voice to local and national government.

Prototypes for this type of co-operation exist already. PECAN is an evangelical network linking the churches of North Peckham in south-east London. Established in 1989, it employs volunteers to visit people in their homes on local housing estates and recruit those who are without jobs on to their Employment Preparation Courses. By this means they trained over 1240 people during their first five years of operation and saw over 400 gain employment.

PECAN also runs a Job Club and a 'One to One' literacy scheme for those unable to read or write. Like many inner-city areas Peckham has a large number of refugees from all over the world. Many struggle to learn English and so are socially excluded from the workplace. PECAN's English for Speakers of Other Languages courses are designed to help this group. In 1993 they were given the prestigious 'Investors in People' award.[9] In a full year they now train 500 people, which is equivalent to 10 per cent of the unemployed in North Peckham.[10]

In the London Borough of Hackney, the Churches' Unity Project built an effective network of black-led churches. Jointly funded by the Hackney Task Force and the Evangelical Alliance, it joined with other Hackney evangelical churches to form the Hackney Employment Link Project. This operates on similar lines to PECAN and has established a policy of visiting over 4,000 homes up to four times a year.[11] Support for this type of initiative stemmed originally from the Evangelical Alliance's Community Initiatives Unit which continues to see new projects established in urban areas.

Many other bodies involved in urban mission share this concern for urban regeneration. The Evangelical Urban Training Group and the Alliance's non-book group concentrate on reaching people from a non-book culture and train others to do the same. Frontier Youth Trust, a department of Scripture Union, organizes outreach and training for inner-city young people. Evangelicals and non-evangelicals work together in the Churches' National Housing Coalition creating emergency hostels and drop-in centres for the homeless. Individual hostels and centres are also operated by a variety of evangelical churches and organizations. The list continues to grow.

Not all initiatives of this kind are either local or new. The 'Noble Earl' could scarcely have anticipated that his Ragged School Union would develop 150 years later into the Shaftesbury Society of today. Nor could John Groom have been expected to realize that the flower sellers for his Crippleage would become the foundation for the John Grooms Housing Association. Would Charles Haddon Spurgeon have believed that his orphanage could develop into the Child Care Association that bears his name? Each of these organizations has experienced a major renaissance and fresh impetus for growth in the 1980s and 1990s. Their contribution in housing, care for the elderly, churches and mission centres, special schools, urban action and support for the disabled has been enormous and represents evangelical social concern at the highest level.

The 1980s were also to herald the emergence of other significant new evangelical initiatives. AIDS Concern for Education and Training (ACET), with its emphasis on caring for the sufferers of AIDS, the Christian Childcare Network caring for, or counselling, children and families, and the various initiatives of the Jubilee Centre at Cambridge all provided ample evidence of a change in the evangelical climate.

A commitment to philanthropic ideals was now being positively wedded to an active political involvement. Through its Keep Sunday Special Programme, Jubilee Centre promoted an active, though ultimately unsuccessful, campaign to avert the legalization of Sunday trading. Care Trust, which had developed out of the old Nationwide Festival of Light, fought to resist changes to liberalize the law on abortion and to ensure that the sanctity of life is respected at the frontiers of medical research and practice. Parliamentary research on a number of issues was promoted by both organizations in order to support Christian parliamentarians and influence their secular counterparts.

The gathering of information and attempts to address issues from a Christian perspective were a direct response to the challenge issued by John Stott for the development of a 'Christian mind'. He called for biblical integrity and contemporary relevance in relation to issues confronting secular society. The publication of *Issues Facing Christians Today* was one of the greatest single influences on the attitude of evangelical thinking in the last 20 years.[12] The emergence of the London Institute for Contemporary Christianity was Stott's brainchild and one of the young men he had deeply influenced, the economist Roy McCloughrey, developed the work of the Kingdom Trust to support individual churches in their understanding of these issues.

Meanwhile the Evangelical Alliance did not remain impervious to these issues. Having grown to become a more influential body representing some 5,000 churches and 700 parachurch societies in its membership, the Alliance adopted a definite stance on socio-political issues. While its member societies like Care and Jubilee actively lobbied Parliament to achieve specific objectives, the Evangelical Alliance sought quietly to represent evangelical opinion to Government, Opposition and the media on a wide range of issues. Its Salt and Light programme endeavoured to enable evangelicals of different political perspectives to understand each other. Its Public Affairs Department joined with *The Church of England Newspaper* in producing 'Westminster Watch' as a regular digest of parliamentary affairs coupled with informed evangelical comment.

None of this would have achieved significance without the increase of caring initiatives among evangelicals. Inevitably one will be guilty of failing to mention several important new projects. However, four can serve as illustrative of the new mood which has pervaded evangelical thinking.

Credit Action, a work pioneered by Keith Tondeur, addresses the whole question of personal debt. Building societies have adopted its counselling service. Advice is given to those who have become embroiled in financial difficulties. With 37 million credit cards held by citizens of the United Kingdom, debt has become a major issue for the church and the community.[13]

Care for the Family, a section of the influential ministry of Care, offers support and guidance on parenting and family issues. Care's wider ministry gives help to single-parent families, advice and counsel on abortion, and spearheads a vigorous campaign on the issue of euthanasia.

Evangelical Christians for Racial Justice (formerly the Evangelical Race Relations Group) focuses its attention on racism in Britain. It boldly declares:

> Over the past 40 years the ties between Britain and its Empire have been cut in favour of those with the European Community. During this time Black communities have had to defend themselves against economic exploitation and physical, cultural and political attack, all underpinned by unjust laws and administrative practices.

ECRJ has therefore committed itself to raising awareness of the dangers of this attitude within the evangelical community and rooting out this problem wherever it occurs.[14]

The strengthening of links between black and white churches is being fostered by the African-Caribbean Evangelical Alliance which encourages partnership between churches wherever possible. The Alliance of Asian Christians performs a similar role for churches within the Asian community.

Cause for Concern was founded in the 1980s by David Potter, a Free Church pastor and his wife Madeleine. It concentrates on providing care and accommodation for some 85 adults with mental disabilities. At the same time this organization seeks to create a wider awareness within the evangelical community of ways in which those with learning difficulties may be integrated within the life of the local church.[15] This advocacy is visibly demonstrated in the special programme they have created during each year's Spring Harvest event. By running separate seminars for those with learning difficulties, whilst integrating them within the plenary celebration meetings, members of the wider Christian community can see a model to replicate in their own church.

All this, together with much more which could be mentioned, serves to illustrate a radical development in evangelical social concern. It denotes much activity – but how effective is it?

It is true that many of the initiatives that have been introduced remain the province of a small number of committed specialists. Each retains its own emphasis and area of concern, but the majority remain relatively small and poorly funded. Nevertheless, without doubt general evangelical awareness has been heightened. Much good has been achieved for individual recipients of care and concern. Prejudices have been challenged – by groups like ACET and the Mildmay Hospital in relation to AIDS, and many others in areas of racism, drug abuse and so on. Yet still the evangelical response remains a drop in the ocean of the vast sea of contemporary social need.

One is entitled to enquire whether long-term gains have been achieved of lasting value and whether the grapeshot of varied individual endeavours will make an important contribution to national life.

It is possible to argue that these are early days. The 1980s may mark a watershed in the transition of evangelical attitudes towards issues of social responsibility. Yet what evidence exists for the claim that evangelicals are now prepared to adopt a strategy for committed community involvement at both the local and the national level?

Five factors merit serious consideration at this point:

1 Embryonic new organizations which emerged in the 1970s and 1980s are maturing in the 1990s. Established operations like the Shaftesbury Society and the Salvation Army have now been joined by groups like Care, Jubilee, ACET and Tear Fund which are becoming nationally significant and recognized by major secular institutions.

2 The earlier twentieth-century days of evangelical disillusion with direct involvement in secular affairs appear to be receding. Committed evangelicals are being appointed to high positions in Government, Civil Service, education, social welfare, national and local politics, medicine and the media. Moreover they are no longer being ignored by their fellow Christians: many churches are now providing active prayerful support for their vocational commitments.

3 Evangelistic organizations like the Oasis Trust (sponsors of the Christmas Cracker Project), Youth For Christ, Scripture Union and the bodies involved in March for Jesus have succeeded in combining a commitment to social responsibility with a passion for evangelism. Once these would have

been regarded as being mutually exclusive, but today it is argued that they should be viewed as complementary functions of Christian ministry.

4 The Church can so often be regarded as an iceberg because most of its bulk remains invisible beneath the surface. While societies and organizations represent the more visible aspect of evangelical social action, much more is happening nationwide through local churches and fellowships. Denominational offices dealing with these issues now have a strong case to make because of growing involvement from their churches.

5 Once evangelicals were branded as being preoccupied with moral but not with social issues. Today this accusation is heard less frequently. For while moral matters are still a major cause for evangelical concern, so also are poverty, unemployment, homelessness and urban action. Indeed, as early as 1989, Kenneth Clarke (now Chancellor of the Exchequer) commented on the duality of evangelical social and moral concern. He even had to ask me, 'What are you evangelicals, are you left-wing or right-wing?'

Certainly the stereotypical image of evangelicals as being automatically right-wing is less true in the United Kingdom than in the USA. Normally, evangelicals who owe an allegiance to differing political parties are prepared to work together. Frequently they are prepared to join in broader ecumenical frameworks on social issues where doctrinal differences are seen as being less directly relevant.

This is not to suggest that evangelicals will always agree with each other. Educational issues provide a vivid illustration of an instance where some will endorse Government policy and others will disagree. On the matter of a daily act of worship there are those who will declare it to be unworkable, while others demand that the principle of adherence to the law must remain inviolate. Where evangelicals unite is in their attempt to make acts of worship as meaningful as possible – even though they may disagree over their frequency.[16]

In an attempt to produce a more united voice on major issues, the Evangelical Alliance has fostered the creation of a

large number of coalitions and consultations from within its
membership. Widespread concern amongst Christians on 'green
issues', especially among young people, led Youth For Christ
and Tear Fund to generate the 'Whose Earth?' initiative which
enjoyed the support of Dr George Carey, the Archbishop of
Canterbury. This was to lead to the publication of *Creation
Care*, a booklet, from a coalition of interested parties, designed
to encourage Christians to live in a more environmentally
friendly fashion.[17]

Similarly, the Evangelical Coalition on Drugs and Substance
Abuse drew together prevention bodies like the Band of Hope,
large rehabilitation centres like Yeldall Manor, and a host of
smaller organizations. Formed in 1990 this group was able to
encourage the work of Freedom Line which offered support to
those seeking to break free from tranquillizer addiction. Through
its annual conferences, it encouraged links of support and
friendship between its members. Faced with serious consequences from impending Government legislation, its members
were able to join with Martyn Eden, the Evangelical Alliance's
Public Affairs Director, in making successful representations
for a change in Government policy. They also obtained the
membership of one of their number on the relevant Government monitoring committee.

A parallel coalition of those working on disability issues was
also able to make a submission to a Government consultation
on issues of discrimination against disabled people.[18]

Similar representations were made by the Alliance, from its
involvement in the Video Standards Council, about the degree
of violence in many video productions. The Home Secretary,
Michael Howard, eventually acquiesced in a change in the
Government's stance. He exceeded all expectations by determining to prosecute those who distributed such videos to
under-age children.

While these representations indicate that a significant step
forward has been taken, the initial parliamentary victory in
1986 of Jubilee's Keep Sunday Special campaign remains the
only clear illustration of what could eventually be achieved. So
much more needs to be built, undertaken and achieved.

This does not apply only to the United Kingdom. The
European dimension remains to be explored and the sharing of

a Brussels office by Care and the Evangelical Alliance may well be a harbinger of future development. The European Evangelical Alliance has begun interaction with European Union bodies to develop an awareness of the evangelical position on key issues.

In 1985 Mike Morris, later Executive Secretary of the World Evangelical Fellowship's Religious Liberties Commission, made a visit to Turkey. He went to accompany Sir Fred Catherwood as a delegation from the Evangelical Alliance in order to protest at the imprisonment of the pastor and members of an evangelical church. They obtained assurance that restrictions on evangelicals in Turkey would be lifted. It is significant that they were able to draw attention to similar visits from the Alliance in the nineteenth century to the same country! This was to be the precursor of many other initiatives on behalf of the persecuted by many evangelical groups in the United Kingdom that enjoyed varying degrees of success.

I freely acknowledge that many subjects and organizations will have been neglected in this brief study. Nevertheless a firm impression remains. Evangelicals in the closing years of the twentieth century possess a firm desire to recover the identity and emphasis of their predecessors.

Who knows how historians, a century later, will evaluate this period of time. Perhaps it will be recorded as a time of transition – a moment when evangelicals returned to their roots and a commitment to evangelical social action was reborn.

Until more concrete gains have been achieved the question of the ultimate value of what has been begun remains unanswered. Yet it can be argued that every major development originates in a small way. One thing is clear, a fresh passion for community involvement and socio-political responsibility has emerged – and God alone knows where it will end. Evangelical heads are again being lifted from the sand: history will one day record the result!

Notes

1 S. Turner, *Nice and Nasty* (London: Razor Books, 1980).
2 For an expansion of these points see C. Calver 'The Value of the Christian Past: History and Christian Witness' in *Christianity and*

History Newsletter, No. 13 (Leicester: The Study Group on Christianity and History, 1994).

3 D. W. Bebbington, *Evangelicalism in Modern Britain: A History from the 1730s to the 1980s* (London: Unwin Hyman, 1989).

4 See C. Calver, P. Meadows, S. Gaukroger and S. Chilcraft, *Dancing in the Dark* (Tring: Lynx, 1994).

5 M. Eden, 'Introduction' in M. Eden ed., *Britain on the Brink* (Nottingham: Crossway, 1993).

6 Tear Fund, 'Introducing the Guidelines for Tear Fund Partnership'.

7 Christmas Cracker, Annual Report, 1993–94.

8 From an unpublished paper, 'Tear Fund/Evangelical Alliance United Kingdom Fund', February 1994.

9 *Employment News*, No. 236, December 1994.

10 *South London Press*, 1 March 1994.

11 *HELP Annual Report 1993/4*, HELP Ltd (Hackney Employment Link Project), Frampton Park Baptist Church.

12 J. R. W. Stott, *Issues Facing Christians Today* (Marshalls, 1984).

13 K. Tondeur, *A Student's Guide to Better Money Management* (Cambridge: Credit Action, 1994); K. Tondeur, *Escape from Debt* (Evangelical Alliance/Credit Action, 1993).

14 ECRS, 'Manifesto for the 1990s'.

15 David and Madeleine Potter, *We're All Special to God* (London: Scripture Union, 1990).

16 For further details, see Evangelical Coalition for Educational Issues Briefing Paper, 4 December 1994, and Press Release from Christian Institute, Newcastle-upon-Tyne, 8 December 1994.

17 C. Seaton and G. Dale, *Creation Care* (Evangelical Alliance, 1994).

18 Details contained in 'The consultation on Government measures to tackle discrimination against disabled people. Submission from the Evangelical Alliance'.

Index

211